MINIATURE MESSAGES

Jack Child

MINIATURE MESSAGES

The Semiotics and Politics of Latin American Postage Stamps

DUKE UNIVERSITY PRESS
DURHAM AND LONDON 2008

Printed in the United States of America
on acid-free paper ♾
Designed by Amy Ruth Buchanan. Typeset in
Quadraat by Tseng Information Systems, Inc.
Library of Congress Cataloging-in-Publication
Data appear on the last printed page of this book.
Duke University Press gratefully acknowledges
the support of the College of Arts and Sciences
of American University in the production of
this book.

For Alex, Zach, Jack,

Katie, Evita, Peri, and Mayo

May you (or at least

the bipeds among you)

someday also be philatelists

CONTENTS

ILLUSTRATIONS

Maps

Tables

Plates

Plates appear between pages 108 and 109.

PLATE 1

PREFACE

This book is in a sense the culmination of a project begun six decades ago in Argentina. Or as a colleague put it, "a sixty-year-old hobby gone pedantic." I grew up in Argentina during the Perón years as a dual U.S.-Argentine citizen. Like others, in early boyhood I collected stamps, and remember being fascinated by the changes from the older and rather undistinguished pre-Perón stamps to the larger, more colorful, and far more interesting ones of the 1945–1955 period. When I entered high school my interest in philately diminished as I discovered rugby, swimming, fishing, amateur radio, and girls. But I never got rid of my stamp collection, and it accompanied me to the United States as I began college (and evaded being drafted into the Argentine army).

My philatelic interests remained dormant until I began graduate school at American University's School of International Service, where as something of a lark, and with the encouragement of my friend and mentor the late John Finan, I wrote a term paper titled "Argentine Politics through Its Postage Stamps" (it was never published). The technology was primitive: the actual stamps were mounted on paper with brief captions below. In the last semester of my M.A. program the paper was expanded, and more serious research at the Library of Congress and the Columbus Library of the Organization of American States began. The second paper used more sophisticated technology (photocopies of stamps) and some analytical tools picked up in graduate seminars.[1] I began to make connections between the stamps and historical and sociopolitical events in Latin America. In some cases, such as the conflict situations described in chapter 4 of this book, it was evident that the stamps themselves were potential contributors to international tension. Further, contrary to what I had been taught in Argentina, the rest of the world did not necessarily agree that the Malvinas Islands and a big piece of

Antarctica belonged to Argentina, and there were stamps available to show these differences of opinion on both sides.

In subsequent professional activities and doctoral work (also at the School of International Service) I continued to develop linkages between postage stamps and events in the hemisphere, and used 35 mm slide technology to make presentations at various conferences and other events using postage stamps as illustrations. Interestingly, most postage stamps, being government documents, are in the public domain and are thus not subject to copyright limitations. This moved me to use them as illustrations in several books and articles. Editors were not always understanding or helpful, and the quality of some of the reproductions was embarrassing: one article printed several of the stamps upside down; the editor responded, "Well, they are in the Southern Hemisphere, aren't they?" Another editor mutilated the stamp photographs by trimming off the perforations and showing the stamps against a white background, making it difficult to perceive that they were postage stamps.

My tenure-track academic career at American began just as the 1982 Anglo-Argentine War broke out, and in a number of presentations and publications relating to the conflict, stamps were used as illustrations of the positions and goals of Argentina and the United Kingdom. By now the technology had shifted to the computer and a breakthrough combination of digital scanning, graphic manipulation software (Photoshop), and computer-assisted teaching tools on the Web such as Blackboard. Although my three-thousand-plus 35 mm stamp slides are now increasingly obsolete, their replacement by digitized scanned images is well under way, and their use has now extended to class lectures and presentations by students.

My Malvinas/Falklands stamp lectures soon included others linking Antarctica to the islands of the far South Atlantic, and this in turn led to some dozen trips to Antarctica and the Falklands/Malvinas on which, as a guide and lecturer on board expedition cruise ships, I used stamp slides extensively. Membership in key philatelic associations soon followed: the American Philatelic Society, the American Society of Polar Philatelists, the Falkland Islands Philatelic Study Group, and the Carto-Philatelic Society.

About five years ago these various pedagogical, academic, and philatelic threads came together with an analytical framework focusing on semantics and semiotics. Serendipitously, I ran across David Scott's work dealing with a semiotic approach to European stamp design and wondered if something similar could be done for Latin America.[2] I also was exposed to the use of fake postage stamps for political, satirical, and humorous goals by authors such as Garry Trudeau and the Michael Thompson–Michael Hernández de Luna duo.[3] In the Latin American context the work of author-philatelist Ríus provided the confirmation that yes, this was a fruitful field of study.[4]

And so began extensive research in the Organization of American States Library, the Library of Congress, and the libraries of the Smithsonian's National Postal Museum and the American Philatelic Society. There were some setbacks: American University's Research Committee turned down a request for funding on the grounds that while the approach was interesting, it fell short of their funding criteria. A sympathetic dean (Kay Mussell of the College of Arts and Sciences) stepped in with funding for a weeklong visit to the American Philatelic Society's extensive library in State College, Pennsylvania, which also was the basis for a research note in the society's *Philatelic Literature Review*.[5]

In mid-2003 I tested the waters of academic legitimacy by submitting an article on the semiotics and politics of Latin American postage stamps to the premier journal in the field, the *Latin American Research Review* of the Latin American Studies Association. To my delight their response (and that of their referees) was quick and encouraging, and I very much appreciate the support of their editor Peter Ward and their managing editor Shannon Halley. After some relatively minor changes, it appeared in February 2005, and became the first article to be published by the review with color illustrations.[6] The twelve stamps featured were prepared using scanning and graphic manipulation technology. The linkage to Latin American popular culture was also significant in that starting in fall 2003 I have taught a course each semester on the subject, using postage stamps as one element of popular culture that is available for analysis. In preparing the *Latin American Research Review* article I discovered something that is also true for this book: the process of finding, analyzing, scanning, and manipulating the stamps and their digitized images can be more time-consuming than the actual writing of the manuscript. To paraphrase my friend and colleague Richard Millett, we don't enjoy writing, but we enjoy having written, and spending time with the stamps involved.

One by-product of this project is a CD-ROM containing approximately two thousand images of Latin American postage stamps, including all the ones cited in this book. They are available in JPEG format as well as on PowerPoint slides that provide a brief note on the historical, political, and cultural significance of the stamp. These images are copyright-free since they are government documents in the public domain, and are thus available for use in lectures, publications, and student presentations. The CD-ROM is available at no charge as shareware from the author: Dr. Jack Child, Department of Language and Foreign Studies, American University, Washington, DC 20016; tel. 202–885–2385; email: jchild@american.edu. Although there is no charge for the CD-ROM, we request that a small donation to support reproduction and handling of the CD-ROM and updates be made to Spanish-Latin American Studies Restricted Fund, Department of Language and Foreign Studies, American University, Washington, DC 20016.

ACKNOWLEDGMENTS

Many friends and colleagues generously contributed to this project through their encouragement and their time reading the manuscript and making suggestions. They include American University's interim provost, Ivy Broder; Dean Kay Mussell of the university's College of Arts and Sciences; Language and Foreign Studies Department chairs John Schillinger, Naomi Baron, Alina Israeli, Olga Rojer, and Nadia Harris; librarian Paul McCutcheon of the Smithsonian's National Postal Museum; Barbara Boal and librarians Gini Horn, Ellen Stuter, and Roseann Staie of the American Philatelic Society's Research Library; and colleagues Amy Oliver, Consuelo Hernández, Ana Serra, Brenda Werth, Consuelo Gall, Jeannie Downey-Vanover, and Florencia Cortés-Conde of our Department of Language and Foreign Studies. My brother Ted gets credit for help starting my stamp collection in Argentina in the 1940s. A number of colleagues and friends also assisted greatly by reading the manuscript and providing corrections, suggestions, and editing: John Splettstoesser, Debra Luff, Paul Goodwin, David Bushnell, Frank Nuessel, Steve Pendleton, Pope Atkins, Florene Memegalos, Joseph Scarpaci, Guy Shaw, and María Manzana. Student assistants Katie Baldwin, Leah Sand, Sarah Hughson, Rachel Labruyere, and Jody Burghardt gave generously of their time to edit and comment, and students in various courses were subjected to required readings of some of the chapters, especially those dealing with Argentina, Antarctica, and the Falklands/Malvinas. I am especially indebted to former students Vanessa Mueller and Marissa Newhall (both editors of the American University student newspaper *The Eagle*) for their close reading and editing of this text.

The encouragement and support of Duke University Press editors Valerie Millholland, Miriam Angress, and Molly Balikov are much appreciated, as are the comments provided by their anonymous referees and the copy editor, Maura High (to whom I owe an apology for my "minimalist" endnotes).

Finally, and most importantly, I am indebted more than she knows to Leslie Morginson-Eitzen, "colega, compañera y amiga," who endured many crossings of the Drake passage, numerous lectures, and hours of reading the manuscript.

I am grateful to all of these friends and associates for their help and support. Errors and omissions are of course my responsibility, but without the help of these individuals there would have been far more of them.

CREDITS

The Augusto Pinochet middle-finger salute stamp (figure 1.7) comes from *The Stamp Art and Postal History* of Michael Thompson and Michael Hernández de Luna (Chicago: Bad Press Books, 2000) and was provided for use in this book by its creator, Michael Thompson, who generously forwarded other satirical stamp creations, including those targeting former Peruvian president Alberto Fujimori and controversial places such as Chiapas, Vieques (Puerto Rico), and Guantánamo, Cuba ("Puerto de Imperialistas"). Postage stamps issued after the 1978 creation of the U.S. Postal Service are copyrighted, and require a licensing fee to reproduce. I am indebted to Ms. Courtney Loy of the USPS Rights and Permission Program for facilitating this process.

Portions of chapters 1 and 4 appeared previously in my article, "The Politics and Semiotics of the Smallest Icons of Popular Culture," *Latin American Research Review* 40.1 (2005): 108–137. Portions of chapter 5 appeared in "The Politics and Semiotics of Argentine Postage Stamps," *Essays of the Middle Atlantic Council of Latin American Studies* 18 (2005): 1–34. Permission to use this material is gratefully acknowledged.

Unless otherwise noted, all translations in the text are my own.

INTRODUCTION

Stamps can have impact. In late June 2005 the Mexican Post Office released a set of five postage stamps (Scott 2431–2435) portraying the classic comic book character Memín Pinguín, a small and mischievous black boy with pronounced Sambo-like features.[1] The stamps were immediately perceived as portraying a racist stereotype and were harshly denounced by many in the United States, much to the amazement of the Mexicans. President Vicente Fox stated that he was baffled by the indignant reaction across the border and said that he, like many Mexicans, had known and loved this character since he was a boy.[2] Despite comments from the White House that the stamps were offensive, he rejected a request from the Reverend Jesse Jackson that Mexico repudiate the stamps and withdraw them from circulation. In the U.S. Congress a resolution was introduced condemning the Mexican government for "printing and distributing blatantly racist postage stamps."[3] In Mexico there was something of a backlash as post offices were crowded by Mexicans anxious to buy the stamps, and defend their cherished comic character, refusing to be pushed around by their northern neighbor (as they saw the situation). On eBay the asking price for the set of stamps, which had a face value of around three dollars, rose to two hundred dollars, although it is not clear if anyone actually paid that price; after a month the price on eBay had dropped to the high thirties. Mexican intellectuals came to the defense of their government's position, arguing that the character was not racist and was deeply cherished, especially among poorer Mexicans who identified with him.[4] Several Web sites and blogs were launched to address the issue, generally from a viewpoint critical of the U.S. reaction. Although this was an extreme case because of cross-cultural misunderstanding and the sensitivity of race in the U.S.-Mexican relationship, it does serve to illustrate the power that the message on a postage stamp can have. Postage stamps, after all, are official government documents, and their release implies approval by responsible officials. In the Mexican case an advisory commission headed by the nation's postmaster general makes design recommendations, which must be approved by the Office of the President.[5]

A less volatile but also powerful message was contained in the 1997 release of a postage stamp of Che Guevara by Argentina on the thirtieth anniversary of his death in Bolivia (figure 2.6, Scott 1978). Guevara, a hero to the Latin American Left, was reviled in Argentina by conservative sectors, and especially the military, which reacted strongly to the postage stamp. The stamp was denounced by political groups opposed to the government of the Peronista Carlos Menem as a ploy to gain favor from the Left.

A third example of the political impact of a postage stamp concerns the Mexican painter Frida Kahlo, to be discussed further in chapter 1. In July 2001 the U.S. and Mexican postal authorities issued a dual stamp of one of Kahlo's self-portraits (Scott Mexico 2228 and U.S. 3509), with the same design on both the Mexican and American stamps. The Kahlo stamp was released in Arizona amid comments from Hispanic groups in the United States that it was a symbol of diversity that honored one of their own. To the surprise of many in Mexico (and a few in the United States), the stamp was loudly denounced by conservative sectors in the United States, who argued that it was a travesty to put such an American-hating, militant Communist on a U.S. stamp. The fact that she was an avowed bisexual who indulged in drugs, and had had an extramarital affair with Leon Trotsky, did nothing to endear her to the U.S. critics.[6]

The purpose of this work is to examine some of the semiotic messages and the politics (national and international) involved in Latin American postage stamps such as these three examples. The argument will be presented that postage stamps, which can be called the smallest icons of Latin American popular culture,[7] frequently carry miniature messages. These messages are frequently political in nature, involve national cultural identity, and impact a country's citizens as well as the image that is projected abroad of that country.

My use of semiotics to analyze postage stamps follows the pioneering work of David Scott in his *European Stamp Design: A Semiotic Approach to Designing Messages*,[8] although I focus on a different geographic area, and more on the politics involved. I rely on the typology first set up by the noted American philosopher Charles Sanders Peirce, and consider the postage stamp to be a unique kind of sign, with an impressive capacity to convey a number of messages in a very confined space. My use of Peirce's typology, as adapted to postage stamps, is explained in the following chapter. The use of semiotics to analyze advertisements, as epitomized by Arthur Berger[9] and others, will also serve as a model of how the study of messages and signs can be useful in a variety of fields.

The humble postage stamp, introduced in England in 1840, has evolved over the years to the point where an initially secondary function of the stamp deserves serious study, that is, the use of the postage stamp as advertisement or propaganda (domestic or international), with themes as far ranging as nationalism, history, politics, economics, art, culture, and so on. In the particular case of Latin American stamps, the Pan American Union had this to say in 1944: "Postage stamps have long since advanced beyond their original purpose of denoting the prepayment of postal charges. For many years they have been used by the governments of the Americas as publicity media to invite attention to illustrious sons, national beliefs, scenic beauties, and economic opportunities. Selected by the governments themselves, the nationalistic subjects act as windows through which others may view the culture, accomplishments, and ambitions of distant lands."[10]

The postage stamps of Latin America demonstrate an extraordinary variety and range of themes, formats, and design characteristics. Although originally strongly influenced by trends in European (and later U.S.) stamp design, Latin American stamps in the last several decades have developed their own strong identity, which increases their value as a source of information about the area. Particularly noteworthy in this connection are the stamps of Argentina (especially during the Perón era), Mexico, and revolutionary Cuba and Nicaragua.

The value of considering postage stamps as a fresh, alternative window into Latin American reality is demonstrated by the work of the inimitable Mexican humorist Ríus (Eduardo del Río), who frequently uses postage stamps to illustrate his work, and who has written a delightful and entertaining guide to them. Ríus notes that up until recent times there was a tendency to make fun of stamp collectors as "locos maniáticos" ("crazy maniacs"), but that this pejorative approach has been replaced by a grudging acceptance of the cultural and educational value of stamps, even by organizations such as UNESCO.[11] Ríus's use of postage stamps to illustrate many of his works brings out an additional aspect of this project: the systematic search for postage stamps as illustrations in the teaching of Latin American studies. With some few exceptions (current U.S. stamps being the most prominent), postage stamps are in the public domain since they are government documents. Thus, they may be reproduced for educational and academic purposes without infringing copyright laws. The Latin American postage stamps discussed in this volume can be used to illustrate a wide range of themes that are important in studies of this region. With the advent of the computer and the digital scanner, it is now easy to reproduce these stamps, and the CD-ROM produced as part of this project contains several thousand such illustrations, with appropriate indexes and commentary.

It can be argued that postage stamps are frequently taken for granted, with the general public paying only passing attention to their design and messages. But the messages are there, and the postage stamp is one form of art that is seen daily or frequently by almost all citizens. The messages carried may be subconsciously and subtly conveyed, and it can be argued that the process of repetition (i.e., seeing the same design many times) further consolidates the process of delivering the message.

Furthermore, the aesthetic and design features of postage stamps merit our attention and respect, for a well-designed stamp represents the creative effort of one or more specialists who have to be carefully attuned to a number of sometimes competing factors: the legal requirement that the stamp show how much postage has been prepaid, the country of origin, the typography, the graphic element (since almost all postage stamps now carry some kind of image), and the artistic presentation of something that is both useful and attractive, all the while working in the confines of a very small surface area.

The sheer numbers of different designs and visual images are staggering. Stamp catalogues list approximately six hundred different stamp-emitting "entities," "authorities," or "stamp issuers" (including countries, colonies, dependencies, offices abroad, etc.), which over the last century and a half of stamp usage have produced an estimated 250,000 different designs; from 1984 to 2004, an estimated 10,000 to 18,000 different new stamps were issued yearly worldwide.[12] For Latin America alone, the total since the first stamps in 1843 is over 50,000, with around 20,000 different designs. Almost every conceivable theme and image has appeared in some form on a postage stamp, and the variety of forms, styles, and themes is very large.[13] The range of printing methods and typography adds to the total volume of different varieties. A number of basic technical problems inherent in the printing process have been resolved, and even the less sophisticated stamp-emitting countries have in recent years improved their product, although blunders, errors, and aesthetic disasters still occur.

My research for this book began with a thorough literature review to identify Latin American postage stamps with significant messages. The literature was located using appropriate Web search engines and the catalogues of several university libraries, as well as the Library of Congress, and the specialized libraries of the Smithsonian's National Postal Museum, the Organization of American States, and the American Philatelic Society. Most of the materials in these libraries consisted of secondary sources, but available government decrees and explanations of why certain stamps were issued were important primary sources. One key resource was the publications of philatelic associations of the larger countries, mainly Argentina, Mexico, and Brazil; these frequently contained analyses of the historical and political significance of stamps issued by the nations of Latin America.

The second focus of my research was postage stamps as primary source materials; I examined a significant number of the approximately twenty thousand different varieties of Latin American postage stamps since the first ones appeared in the mid-nineteenth century. One could question whether these postage stamps are truly primary documents, but as they are produced by the governments concerned and are usually designed with specific political and aesthetic considerations in mind, they do meet criteria for primary documents. Some of the stamps I examined come from my personal collection; others are from the *Scott 2006 Standard Postage Stamp Catalogue*, which is the authoritative source of information for philatelists. Although the examination of this many postage stamps might seem daunting, it was made easier by the fact that most nineteenth-century stamps have few variations in theme and can be visited rather quickly. For twentieth-century stamps the process was much more time-consuming, although it was facilitated by the brief descriptions of the stamps' subject contained in the *Scott Catalogue*. My initial survey turned up a number of stamps that would be candidates for inclusion in the color plates of this book. Many were already in my personal collection, and for those that were not, I placed an order with specialized stamp dealers, who in most cases were able to provide them. In the case of Argentina, Mexico, the Falkland Islands (British), South Georgia, and the British Antarctic Territory, I have had for some years a standing order for all new issues, and this greatly increased the number of stamps available for analysis.

I begin the book with some general considerations: first, a brief discussion of semiotics as applied to postage stamps across the board, with an emphasis on the work of Peirce, and next, a consideration of postage stamps as popular culture. Postage stamps are produced by governments, but they are also important symbols of national identity in which citizens have an input and are in turn influenced by the messages. Postage stamps also have an educational function and carry political implications and consequences, as we see in some important stamp issues, including several from non-Latin countries and the United States. As an object, the postage stamp can be viewed in terms of its many functions, its impact, and the limitations and challenges involved in producing stamps, as well as aesthetic and design features. We can look at the stamp as art form, and examine the use of the stamp format by established artists who may be contracted to create stamps used for postage, or may simply create stamp-like art not intended for postage, but which imitates the real thing. Some of these can be quite creative and complex, using a fictitious country ("La República de Banana") to convey humorous and sometimes stereotypical insights into a region and its culture. Other imaginary stamps may be prepared by entities such as guerrilla movements seeking to gain greater political legitimacy, most notably the Mexican EZLN (Zapatista Army of National Liberation). Real or imaginary stamps have also been used for propaganda purposes in conflicts such as World War II or the cold war: for example, the Hitler death's head issue (figure 1.5), or Vietnamese and Cuban stamps bitterly attacking the United States during the conflict in Southeast Asia (figure 4.10, Scott Cuba 1163).

Latin American postage stamps have a long and fascinating history, which I outline in chapter 2. Each of the countries of the region has produced numerous different stamps over the past century and a half, and their designs and functions have evolved over the course of time. The first stamps—the Brazilian so-called bull's-eyes in 1843 (figure 1.1, Scott 1)—were followed by classical issues late in the century (e.g., figure 1.3, Scott El Salvador 103), and the arrival of commemorative stamps focusing initially on the 1810 centennial of independence of most of the Spanish-speaking nations of the hemisphere. The Bolivian "Gate of the Sun" issue (figure 1.9, Scott Bolivia 450) is a case study of the problems caused by irregularities in the preparation and issuing of postage stamps, compounded by the impact of inflation in Bolivia.

Domestic politics influences the selection of stamp themes in a few countries, and I look at these in chapter 3, including the United States for comparison. The goals of governments in this process include the governments' use of the postage stamp to portray a favorable (and possibly distorted and even false) image of the nation and its leaders. Other topics are good citizenship, women and gender issues, economics (exports, tourism), disaster relief, internationalism, national identity, and the presenting and sustaining of notions of sovereignty. Specific examples of internal political messages carried by stamps include their use by dictatorial regimes, such as those of General Jorge Ubico of Guatemala, Rafael L. Trujillo of the Dominican Republic (figure 2.3, Scott C185), Alfredo Stroessner of Paraguay (figure 2.1, Scott 1453), and the Somozas of Nicaragua. The case of Chile provides an interesting contrast between the stamps of the leftist government of Salvador Allende and the rightist dictatorship led by General Augusto Pinochet that followed (figure 2.4, Scott 423; figure 2.5, Scott 496). Reformist and revolutionary regimes, such as those of Mexico in the early part of the twentieth century, Cuba starting in 1959, and Nicaragua in 1979, have made ample use of their heroes and icons in the stamps produced during their tenure.

These topics have implications beyond a country's borders and impinge on the cooperative and conflictual aspects of interstate relationships. A number of significant interstate conflicts in Latin America are portrayed on postage stamps. In most cases the stamp simply reflects an existing conflict, but in a few special cases the stamp itself was the cause of a conflict, or of its intensification. This is especially true for border conflicts where a stamp includes a map, which inevitably (and understandably) portrays the issuing country's perception of how the border issue should be resolved and provokes a reaction by the other party involved. An example is the 1935 Argentine stamp of South America (figure 4.1, Scott 445), which produced diplomatic protests from Peru (over the border with Ecuador), Chile (over the border around the Magellan Strait area), and Great Britain (over the representation of the Malvinas/Falkland Islands as being Argentine). Another example is the Nicaraguan stamp (figure 4.8, Scott 129) showing an erupting volcano, which was used by Philippe Bunau-Varilla as one element in his successful attempt to get the U.S. Congress to move the proposed Isthmian Canal from Nicaragua to Panama. Long-standing border conflicts between Bolivia and Paraguay, Haiti and the Dominican Republic, Guatemala and Belize, Venezuela and Guyana, and Chile-Bolivia have resulted in stamps, especially map stamps, which present each country's views on the correct demarcation of the border, and which frequently result in a quick philatelic response by the other nation involved. Strains between the United States and Cuba have led the Cubans to deliver numerous miniature messages celebrating their triumph at the Bay of Pigs (figure 4.9, Scott 3308), condemning U.S. actions in Vietnam (figure 4.10), and supporting guerrilla movements which formed part of their opposition to U.S. imperialism (as they saw it) on a worldwide scale. Not all international stamp messages have been critical or hostile, however; some commemorate friendly presidential visits, conferences, disaster relief, and support for victims of terrorism, such as the Costa Rican stamp memorializing those who died in the 9/11 attacks on the United States (figure 5.9, Scott 560).

The country of Argentina, which I consider in chapter 5, is of particular interest because of its blatant insertion of partisan politics into Argentine stamps in 1930, beginning a tendency that continues to the present. This specific series of stamps celebrated the September 1930 coup, which ended the regime of the unpopular radical president Hipólito Yrigoyen. The stamps (figure 6.3, Scott 376) show intermingled civilians and soldiers marching heroically under a sky filled with the Argentine flag and various weapons, delivering the message that this was a combined military-civilian action against a president who had lost credibility and popular support. The first Perón era (1943–1955) witnessed a sophisticated use of postage stamps to convey the political messages pushed by the Peronista regime. The annual totals of new stamps increased dramatically in this period, as did changes in design, quality, and repetition of semiotic messages. Examples include a stamp celebrating the 1943 coup (Scott 508); stamps issued to raise funds for the victims of the 1943 San Juan earthquake, which brought Juan and Evita Perón together (figure 6.4, Scott B6–9); the Perón presidential inaugural in 1946 (figure 6.5, Scott 552); Peronista "loyalty day" (figure 6.7, Scott 556); the "descamisado" voluntary stamp issued to raise funds for a monumental statue which was never built (figure 6.8, not catalogued by Scott); and a number of stamps promoting the Peronista five-year plans. The death of Evita in 1952 led to a unique requirement that for one year, only stamps commemorating the deceased first lady could be used; the stamps created a difficult situation for postal clerks who were instructed to be careful that the black ink cancellation marks not touch the face of Evita (figure 6.9, Scott 616). When Perón fell in 1955 (an event celebrated by several stamps, such as figure 6.11, Scott 647), Argentina went into a long period of alternating military regimes and failed civilian presidencies marked by stamps noting the inaugurals of elected presidents and (when the military took over) stamps celebrating the armed forces.

Argentina has major interests in its Antarctic claim and the Falkland Islands (or Malvinas), and its stamps reflect those interests. The postage stamps issued by the Falklands and South American countries with a presence in Antarctica both reflect and stimulate currents of interstate conflict and cooperation in these two regions linked to Latin America by geography and geopolitics. British Falklands Islands stamps were relatively uncontroversial until the 1933 series celebrating the centennial of the British occupation of the islands (figure 8.4, Scott 70; figure 8.5, Scott 69), followed by stamps of the Falkland Islands Dependencies (figure 8.1, Scott ILI), which clearly showed the British perception of the relationship between the Falklands, other South Atlantic islands, and the British Antarctic claim. A similar Argentine stamp (figure 8.2, Scott 758) shows their blue-and-white flag on all the relevant islands, as well as Argentina's parallel Antarctic claim. The short but bitterly fought 1982 war produced a number of stamps featuring key military events on both sides, as well as a 1983 Argentine stamp noting the "first" recovery of the Islas Malvinas (figure 8.9, Scott 1411), suggesting that their efforts to obtain effective control of the islands would continue. In the case of Antarctic stamps, a number of other players join Argentina and Great Britain in using postage stamps to put forth their Antarctic interests. Map stamps play a significant role here, with Chile issuing ones showing its claim, which overlaps the British and Argentine ones to a considerable degree. Brazilian, Uruguayan, Peruvian, and Ecuadorian Antarctic activities are well represented in their stamps, although none of these countries has an Antarctic claim, and thus maps are generally not used. All the major Antarctic expeditions have been celebrated in stamps of the relevant European countries as well as the United States, with the British using numerous stamps to present the detailed history of their Antarctic heroes, such as Captain Robert F. Scott (figure 11.7, Scott BAT 140) and Sir Ernest Shackleton (figure 9.7, Scott Falkland Is. 760). The latter explorer's epic story of survival and final rescue by a Chilean ship is told in numerous stamps issued by Chile (e.g., figure 10.8, Scott 361).

The stamps of a number of other Latin American countries can be viewed in many respects like those of Argentina. Brazil's stamps are distinguished by their excellent design features, especially in recent years, and their attention to controversial themes such as deforestation and conservation and HIV/AIDS prevention (the latter stamp featuring a condom, figure 12.1, Scott 2624). The story of the Cuban Revolution has been told numerous times through Cuba's postage stamps, from the 1953 raid on the Moncada Barracks to the landing of the *Granma* in 1958 and the triumph of the Castro guerrillas in 1959 (figure 12.8, Scott 613; figure 12.9, Scott 626). Major icons of the revolution such as Camilo Cienfuegos and Che Guevara have made numerous appearances (e.g., figure 12.11, Scott 4069), although the philatelic coverage of Fidel Castro has been relatively restrained. The Sandinistas in Nicaragua did place Castro (along with Augusto Sandino, Simón Bolívar, and José Martí) in a stamp celebrating the thirtieth anniversary of the Cuban Revolution (figure 14.2, Scott C1161). The years of Sandinista rule in Nicaragua produced stamps following the Cuban pattern, with annual issues noting the triumph of their revolution and the major iconic figures of their struggle (figure 14.1, Scott C973). This came to an abrupt end with the electoral triumph of Violeta Chamorro in 1990, whose administration promptly issued a stamp honoring her murdered husband; stamps of Mrs. Chamorro herself followed (figure 14.3, Scott 2199), as did traditional Catholic themes at Christmas time. Mexico's stamps have made effective use of the country's artistic heritage to illustrate the 1910 Revolution, with special emphasis on the contributions of the muralists such as Diego Rivera (figure 13.9, Scott 1464), as well as his precursors, such as José Guadalupe Posada and his *calaveras* (figure 13.7, Scott C278). In Venezuela, the cult of Bolívar is evident in the country's postage stamps, as are some themes of current political economy such as OPEC (Organization of Petroleum Exporting Countries; figure 14.8, Scott 1339) and SELA (the Latin American Economic System, which includes Cuba but not the United States; figure 14.9, Scott 1337).

Having described the book's purpose and scope, I should also perhaps specify what it is not, in order to avoid confusing the reader who is expecting a more traditional philatelic approach to Latin American stamps. For the nonphilatelic reader, the following clarification may be necessary: there is a rich lode of philatelic research produced by serious stamp collectors, which is published in journals such as the American Philatelic Society's monthly *The American Philatelist* and its quarterly *Philatelic Literature Review*, as well as a number of specialized study groups focusing on individual countries or areas such as the polar regions and the Falkland Islands. This present work is not subsumed under the category of "philatelic research" described above, which focuses on the details of a particular stamp issue, with emphasis on idiosyncrasies, irregularities, and errors. It also is not postal history (the study of postal rates, covers, cancellations, and items actually carried in the mails). Neither is the project in the category of "History of X as Told in Postage Stamps," where X can be a country, notable personality, or specific topic or theme. It also is not a topic or theme of the type studied by the various topical associations, such as an analysis of the Olympics through stamps, or animals, scientific phenomena, and so on.

The skeptic is entitled to ask whether this project has academic or scholarly validity. It is, after all, an unorthodox topic for a monograph, and the first reaction of associates who hear of the project may be to equate it with a hobby or pastime until its grounding in semiotics and politics is explained. In this connection, one could perhaps fall back on G. P. Murdock's contention: "Most of the sciences and humanities first began, of course, as hobbies, and some activities which were once valued and supported, like astrology, have subsequently declined once more to the status of hobbies. As culture changes, in short, the values of different intellectual hobbies fluctuate."[14]

Another perhaps useful observation is that there is a certain parallel between the serious academic study of postage stamps and that of comic books. Both lie outside the original and traditional bounds of academic disciplines, and yet comics have begun to be respected as a valid manifestation of popular culture and worthy of such study.

Recent scholarly books and journals dealing with popular culture have included chapters or articles on postage stamps as legitimate examples of popular culture. The noted Latin Americanist David Bushnell has been the author of several such contributions, and is himself a collector of Latin American postage stamps as well as a scholar focusing on their contribution to the history and politics of the area. Bushnell has used photographs of relevant stamps from his personal collection to illustrate journal articles, as has John Reid.[15] I must also confess to a similar (although more modest) orientation, having used postage stamps from my collection to illustrate various publications and, perhaps more important, to illustrate lectures and presentations.

Charles Ekker has argued that stamps, as government documents with important content, should be accepted by scholars as legitimate primary source materials for research purposes.[16] While recognizing the limitations imposed by its focus on a single geographic area, this book will attempt to validate Ekker's argument, using semiotics and politics as the academic tools by which postage stamps can contribute to the field of Latin American area studies.

Another aspect of the argument for academic interest in the study of postage stamps has to do with the fact that notable figures in the Americas have devoted considerable time and attention to philately, sometimes as collectors, but also as students of the area, noting the contribution that such study has made to their understanding of a variety of interdisciplinary endeavors. Historians have noted the great interest that Franklin D. Roosevelt took in philately. Less well known is the fact that Roosevelt personally participated in the design of several U.S. stamps, most notably the 1933 commemorative honoring Admiral Byrd and his exploits in Little America (Antarctica), and during his administration encouraged Nelson Rockefeller and others to use stamps as a vehicle for greater inter-American understanding and cooperation. I have noted above the use made of postage stamps by the Mexican humorist Ríus. A countryman of his, Porfirio Díaz, had what was considered the best collection of Mexican stamps of his generation, a collection that came to a tragic end when it was tossed into a bonfire as the Díaz regime fell.[17] President Juan Perón once told a visiting American journalist that he had an interest in postage stamps, and had influenced the design of some Argentine stamps during his years in office.[18] More recently, the Peruvian U.N. secretary-general, Javier Pérez de Cuéllar, discussed his own philatelic interest and the role that postage stamps play in achieving the United Nations' goals: "Stamps are a form of communication and culture. They carry a message of their own and lead to world understanding."[19]

1 SEMIOTICS, POPULAR CULTURE, POLITICS, AND STAMPS

Semiotics is the study of signs and the messages they contain. The discipline has acquired numerous adherents in the last hundred years as a scientifically based approach to the myriad of pieces of information we are bombarded with on a constant basis. There is a rich and complex theoretical component to semiotics, and an equally rich and diverse field of applied semiotics that attempts to relate these theoretical aspects to concrete areas of human activities such as advertising, propaganda, popular culture, the arts, and cultural studies generally. In this work I will apply some basic semiotic notions to the study of Latin American postage stamps, following the work on the semiotics and designs of European stamps that was pioneered by David Scott.[1]

At the simplest level of definition, signs are things that stand for other things. Thus, they have meanings and combinations of meanings derived from the things they stand for and the way they are presented. Words are the most basic and common signs, but they are by no means the only kinds of signs. As Arthur A. Berger points out, a theatrical performance (or a movie) relies on many semiotic signs beyond words. There is scenery, music, and costuming. The western villain's black hat is a sign with a certain meaning, as is the white hat worn by the hero.[2]

One American philosopher stands out as the pioneer of the American (as opposed to the European) tradition of semiotics: Charles Sanders Peirce (1839–1914).[3] A native of Cambridge and a graduate of Harvard, Peirce did not pursue an academic career, preferring instead to work for many years in the U.S. government's Geodetic Survey. His contributions, however, encompassed many fields, including philosophy, psychology, engineering, and logic. He published relatively little, and it was only after his death that his major essays were collected in one publication.[4] His writing is dense, theoretical, and hard for the layman to grasp. Nevertheless, his basic ideas regarding semiotics and signs were to have wide-reaching impact. Peirce's view of the world was pansemiotic, and he believed that "the entire universe is perfused with signs, if it is not composed exclusively of signs."[5] This pervasive presence of signs meant to Peirce that any field he studied could, and indeed must, be approached through the discipline of semiotics and the search for the signs that gave it meaning. As part of his approach to semiotics Peirce created a comprehensive and complicated typology of signs. Starting out with a relatively simple three-class typology, Peirce multiplied and compounded the categories until he arrived at ten major classes of signs, then sixty-six, and finally almost sixty thousand.[6] In our approach to the semiotics of postage stamps we will limit ourselves to his original trichotomy, as Scott did in his semiotic study of European stamps.

The first semiotic message a postage stamp delivers is self-referential: it must identify itself as a postage stamp. The conventional way of doing this, and confirming that a postage stamp is indeed a postage stamp, has to do with its relatively small size and the perforations that surround it. If it is affixed to an envelope in its accustomed place in the upper right-hand corner we further confirm its identity. And if it arrives as part of a mail delivery and has been canceled with a date/time/city black-ink mark, then the message is clear and firm.

We should note that there is a fairly complex semiotic language associated with how the stamp is placed on the envelope. In addition to the four corners and the four sides of the envelope's front, stamps can also be placed at a large number of angles ranging from the conventional right side up to fully upside down. In the late nineteenth century elaborate codes were prepared with "secret" romantic messages associated with these various positions and angles. These messages ranged from "Do you love me?" to "I have my doubts" and "Write no more."[7]

The next semiotic message is the identification of the country of origin. As we will see below when we apply Peirce's typology, there are a number of ways of delivering this message, starting with a simple typographical statement spelling out the name of the country. Most mail we receive is from our own country, so this important function is sometimes overlooked. The next message is a quantitative one: has the correct amount of postage been paid? This is confirmed by a number on the stamp specifying the prepaid value of the stamp, and presumably the weight of the letter or package delivered is covered by its value. This seemingly everyday function is crucial because the basic postal purpose of the stamp (leaving aside the various political and other purposes we will be exploring) is to carry the mail by validating the payment for delivery. Indeed, the invention of the adhesive postage stamp was due to the inconveniences and inefficiencies of the earlier system under which the recipient of the letter had to pay the cost of carrying it.

At deeper levels of semiotic meaning, messages common to most stamps are carried by features of design, to include color, typography, layout, and, of singular importance to our study, any representational drawings, engravings, photographs, or other graphics. These can deliver increasingly sophisticated messages of a cultural, historical, political, or economic nature.

Peirce called his three-part typology "the trichotomy of signs," in which he classified a sign as either an index, an icon, or a symbol.[8] Signs that combined these features were also possible, and indeed Peirce argued that most signs were complex blends of these three categories. In layman's terms the three elements of the typology can be defined as follows:

Index: a pointer taking the viewer somewhere. An example would be smoke, which is an index to the fire that released it.

Icon: a graphic pictorial representation such as a picture, a design, or a photograph. It can be observed for its own aesthetic sake or, more important for our semiotic analysis, analyzed to see what the message of the picture is.

Symbol: a conventional sign in which elements stand for something else. Thus the symbol "$" stands for dollar, and the post horn is a common symbol for postal service.

Some examples will serve to illustrate how this semiotic analysis works. One such example concerns the indexing semiotic function of a postage stamp by which the viewer is given the message concerning the country of origin. The simplest solution to this requirement is to use typography (print) to identify the country, and indeed most postage stamps today carry the name of the country as text. However, the first postage stamp produced (by England in 1840) did not carry the name of the country.[9] Instead, a profile of Queen Victoria was used. The only typographic elements on the black stamp were the words "postage" and the spelling out ("One Penny") of the amount of prepaid postage, which explains the popular nickname, "Penny Black." To this day British stamps do not carry the name of the country. Instead, the head of the reigning monarch is used, sometimes dominating the design (and thus becoming an icon in Peirce's typology), and sometimes discreetly placed in one of the upper corners.[10]

The earliest Latin American stamps, those of Brazil in the year 1843, carried no index sign, and consisted simply of a numeral indicating the postage paid, along with an abstract ornamental design intended to make it difficult to forge the stamp (figure 1.1, Scott Brazil 1). In part this was because it was assumed that the stamps would be used only for internal mail within Brazil. But the reasons sometimes given for not placing the head of Emperor Dom Pedro of Brazil on early stamps included the argument that it would be undignified to blacken the royal face with an ink cancellation. It was not until the issues of 1866 that Dom Pedro appeared on Brazilian stamps.[11]

The indexing function is sometimes accomplished with more abstract iconographic signs, such as Marianne, the national symbol of France, or a flag. In the case of countries with long names (United States of America, for example) initials or acronyms are frequently used, with a flag or national symbol such as the presidential palace as iconographic indices.

The iconographic semiotic message is the one that is more subtle and complex, and will be the main focus of our analysis. It is in the selection of the icon that a government frequently makes a conscious choice of what message is to be delivered, and how. The challenge of selecting meaningful icons is compounded by the extremely small surface area involved, and technical limitations such as printing methods (engraving vs. lithograph, etc.), inks, colors, and paper. The Universal Postal Union also imposes certain standards and requirements, which governments ignore at their peril.

When analyzing the iconic function of postage stamps an important distinction must be made between "definitive" and "commemorative" stamps. Definitive (sometimes also called "ordinary") stamps tend to portray general iconic messages that are not time-sensitive. They are usually smaller in format and simpler in design, and are intended to carry the mails for an extended period of time, which can be several years. In recent decades the ravages of inflation and the increase in postage rates have required fairly frequent changes in definitive stamps (witness the changes in United States definitives due to budgetary problems in the U.S. Postal Service). It is of course possible to use the same definitive stamp and simply change the numerical value. In fast-moving inflationary situations this is commonly done by overprinting the new value. The classical case is Germany in the 1920s, when definitive stamps increased their denomination several millionfold in a short period. Latin American cases include Bolivia, Argentina, and Nicaragua under the Sandinista regime.

Commemorative stamps, on the other hand, are issued to celebrate a special time-sensitive event, frequently an anniversary of some historic or cultural landmark. Visits by heads of state and border disputes are examples of commemorative stamps with strong political iconic messages. Commemorative stamps are usually issued for short periods (as brief as the day of a special event), but more commonly are sold for several months and used until the supply runs out. They are generally larger in format and often are clearly aimed at international postal service as well as internal, as can be seen from the postal rates they carry. The commemorative stamp is usually of greater interest to the collector than the definitive stamp, and this has led to abuses where nations issue many large and colorful stamps whose iconic semiotic message bears little or no relationship to the country involved. One class of stamp collector is the "topical" philatelist, who collects only stamps of ships, flowers, butterflies, and so on, from whatever country issues the stamp, and these topical collectors are sometimes the victims of unscrupulous postal administrations that issue such stamps knowing full well that they will rarely, if ever, be used to carry the mail. A classical example here is the stamp of an Antarctic penguin issued by a tropical country (Nicaragua).

Stamps with a strong iconic content are also usually quite clear about the semiotic indexing function, since when these stamps travel abroad it is essential that the country of origin be unambiguously identified. They are also frequently symbolic when a national, monetary, or linguistic symbol is used as well. This combination of Peirce's three typological elements, plus an array of design limitations and features, makes the commemorative stamp a complex sign with several levels and affording several degrees of analysis. Because of the larger format of commemorative stamps with a strong iconic component, these are where we tend to find the greatest range of pictorial and graphic elements, to include scenes of battles or other important events, illustrations of a nation's major economic products (especially those that are exported), famous buildings, celebrated citizens, scenic terrain or landscapes, tourist attractions, sports triumphs, and important works of art. Many of these categories, as we shall see below, carry intentional messages of a political, propaganda, nationalistic, or cultural nature.

As an example of a commemorative stamp with a rich mixture of indexing, iconic, and symbolic elements, Scott describes the 1994 French stamp celebrating the opening of the Channel Tunnel to Great Britain.[12] The stamp, designed by the Englishman George Hardie, shows two icons (also national symbols): the British lion and the French rooster (*le coq gaulois*) reaching out from their shores over the Channel to touch claws (hands) while the rail tracks of the tunnel are shown uniting the two countries. The iconic element is strengthened by typography ("Tunnel sous la Manche"—"Tunnel under the Channel"), and the indexing element is explicitly confirmed by the French words "La poste." A parallel stamp (sold in a pair with the previous one) is by the French designer Jean-Paul Cousin, and shows the hands of Britannia and Marianne, wearing appropriate national rosettes as rings on their fingers, touching over the stylized icon of a train making the underwater run between the two countries.

The Peircian typology is completed with the symbol. For several European countries their long existence as nation-states, and their extensive empires, have allowed them to develop national symbols that are almost instantly recognized around the world. Such is the case of the British monarch (especially those with very long reigns such as Victoria and Elizabeth II) and the French Marianne (celebrated early on in the Eugène Delacroix painting *Liberty Leading the People* [1830], now in the Louvre). Supplementary national symbols would include the British lion, and flowers associated with the major national components of the United Kingdom. The French supplement Marianne as a national symbol with Ceres, the goddess of agriculture, and the *coq gaulois*. The Japanese use the chrysanthemum or the rising sun, while the Communist states associated with the former Soviet Union used a rich variety of national symbols derived from their common ideological roots (hammer and sickle, red star, head of Lenin, etc.).

A Peircian semiotic symbol can also take the form of linguistic expressions such as words, numbers, abbreviations, or acronyms. For many years Dutch definitive stamps were characterized by an austere simplicity in which the only elements on the stamps were the indexical name of their country, "Nederland" (also now a symbol because of linguistic considerations), a numerical symbol showing the denomination of the stamp, and some abstract calligraphic decorative elements. Scott notes the interesting case of Switzerland, which has four national languages (German, French, Italian, Romansch).[13] It would be impractical to use all four languages as the typographical indexing sign, so the Swiss use the Latin word *Helvetia* to identify their federation. "Helvetia," honoring the Helvetii who resisted Roman conquest, is also an icon, which in this case serves the Peircian function of symbol of nation. The Swiss also use distinctive landscapes, such as the Jungfrau, as national icons.

Postage stamp designers frequently resort to pleonasm, the use of redundancy or repetition to get their point across. Thus, the figure of Marianne on French stamps is sometimes reinforced by stripes of color across her face to represent the national three-colored flag. Flags themselves are frequently used as index, icon, and symbol, especially by newly independent nations breaking free from colonial empires, and also in the case where a flag is redesigned, such as the United States with the addition of new states, or the Canadian adoption of the maple leaf flag to replace the British Union Jack.[14]

When many of the old European colonies in Africa gained their independence in the 1960s, there was a concerted effort to replace the old colonial icons on postage stamps with new ones reflecting their independent identity. President Nkrumah of Ghana explained why: "Many of my people cannot read or write. When they buy stamps, they will see my picture—an African like themselves—and they will say, 'Aiee, look, here is my leader on the stamps. We are truly a free people!'"[15]

Semiotic analysis also is useful in identifying the economy (or scarcity) of symbols employed by some designers, especially in the definitive issues of stamps. Probably the most extreme case is a long series of standard British definitive stamps that have only two elements in addition to color variations: a portrait of the monarch and the abbreviated notation of the value, such as "1d." The icon of the monarch is also indexical, since the British assume, with considerable justification, that any educated and aware person would recognize it, and know it is British. In the case of Elizabeth II her face or profile has now become the most reproduced and recognized individual face ever printed, since it appears not only on British stamps, but also on those of British crown colonies (now reduced to a very few, including the Falkland Islands). The notation giving the denomination "1d" is a symbol that requires knowledge of what the letter "d" means (Latin *denarius*, penny), and an understanding of how the decimal system has replaced the old British coinage system consisting of pennies, shillings, and pounds.

To put the issue of economy another way, we can cite the concept of "semantic density" developed by Kristi S. Evans in her piece on the Polish underground movement Solidarity, in which she uses stamps to establish Solidarity's legitimacy and delegitimize the pro-Soviet Marxist regime.[16] Postage stamps are indeed "semantically dense" in that they accomplish multiple functions in an extremely small space. Because of the relatively heavy semiotic load they carry in a reduced area, they are among the densest and most semiotically economical of the many signs Peirce feels our universe is perfused with.

YES, BUT IS IT POPULAR CULTURE?

In the opening pages of this book I described postage stamps as the "smallest icons of popular culture." In so doing I wanted to introduce the argument that postage stamps, and specifically those of Latin America, should be considered legitimate objects of study subsumed under "popular culture." In this section we will consider the problem of defining popular culture, and the extent to which postage stamps should form part of that field of study.

Popular culture and its definitions

A major figure in Latin American cultural studies warns of the risks any scholar takes in making an academic approach to popular culture because "the field is regarded as an amorphous, ill-defined, and even dubious area by the academic establishment."[17] This attitude apparently stems from the rather arbitrary division of culture into three categories that (to some) possess sharply defined boundaries: folk, mass (or popular), and high. In this typology, folk culture is that created by lower-class artisans and craftspeople, while mass or popular culture is that favored and enjoyed by large segments of the population. This leaves "high" culture as the province of the elite and the corresponding highbrow intellectuals and curators of the treasures of literature, music, and art (among other fields). This arbitrary division has come under increasing criticism in recent years by those who argue that the boundaries are permeable and impossible to accurately define.[18] Furthermore, as Chandra Mukerji points out, a number of traditional academic disciplines and scholars and critics (especially in literature, art history, music history, and cultural studies) have been among the strongest defenders of the elitist approach, reserving for themselves the right to define taste and value.[19] A strict and narrow definition of popular culture would limit this category to culture created by and for the people, which would presumably include folk and possibly mass culture, but would exclude elite high culture. This narrow definition would also exclude postage stamps, since they are the creations of governments, not the masses.

The definition of popular culture I prefer to employ is that suggested by Jean Franco: that it should include all aspects of culture except those institutionalized as "high culture."[20] This would include folk culture, popular and mass culture, and related areas such as entertainment, the media, communications, and the "culture industry." This broad definition also can be extended to include a multitude of aspects of daily life among the general population, that is, the things that ordinary people do for pleasure and to enrich their existence. Popular culture becomes, then, a mirror by which societies can grasp and perceive the entertainment, pastimes, pleasures, and activities of everyday life, which collectively contribute to the national identity of a people.[21]

The extraordinary range of possible topics subsumed under this broad definition of popular culture can be seen from a list of chapter titles in the comprehensive three-volume *Handbook of American Popular Culture*: almanacs, jazz, leisure vehicles and the automobile, magazines, magic, newspapers, physical fitness, pornography, records, popular science, trains, advertising, bestsellers, the circus, death, comics, editorial cartoons, games and toys, the occult and supernatural, photography, religion, romantic fiction, gothic novels, verse, women, animation, children's literature, film, popular music, the pulps, radio, science fiction, television, and the western. We should also note that John Bryant's chapter in the third volume of this series deals with stamps and coins as objects of popular culture.[22]

A closely related field consists of the impulse to collect, organize, trade, and catalogue objects of popular culture, and the study of this activity has also been included in academic treatment of the broadly defined approach to popular culture. As one scholar has put it, "Collecting is a way of creating self-identity."[23] Obviously, stamps lend themselves to this collecting impulse, and as a result, philately will be considered in the sections that follow.[24]

But vehicles for presenting a particular vision of popular culture and national identity can be manipulated and controlled by ruling elites, populist leaders, or authoritarian governments. The political and propaganda functions of popular culture (and of postage stamps as one element of popular culture) thus merit our consideration as mechanisms for control and governance.

The study of Latin American popular culture

Within the field of Latin American studies, there is a parallel to Thomas Inge's pioneering *Handbook of American Popular Culture* and to the *Journal of Popular Culture*: the work of Harold E. Hinds and Charles M. Tatum, who in 1985 published the *Handbook of Latin American Popular Culture*. As the editors recognized, their effort was "a modest, yet sound beginning," in which ten chapters by different authors explored a number of areas of Latin American popular culture including music, sport, popular religion, comics, television, photo novels, film carnivals, cartoons, and newspapers. Postage stamps were not included. The editors noted that the scholarship on Latin American popular culture "is in its infancy," a situation they found unsurprising given that the field as a whole was relatively new.[25]

Hinds and Tatum were also the editors of the only specialized publication in this field, *Studies in Latin American Popular Culture*, which began publication in 1981. The journal has carried a few articles on postage stamps as elements of Latin American popular culture, most notably by David Bushnell.[26]

In that journal Hinds and Tatum noted, as several scholars had done previously, that no widely accepted definition of popular culture exists, although they tentatively advanced their own definition: "some aspect of culture which is accepted by or consumed by significant numbers of people. Acceptance or consumption may take the form of (1) widely held artifacts, symbols, beliefs and myths, or (2) direct participation as a viewer of, reader of, listener of, or some other sensory response to some aspect of popular culture." They go on to warn that the English term "popular culture" does not mean the same thing as its Spanish cognate, *cultura popular*, because the Spanish term is usually associated with folk art.[27]

Other scholarly sources of information on Latin American popular culture include the work of William Beezley, William Rowe, Néstor García Canclini, and Eva P. Bueno. Although he is primarily a journalist and cartoonist, Ríus (Eduardo del Río) should be included in this category because of his pioneering work on philately as a vehicle for popular culture.[28]

Postage stamps as objects of popular culture scholarship

Hopefully the broad definitions of popular culture explored above leave adequate room for a scholarly approach to the postage stamps of Latin America as subjects of the analysis undertaken in this work. With the exception of the aforementioned articles by Bushnell, and one by Frank Nuessel, there have been almost no scholarly publications on Latin American postage stamps as icons of popular culture.[29] Two such articles by the present author were published in 2005, and are in effect a forerunner of this book.[30]

In a sense the difficulty postage stamps experienced in achieving general acceptance as icons of popular culture parallels the experience of comics.

Comics for many years were seen as trivial elements in the popular culture scene, but in recent years have become legitimized. Comics, like postage stamps, can be (and have been) subjected to the theoretical framework of semioticians such as Peirce in this process.[31]

In his chapter in the *Handbook of American Popular Culture*, Bryant notes that philatelists (i.e., those who collect and study stamps from a technical perspective focusing on identifying, cataloguing, and pricing) have published a substantial body of literature, much of which rises to the standard of scholarly research. Bryant continues: "Yet the amount of material published by our universities' cultural historians on these subjects is minute."[32] Bryant goes on to note that "the scholar interested in postage stamps as art object, social icons, or historical evidence stands before a field virtually untouched by the cultural historian."[33] For a variety of reasons Bryant is not optimistic over the value of postage stamps to the cultural historian until a methodology of analysis is established. Hopefully the work of David Scott on European stamps, and this present work dealing with Latin American stamps, will move toward that goal.

STAMPS: THE POLITICS AND PROPAGANDA

The discussion in this section will be general, using examples from countries outside of Latin America, since the political and propaganda aspects of Latin American stamps will be more extensively addressed in chapters 2 and following. Politics and propaganda involved in postage stamps have been treated in a fragmentary manner in the literature, usually in the form of a brief article when a particularly compelling postage stamp catches the writer's eye. The most comprehensive treatment is a brief monograph by Carlos Stoetzer, which, although dated, contains much useful information. Stoetzer opens his treatise with these comments:

> The postage stamp and the postage cancellation constitute a comparatively new propaganda medium of which people are little aware. Today this medium is being used extensively. However, since propaganda on postage stamps is of a more subdued and discreet nature than that exhibited by other media, it has been given surprisingly little attention. Yet the fact that the postage stamp is widely circulated and that it does not have an obvious message enhances its peculiar effectiveness.
>
> The stamp itself is ideal propaganda. It goes from hand to hand and

> town to town; it reaches the farthest corners and provinces of a country and even the farthest countries of the world. It is a symbol of the nation from which the stamp is mailed, a vivid expression of that country's culture and civilization and of its ideas and ideals. By the use of symbols, slogans, pictures, even loaded words, it conveys its message far and wide.[34]

Stoetzer notes some of the elements that affect the efficiency of the propaganda on stamps.[35] The stamps must have wide circulation in the target country (be it the issuing nation, or a different one). The face value (denomination) should be carefully chosen in relation to current postage rates so as to make it more likely that it will be used on many letters. The temptation to add a special surcharge for fund-raising purposes should be resisted, as should the tendency to put out too many stamps. Finally, the designs should be attractive and appealing, with due attention to design features. Although Stoetzer did not use Peircian language, it is clear he is addressing the interrelationship between the various aesthetic and functional characteristics associated with Peirce's typology of index, icon, and symbol.

In a study that applies psychological concepts to the propaganda use of postage stamps, Harlan J. Strauss argues that they work at the subliminal level, with reinforcement each time the stamp is encountered. He believes that postage stamps are a particularly efficient form of psychological propaganda because they are unitary (i.e., they operate in a single medium—the visual). He concludes by presenting a set of twenty-seven working hypotheses that could be subjected to testing.[36]

Civil wars and interstate conflicts frequently produce significant numbers of postage stamps with political and propaganda messages. In the Spanish Civil War (1936–1939), for example, both sides resorted to the use of slogans and national icons on postage stamps to support their cause. In its appeal to supporters in the United States the Republican side used a stamp linking the U.S. Statue of Liberty to the Republican cause by surrounding the statue with flags of the United States and Republican Spain. The Nationalist side countered with stamps featuring historical icons of Spain's glorious past ranging from El Cid (the hero of the reconquest of Spain from the Moors) to King Ferdinand and Queen Isabella I.[37] After the Nationalist victory the face of Francisco Franco dominated Spanish postage stamps for decades. In a related episode, the Franco regime refused to accept mail from Czechoslovakia carrying a stamp showing Pablo Picasso's *Guernica*, which depicted the bombing of a Republican town in northern Spain by German aviators on Franco's side during the civil war.

Totalitarian and authoritarian states are especially attracted to the use of postage stamps for political and propaganda purposes. A basic feature of fascism is the cult of the leader, and thus it is no surprise that Adolf Hitler's portrait dominated the stamps of Nazi Germany.[38] A similar phenomenon occurred in Mussolini's Italy, although the Italians also made heavy use of fascist symbols and the icons of Italy's past. The Soviet Union, and its associated satellites, can be counted among the nations with the largest number of individual stamp issues—many of which carry heavy political overtones[39]—to include portraits of famous citizens, calls for world peace, and the successes of the various five-year plans. As we shall see in chapter 5, a design team from Italy had considerable influence on the stamps of Perón's Argentina in the 1940s and 1950s.

The value of postage stamps and postal systems for propaganda purposes was not lost on the Allies in World War II. The U.S. Office of Strategic Services (OSS—precursor to the CIA) in 1944 produced large quantities of fake German stamps bearing the effigy of Hitler and used them on letters containing anti-Nazi propaganda mailed to some fifty thousand legitimate addresses in Germany.[40] A similar effort was made by the Allies in Italy, using a parody of the World War II Hitler-Mussolini stamps that had been issued simultaneously in Berlin and Rome.[41] One category of postage stamp propaganda used in World War II consisted of imitating (but changing) German stamps in ways that attacked the Nazi regime or Hitler personally. In the best-known of these, the OSS created a mock stamp similar to the Hitler six-pfennig and twelve-pfennig stamps, but with Hitler's head distorted and morphed to show a death's head skull (figure 1.5, not catalogued by Scott). The words "Deutsches Reich" (German Empire) on the legitimate stamp was changed to "Futsches Reich" (lost or broken empire).[42] The Germans retaliated, modifying standard British stamps showing King George VI in a variety of ways: inserting a small star of David to replace the Christian cross on the British crown; and replacing the "d" for pence with a hammer and sickle. A more blatant variant replaced the queen with the face of Stalin next to King George VI, with the legend "This war is a Jewish war."

It would be an error to assume that only nation-states issue postage stamps. We have many examples of guerrilla movements or governments in exile issuing postage stamps with a heavy political component. Since the issuing of a postage stamp is generally considered an attribute of a sovereign nation-state, a separatist or guerrilla movement can attempt to portray itself as such by issuing stamps. Where the movement controls territory it can claim that it has a legitimate right to issue postage stamps for use in areas under its control. Such was the case of the Vietcong National Front for the Liberation of South Vietnam, and the breakaway Indonesian province of the South Moluccas in 1951.[43] During the Central American conflict of the 1980s the American cartoonist Garry B. Trudeau used his *Doonesbury* strip to humorously criticize the Reagan administration's support of the contras in their struggle against the Marxist Sandinista regime in Nicaragua. In an August 1986 strip a CIA representative engages a contra leader and urges him to have his troops leave their Honduras base camps, cross the border into Nicaragua, and declare a provisional government, saying: "Then we can recognize you, and support you with troops if necessary. But first you folks have to start acting like a serious, legitimate government." When the contra leader asks for suggestions on how to do it, the CIA agent replies, "Hell, I don't know. Issue a stamp. Enter the Olympics."[44]

Linguistic politics

I noted previously that in terms of Peircian semiotics the use of the printed word on a stamp can be an index (identifying the country) or a linguistic symbol. This can pose a political problem in nations where two or more languages compete or are in use. Canadian stamps, for example, must carry the indexing and explanatory typography in both English and French.

The problem of postal linguistics is especially sensitive in Spain, where there have been historic tensions between the dominant Castilian (Spanish) language, and the main languages of several areas, some with strong separatist movements such as Catalonia and the Basque Provinces. During the Spanish Civil War most of the municipalities in the Catalonia region (including the major city of Barcelona) issued local stamps using the Catalan language. The Nationalist Franco regime moved firmly to repress the Catalan separatist movement, to include prohibiting the use of the Catalan language in official documents, street signs, and advertisements. The use of any words in Catalan, Basque, or Galician was strictly avoided on postage stamps until recent years, when these regions have been granted a somewhat greater degree of autonomy. In 2000 several regional parliaments (including that of Catalonia) passed bills supporting multilingualism on Spanish stamps, and an Organization for Multilingualism was formed to support this initiative, among other projects that would recognize several languages other than Castilian as official languages of Spain.[45] The organization noted that some eighty nations have issued stamps in more than one language, and that some seventy entities below the level of nation-states have postal autonomy, which allows them to issue their own stamps and choose designs as well as languages.

The cold war's postal politics

The cold war provides many examples of the propaganda and political use of postage stamps on both sides. I noted previously the heavy use of political themes among the stamps of the Soviet Union and its allies. These were sometimes blatant paeans to the glories of the socialist world and ideology, and sometimes more subtle celebrations of the achievements of the Soviet Union in space. Every major accomplishment by Soviet astronauts was celebrated not only on Soviet stamps, but also on those of most of the Soviet bloc nations.[46]

The United States was not unaware of the value of the postage stamp in cold war politics. A 1957 meeting between representatives of the U.S. Information Agency and the U.S. Post Office explored ways in which the messages of the U.S. side of the cold war could be more effectively conveyed to other nations. In the words of Postmaster General Arthur Summerfield, "Postage stamps reach many persons cut off from the normal free press to which we are accustomed, and many other millions who seldom read newspapers and periodicals, or listen to the radio, even if they are available. But the remote receiver of a letter looks at the foreign stamp and studies it."[47] The vehicle chosen as a result of this meeting was the extensive "champion of liberty" series from 1957 to 1961, which featured the portraits of individuals who, in the judgment of the U.S. government, had upheld the ideals of freedom and democracy. The first individual so honored was Philippine president Ramon Magsaysay, who had put down a Communist rebel movement after World War II, and had just died in an airplane crash. Latin American "champions of liberty" included liberators José de San Martín and Simón Bolívar; no contemporary figures were selected. A more direct use of a U.S. postage stamp in the cold war was the 1952 NATO stamp, which was kept in circulation for an extended period of time, and issued in very large quantities as a vehicle for consolidating the rather weak public support for the alliance.[48] Not surprisingly, many pieces of mail carrying these politically influenced stamps were rejected outside the United States, and it seems doubtful that many reached individuals in Soviet bloc states as predicted by Postmaster General Summerfield.

The Hitler falsifications of World War II had a cold war parallel when the CIA prepared stamps to be infiltrated into East Germany with the "Deutsche Demokratische Republik" legend replaced by "Undeutsche Undemokratische Diktatur" (a dictatorship that is neither democratic nor German).[49] The use of postage stamps for propaganda purposes on both sides was supplemented by the use of propaganda cancellations and rubber-stamped slogans on the front or back of the envelope. The themes on such envelopes coming out of the Soviet bloc ranged from banning nuclear weapons to attacking the U.N./U.S. actions in the Korean War. Western nations used similar cancellations, but many of these were rejected or destroyed before the recipient had a chance to see them.[50]

Some of the most virulent postal propaganda was produced by nations (or subnational liberation movements) engaged in conflicts with the United States, especially Vietnam, the associated Vietcong National Liberation Movement, and North Korea. A conference of anti-imperialist journalists meeting in Pyongyang was commemorated in a stamp portraying an evil-looking Richard Nixon being stabbed with pens.[51] The North Vietnamese regularly issued stamps noting the downing of U.S. aircraft, and one especially effective stamp showed a diminutive Vietnamese soldier (equipped with a rifle) escorting a large and disheveled captured U.S. airman with downcast face and a demeanor of defeat.

Postal politics in the Middle and Far East

The volatile political situation in the Middle East (and its repercussions in the United States) has a postal aspect. As might be expected, the level of intensity and emotion is high. Here is an illustrative preface to a work from the Israeli side: "Arab and Moslem propaganda against Israel had made use of stamps for almost half a century. From 1945 on, with no sign that recent developments are about to change this practice, historical dates and events, wars and battles, killings and uprisings have all become subjects for a long smear and hate campaign directed at the Jewish State by Arab and pro-Arab regimes and organizations."[52]

One philatelic aspect of this conflict has been the use of postage stamps to support the existence and identity of a Palestinian state. In 1998 the authoritative Scott Publishing Company's catalogue listed Palestinian Authority stamps for the first time, thus elevating that entity from the status of an unrecognized group printing local stamp "labels" (also called cinderellas) to a legitimate stamp-issuing entity.[53] One factor in this decision is that Palestinian Authority stamps did indeed carry the mails to and through Arab states such as Egypt and Jordan, and thus met the criteria for recognition. Other recent postage issues with political implications include Israel's stamp honoring the late King Hussein of Jordan (judged to be the most respected Arab leader in Israeli public opinion), and Jordan's 2001 issuing of a stamp honoring the "boy-martyr" Mohammad al-Durra, who was killed by Israeli rifle fire while being held in the arms of his father, trapped in a street fight in the Gaza Strip.[54]

Iraq under Saddam Hussein issued numerous stamps portraying him variously as a military leader in uniform, a father figure caressing children, a pious Muslim on pilgrimage, a shovel-carrying reconstructor of cities destroyed during the war with Iran, and a traditional Arab leader in kufiyya headdress. One macabre stamp shows an animal claw adorned with the Iranian flag holding the bloody detached head of an Iraqi child killed during an Iranian missile attack.

In the Far East a seemingly innocuous set of South Korean stamps showing the flora and fauna of the disputed Tokdo islands raised tensions with Japan, which claims them. The islands, located halfway between Japan and South Korea, were under Japanese control when it colonized the Korean Peninsula from 1910 until the end of World War II. After 1945 ownership has been disputed by both countries, although they are uninhabited except for small South Korean military patrols. The Japanese vigorously protested the issuing of the stamps, and in Korea this produced a backlash, demonstrations, and a strong demand for the stamps, whose stock of over two million sold out in a few hours. In a rare moment of agreement, North Korea supported Seoul in the dispute against the Japanese.[55]

On the domestic U.S. philatelic front, a U.S. stamp honoring the Muslim holiday of Eid became the center of controversy shortly after the 11 September 2001 attacks. The stamp was the result of many years of lobbying by Muslim groups in the United States, and was issued a scant ten days before the 9/11 tragedy. *Mekeel's*, one of the leading stamp journals in the United States, printed editorials calling for the withdrawal of the stamp and urged American Muslims to use the "United We Stand" U.S. flag stamp commemorating 9/11 firefighters in its place. A conservative policy group, the Free Congress Foundation, called on Republican congressional leaders to reject the stamp. The White House resisted these requests, and a year later ordered the reissuing of the stamp in time for the 2002 Eid festival, as a parallel to stamps celebrating the holidays of Christmas, Hanukkah, and Kwanzaa.[56] To underscore the politics of the issue, the White House placed the stamp on its Web site shortly after President George W. Bush visited the mosque of the Islamic Center of Washington.

The stamp selection process in the United States

The Eid stamp drew attention to the process by which the U.S. Postal Service (USPS) selects themes for its stamps. The matter is not trivial, since the USPS sells about $160 million dollars' worth of mint (unused) stamps to collectors in a typical year.[57] When they form part of a personal collection they represent simple profit for the USPS, since they are not used to carry the mails. Further, if we accept the premise that postage stamps carry a political message and contribute to national identity as an element of popular culture, then what a nation puts on its postage stamps tells us something about that country. The U.S. selection process is centered on the Citizens' Stamp Advisory Committee, which receives suggestions for stamp themes from the public and various organizations that seek to have their particular icon illustrated on a stamp. The committee was established in the 1950s to put some distance (and political breathing room) between the postmaster general and the individuals requesting themes on stamps. The twelve members of the committee work in secrecy, and select about two dozen themes to be recommended to the postmaster general from the approximately thirty thousand suggestions it receives each year. Presidents and the Congress have over the years attempted to influence the process in favor of their own pet themes, but the committee is remarkably independent and fairly successful in having its recommendations accepted by the USPS. Among the more controversial stamps the committee debated were ones honoring Elvis Presley (the controversy was whether he should be portrayed in his youthful prime or his declining years), and an "end of World War II" stamp that showed the mushroom-shaped cloud of a nuclear explosion, denounced as insensitive in light of the many thousands who died in the bombing of Hiroshima and Nagasaki.[58]

Lobbying for a postage stamp can take many and bizarre forms. The most common method is the straightforward submitting of suggestions to the committee. But these are often accompanied by endorsements from the submitters' representative, or from administration officials. There are few ground rules. One prohibits the placing of an identifiable person on a stamp until ten years after that person's death. An exception is made for former presidents (one year). The ten-year rule caused some difficulties with the "United We Stand" stamp honoring the New York firefighters and rescue personnel who raised the American flag shortly after the World Trade Center towers came down. Although their identity was known, and the stamp was based on a photograph, it was ruled that they were being honored as representatives of their profession, and not as individuals. One example of unorthodox lobbying was the attempt by Mort Walker to get a stamp honoring the one-hundredth anniversary of the newspaper comic strip. He asked his fellow cartoonists to call for this stamp in their regular cartoons for 5 April 1993, and many did.[59]

The most distinguished member of the citizens' committee was the renowned Pulitzer-winning author James Michener, who served from 1979 to 1986, and devotes seven pages of his 1992 autobiography to that experience. He notes: "If this sounds like a fairly routine or even dull task, one should listen in on the quarterly meetings of that group. Few of the collateral operations of the government are more fraught with emotion, logrolling, pressure and even anger than this matter of what agencies and individuals should be honored on our postage stamps. By this device the popular heroes of the republic are identified and in a sense sanctified, so the competition is intense."

Michener goes on to describe the intense lobbying for an Elvis stamp immediately after his death, with appeals to waive the ten-year rule on the grounds that Elvis was more important than a president. Michener reveals the kind of political pressure put on the committee when he quotes the chairman at a key meeting as stating: "El Supremo insists that a stamp be issued honoring a Hispanic, any Hispanic, and it is to be on sale by August fifteenth. The national election will be held, as you know, in November."[60]

As noted in the introduction, a recent controversy involving a U.S. postage stamp surrounds the honoring of the Mexican painter Frida Kahlo. This was to be a joint issue (Mexican and U.S.), with the same self-portrait of Kahlo on each of the two stamps. It was timed to coincide with the June 2001 opening of an exhibit of her work at the Phoenix Art Museum, and the event was intended as a recognition of the importance of the U.S. Hispanic community, as well as a gesture of Mexican-U.S. friendship, since Kahlo had done some of her work in the United States while accompanying her husband Diego Rivera. This was also to be the first time a Hispanic woman (other than Queen Isabella) would be so honored on a U.S. stamp. It did not take long for the protests to be heard, mainly on the usually reserved pages of stamp journals such as *Linn's*. She was declared an unfit subject for a U.S. stamp, and denounced as a Communist, a drug addict, and a bisexual. Senator Jesse Helms criticized the stamp on the floor of the Senate, and the *Wall Street Journal* weighed in against the stamp in an essay titled "The Stalinist and the Stamp: The Wonders of Postal Diversity."[61] One irate collector, upon receiving a letter with the Kahlo stamp, drew a large X across her face and wrote on the envelope: "Return to sender. Contains politically offensive material." His letter carrier, acting either out of political ideology or bureaucratic caution, told the recipient that he could not return the letter on those grounds because it was a legitimate postage stamp. The recipient ended up placing the offending letter in another envelope and spending thirty-four cents to return the letter. One sarcastic critic of what he saw as excessive political correctness quoted Vladimir Lenin ("A postage stamp is a business card of the country"), adding "So the Frida Kahlo stamp is a business card of the United States. Why not Vladimir Lenin or, even better, Joseph Stalin on a U.S. stamp? It would be a great diversity achievement."[62]

EDUCATIONAL CONSIDERATIONS

From the earliest days of philately, which began shortly after the British started issuing the first stamps in 1840, educators and various government officials have noted the possible use of postage stamps as an educational tool, especially among younger children. Professional educators have observed that there seems to be a natural tendency among children in approximately the six-to-ten age group to collect and organize things (shells, baseball cards, rocks, stamps). Why not use this tendency, some have asked, to reinforce class work in relevant fields such as history, geography, culture, art, literature, and foreign languages?[63]

The international political implications of this educational aspect of postage stamps were made evident in the 1940s when it was consciously linked to U.S. policy toward Latin America and the activities of the Pan American Union (now the Organization of American States). The Pan American Union established a Latin American Stamp Section under the energetic direction of Albert Kunze, who wrote numerous articles on the value of stamps in building hemispheric goodwill, and visited many schools in the United States to promote interest in Latin America through its postage stamps.[64]

Nelson Rockefeller, the coordinator for inter-American affairs in the period, was a strong advocate of using cultural contacts in support of U.S. policy goals in Latin America, and had his office send articles on postage stamps of the Western Hemisphere to newspapers in the United States and Latin America.[65]

More recently, the American Philatelic Society (the largest U.S. organization devoted to stamp collecting) has begun an initiative aimed at using stamps as teaching aids in grade school. Although the APS is motivated at least in part by a concern over declining membership and a sense that the number of stamp collectors in the United States is diminishing,[66] this initiative is based on the same perception that children have a collecting instinct, and that this instinct can have pedagogical applications using stamps as visual reinforcement for concepts in a variety of fields. A number of foreign language teachers were especially interested in using postage stamps in their classrooms, arguing that the teaching of a language cannot be isolated from the culture in which it resides, and that the postage stamp could be a valuable icon of that culture.[67] These proponents of the educational value of postage stamps stressed the visual reinforcement that stamps from foreign countries provide, especially in the fields of history, geography, cartography, art, and literature. The foreign languages used on stamps, although present in only brief phrases, were seen as useful in showing the value of learning a foreign language.

In several Latin American nations (Argentina, Colombia, Uruguay) the centralized ministries of education, working with their colleagues in the ministries of communications, and with various philatelic organizations, have gone beyond the simple use of stamps as illustrations to set up proposed model curricula on philately to be incorporated in the school system. Although it does not appear that any of these have resulted in substantial mandatory changes to curricula, they indicate a strong interest in the educational value of postage stamps.[68]

One issue that emerges when educators make copies of postage stamps for educational purposes, or for publications, is copyright. Postage stamps should be in the public domain since they are government documents. But as with coins and paper money, there is understandable government concern over counterfeiting, and as a result statutes have been published governing the reproduction of postage stamps under U.S. law.[69] These laws are especially strict regarding any reproduction and duplication of U.S. stamp designs for another reason: the U.S. Postal Service produces a variety of commercial products (key chains, mugs, T-shirts, etc.) using the images found on American postage stamps, and to protect the sale of these items the Postal Service has copyrighted these images. Any individual or organization wishing to use these images may negotiate licensing fees with the Postal Service for this purpose. These copyright restrictions date from the creation of the U.S. Postal Service as a semiautonomous government agency in 1978; earlier postage stamps may be reproduced for educational purposes. U.S. statutes governing foreign stamps are less rigid, and permit exact-size illustrations. Uncanceled stamps may not be reproduced in the exact size of the original; as discussed below, this restriction now becomes rather meaningless, given the ease with which digitized images can be enlarged or shrunk. This reality is evidenced in the 2006 CD-ROM edition of the standard *Scott* stamp catalogue, which previously was published only in paper form. The digitized CD-ROM images are presented in reduced form using PDF software, but come with instructions on how to enlarge and print them up to a 600 percent increase, including the 100 percent size previously restricted by U.S. statutes.

Another legal consideration concerns the embargo established by the United States against the importing of postage stamps from certain countries. These restrictions form part of general embargoes of merchandise and goods from the countries specified, and despite legal challenges, have remained in effect and have blocked philatelic access to material from these countries. Several stamp catalogues carry illustrations of these stamps, but note that their importation is illegal, and do not cite prices for the stamps. The date of the embargo legislation is significant because stamps issued prior to that date can be imported. Possession of stamps actually used on mail entering the United States from these countries is legal.[70] The countries involved at one time or another are North Korea, North Vietnam, Cambodia, Libya, South Africa, Iran, Cuba, and Nicaragua. Several of these embargoes are no longer in effect (Vietnam, Cambodia, South Africa, Nicaragua). The Cuban embargo was recently loosened to permit the importation and sale of canceled stamps, an event that was seized upon by major stamp outlets to promote them. The availability of large numbers of stamps coming from Cuba, and the pro-revolution themes they carry, make them more than a little suspect, as they provide pure profits in hard currency to the Castro regime, as well as deliver a propaganda message.

In our present digitized age the reproduction of postage stamp images for educational purposes has become far easier than in the past, when it was necessary to make individual photographic images and wait for these images to be developed and returned. With a computer and a scanner it is now possible to make images in a few seconds, and (using a program such as Photoshop) manipulate these images so as to enlarge, shrink, enhance, and cut-and-paste portions of any stamp within the legal provisions stated above. These images can then be inserted into presentation software such as PowerPoint, and used for class lectures and student presentations. As indicated in the introduction, one of the by-products of this current project is a set of assembled, indexed, and organized images that can be used by teachers and students of Latin America to illustrate the instructors' lectures or the students' class presentations and written projects. A supplementary CD-ROM available from the author provides these stamp images along with written material explaining the images used and providing historical and cultural background. Postage stamps selected and presented this way can also be of value to serious academic researchers of the history, geography, economy, politics, and culture of individual countries or regions of the world, both as primary sources (since they are government documents) and as illustrations of a variety of topics to be used in papers, presentations, and monographs.[71]

STAMPS: AESTHETIC AND DESIGN FEATURES

The first and most obvious challenge and physical limitation facing the stamp designer is size. In what may be as little as a one-inch square the designer must comply with the requirements imposed by the Universal Postal Union concerning the indexing semiotic function of identifying the country, specifying the face monetary value of the stamp, and incorporating whatever iconic or symbolic elements are desired and permitted. It also goes without saying that the stamp must be identifiable as a stamp. While the conventions of size and perforations usually accomplish this without any special effort, some stamp issues are so unconventional (odd shapes, colors, and sizes) that this aspect must be attended to with some care.

To make a strong and effective visual statement in this small two-dimensional area the designer uses contrast and color, typography, and symbols to deliver an effective visual message. As Barbara Anderson notes, "Criteria for successful stamp design include ease of production, and ability to survive the mail stream, effectiveness of symbols, visual impact, communication of purpose, appropriateness and the ability to be reduced in dimension and still retain visual clarity. This is a particular challenge to many artists who are used to working larger."[72]

The stamp as art form

Many philatelic writers argue that the postage stamp, properly designed and produced, is an art form in its own right, a sort of miniature version of poster art, with an added set of challenges imposed by the limitations identified above. Several monographs and coffee table books have been produced that attempt to make that case, including what their authors consider masterpieces of the stamp designers' skills.[73] The reward for the designer is the knowledge that the postage stamp may well be the only form of official state art seen (and experienced, through licking and affixing on an envelope) by the average citizen.

Most stamp art is representational, that is, it presents a fairly realistic rendering of the person or object at hand. However, abstract art is also possible, and the use of symbols can take the design in other directions. While there are many mediocre stamp designs,[74] and others are simply formulaic, a good design must rise above these limitations and convey (in addition to all the required elements) the idea that carries the political or cultural message intended by the postal administration involved. David Lidman notes that to the uninitiated observer most nineteenth-century stamps seem to be standardized portrait galleries of monarchs and other chiefs of state.[75] But many of these early stamps, commonly called classic issues, have an aesthetic of their own: they are mainly engraved stamps, and this engraving process was done by hand by skilled craftsmen working with sharp instruments and soft steel to give the raised and seemingly three-dimensional appearance that is the chief feature of these stamps.

The argument that stamps can be art forms is enhanced by a prestigious award given each year by an Italian philatelic association (the Asiago Trophy, named for a popular tourist resort) for the world's most beautiful stamp. The 2001 winner was a stunning British stamp celebrating the centennial of the Nobel Peace Prize.[76] The design was unusual in that it was embossed and thus slightly three-dimensional. The indexing function, as is true for all British stamps, is accomplished by a small silhouette of the monarch (in this case, Queen Elizabeth) in the upper left-hand corner, and the basic idea of the Nobel Peace Prize is conveyed by the Peircian symbolic white dove dominating the central portion of the stamp. The white dove is placed against a white background, and the only color in the stamp is the green olive branch in its beak.

Established artists have sometimes created their own postage stamps (not intended to actually carry the mail) as an art form, and this phenomenon also supports the contention that postage stamps can be art. The best-known of these artists is the American Donald Evans (1945–1977), who created an opus of about four thousand stamps for his forty-two imaginary countries. As might be expected, Evans was a stamp collector as a boy, and his fascination with the world opened up to him through stamps as a pre-adolescent carried over into his adult profession as a commercial and gallery painter. His medium is watercolor, which he used with an extremely fine brush to paint his stamps at life size. He also created realistic stamp catalogues, which included identification numbers, background information on the imaginary country, the color scheme, the date of issue, and the subject. He created perforations for the stamp using the period key of his manual typewriter, and on more than one occasion used his imaginary stamps to illustrate school reports, providing another example of the use of stamps, albeit imaginary ones, for educational purposes. He also received occasional special commissions, such as the ones for the *New York Times* to illustrate topics as diverse as Watergate, the cold war, and the B-1 bomber. He arranged his stamps on black backgrounds to simulate philatelic stock pages, and was able to sell a piece with ten or fewer stamps for six hundred dollars, and one with more than twenty for a thousand dollars.[77] His creations included a series showing a falcon in flight for the mythical Middle East nation of Adjudani; indigenous inhabitants for the French colony of Amis and Amants ("Friends and Lovers") and the South American *guayana* colony of Katibo; stamps with fingers making sign language numbers for the "Islands of the Deaf"; fifteen species of penguins and other animals for the country of "Fauna and Flora"; and surcharged overprints ("Zone Antipaste") during the military occupation of the Kingdom of Mangiare. His Latin American efforts included stamps for the Central American nation of Banana, which he created after he learned of the so-called 1975 Bananagate scandal involving the United Fruit Company in Honduras. Evans's "República de Banana" had its capital in Chiquita (named after the United Fruit Company's Chiquita Banana symbol), and icons of the nation's culture included the Santa Banana cathedral, the Casino Banana d'Oro, and the national lighter-than-air zeppelin "La Banana Grande." His stamps for the República de Banana included a tall palm tree, a scorpion, a shrimp (there is good fishing on the coast), a highly polished military boot from the Presidential Guard Unit, and of course the national icon: a banana.[78]

A somewhat similar, but more modest and irreverent effort at creating imaginary stamps was that undertaken by Bruce McCall, who has done much work for the *National Lampoon*, *Esquire*, and *Playboy*. In a 1982 collection of his work he includes "My Own Stamp Album," with space for categories such as "The Blessings of American Life" (including stamps celebrating heated shaving cream, a cheese-flavored dog food, feminine hygiene sprays, and static-free socks), and stamps from "Backward Nations," "Somnolent Nations," Great Britain ("Rather Decent Occasions Issue"), and "Nations in Transition."[79] In the latter category we find two stamps from the Republic of Sudan, the first dated June 1970 showing scenes of its revolution, and the second showing similar scenes of the counterrevolution dated a month later. The scenes of the counterrevolution include the tank and aircraft of the revolution's stamp, but now destroyed. The Latin American entry is in a similar vein: it shows a stamp of the Bolivian takeover by the fictitious General Varga y Vargas Varga, but the stamp is unfinished because the general was overthrown before the stamp could be completed.

Stamp art, like any art, can also fail the aesthetic test and be ugly, garish, or crudely produced. Some U.S. stamps have been placed in this category, and unfortunately, as we shall see in subsequent chapters, so have a number of Latin American stamps. To cite an example, a 1968 Guatemalan stamp honoring Eleanor Roosevelt was printed but initially withheld from the general public because it was considered too unflattering to the former first lady.[80] In contrast, some recent Brazilian philatelic art ranks among the best in the world with its unconventional designs, humor, and cartoon-like figures such as the seemingly nude muscular soccer player kicking the sun instead of a ball.

An examination of the "stamps as art" books mentioned previously (as well as David Scott's pioneering study) suggests that some of the most aesthetically pleasing and effective stamps are those produced by the European nations that have been in the stamp business the longest, and which devote considerable resources to producing work of high quality: Great Britain, France, Holland, and Switzerland. For those European nations that once had large and far-reaching empires, the range of themes involving history and exotic flora and fauna is exceptional. The two case studies we shall consider in chapters 6 and 7 (on Falklands/Malvinas and Antarctica) are classical examples, with the added irony that the human population of these two entities is minuscule.

Design approaches

As Scott explains, stamp design can involve a number of techniques that might not be appreciated by the casual observer.[81] A basic one is the search for a national icon that performs the semiotic indexing function efficiently and aesthetically. The best examples here are the reigning monarch in Britain, and Marianne in France. Few other nations have had the success of these two countries in defining their nation in so simple a manner. Another indexical technique is pleonasm, which is the repetition or redundancy of the index. Scott gives the example of a French definitive stamp in which France is identified by typography (the name of the country), a national symbol (Marianne), and the three colors of the French flag that appear on Marianne's face.[82] Icons and symbols here have become indices as well.

Other design approaches could involve metonymies in which a part of something is presented to represent the whole. A quarter-circle fragment of the wheel of a bicycle stands for the whole cycle, and subsequently for the Olympic sport identified on the stamp. Collages and patterns (abstract or representational) can be joined together for striking effects.

For many years stamp design in the Western Hemisphere was dominated by the production of a small number of banknote houses in the United States. This tended to give stamps of a number of the smaller countries (especially in Central America) a certain uniformity of appearance, with many of the same decorative elements appearing on stamps of different countries. The notorious Seebeck issues (to be explored in the next chapter) exhibit this characteristic. To save time and money some of these printing houses copied designs and portraits from existing ones; the Brazilian government was not pleased with a commemorative Brazilian stamp in which King João III of Portugal bore a very close resemblance to King Henry VII of England.[83]

Art on stamps

A nation's art treasures are a rich lode of visual materials for stamp design.[84] Here the challenge is to be able to print the image in a way that does not distort the original artist's intent. Metonymy is frequently used, whereby a fragment of a major painting is placed on the stamp with the assumption that the receiving public is familiar enough with the original painting to recognize it. This approach is especially important when working with murals, since the sheer expanse and multiplicity of themes on most murals could not possibly be placed on the small surface area of the stamp. Mexican stamps frequently take this approach using the murals of masters such as Diego Rivera. Another approach is to produce a series of stamps, either as a strip or a block, which then covers a greater area of the mural or original painting.

If one examines the collective body of paintings on the numerous art stamps issued over the years, one gets a fairly comprehensive encyclopedia of art, especially for the European nations that have attempted to put their major artworks on stamps. In the Latin American case, Mexico, Argentina, and Cuba are the leaders in this process. The use of artworks on postage stamps can sometimes create problems. The classic example here is Francisco Goya's *The Naked Maja*, issued by Spain in 1930, along with his *Clothed Maja*. Loud protests were heard complaining that the "naked" stamp would corrupt innocent children who collected stamps. In the United States a related controversy arose in 1959 when United Artists used a reproduction of *The Naked Maja* to advertise a film about Goya. The New York Post Office objected to the visual, prompting the American Civil Liberties Union to challenge the objection, arguing that the image had received wide distribution in the past, including the Spanish 1930 stamp. The Post Office's objection was withdrawn.[85]

Imaginary stamps ("cinderellas")

There is a category of what appear to be stamps, but which are "imaginary" in the sense that they are not really postage stamps although they look like them. Such items, called labels or cinderellas by philatelists, appear to be stamps because they are about the same size, have perforations and gum on the back, and have some of the semiotic elements (index, icon, and symbol) of legitimate postage stamps. Cinderellas differ from the "art stamps" category in that their main purpose is not aesthetic, but rather the support of some cause or agenda, be it political, ideological, ecological, or economic (fund-raising or personal profit). They can also be simply an attempt to provide illustrations or visuals in a humorous, new, or novel format.

As an example, Emmis Books, a small Cincinnati publisher with several titles, provides a sheet of "stamps" with each of its books. These stamps include a set of caricatures relevant to the book, mounted on a perforated and gummed insert at the end of the text.

As noted previously, stamps are sometimes issued by nonstate entities, such as guerrilla or separatist movements, which use the image of a quasi postage stamp to gain political legitimacy. For example, the Mexican Ejército Zapatista de Liberación Nacional (EZLN, Zapatista Army of National Liberation) produced a "stamp" showing a 1977 painting of Subcomandante Marcos by Gerardo Yépez; the sheet of thirty-six stamps sold for fifty dollars on the Internet.[86] But other such labels or cinderellas are produced by designers with a genuine claim to be artists, such as Garry Trudeau, creator of the *Doonesbury* comic strip. In 1990 Trudeau published a *Doonesbury Stamp Album*, with more than 150 labels of this kind. Some of them featured characters from the comic strip, but others poked fun at politicians (George H. W. Bush, Dan Quayle), other well-known figures in American life (Donald Trump), or fictitious characters linked to real organizations. The most famous of these characters is Duke the CIA agent, who in other incarnations becomes President Duke of the Baby Doc Medical School in Haiti, captain of the ship *Rusty Nail* on a cruise to see the fighting in the 1982 Malvinas/Falklands War, and the American neocolonial proconsul in Panama, and later in Iraq. While it is not illegal to produce, publish, and sell such quasi-philatelic items, using them to avoid postage is a violation of U.S. law, and some labels apparently have been used this way, slipping past the detection mechanisms used by the USPS.[87]

More outrageous, mischievous, and frequently charming, is the work of Michael Hernandez de Luna and Michael Thompson, Chicago artists who produce stamp art that is iconoclastic, witty, and sometimes verging on the obscene and scatological.[88] They also have systematically sent envelopes carrying these stamps through United States and international mail, thus violating numerous statutes and laws. They own a small publishing house whose suggestive name provides a clue as to their approach: Bad Press Books. The press has published a coffee table book of their stamp art, ranging from the politically satirical to the frankly obscene. Examples of political themes relevant to Latin America include Nazi symbols on a Uruguayan stamp labeled "Zona Militar"; an Ecuadorian stamp labeled "Justicia," showing two uniformed men beheading a prisoner; Mexican military officers portrayed as skeletons; a British two-pound stamp showing General Augusto Pinochet ("Au guest Pinochet") of Chile raising his middle finger over the caption "British Hospitality" (figure 1.7); a pro-marijuana stamp mailed from the Brazilian Ministry of Agriculture; and a Mexican stamp portraying President Johnson over the legend "El B.J." Pushing the envelope are Monica Lewinsky's blue dress with a white stain on the shoulder; a sequence showing how to put on a condom; "eat whale meat"; "hunt deer"; the naked Maja lying on Napoleon's tomb; Mary Magdalene and Jesus Christ in a sexually suggestive pose; various animals copulating; penises, vaginas, breasts, and a provocative full-frontal nude Lady Godiva.

Philatelic junk

A further category of postage stamp is frequently labeled "philatelic junk" by even the moderately serious collector. These are legitimate postage stamps issued by recognized governments, but obviously intended for the collector sales market, and not for actual use inside the country emitting them. Frequently they are designed to appeal to junior collectors using Disney characters (which are licensed by the Disney organization) or other cartoon figures. Others feature pop culture stars (usually American) of the stage, screen, television, and music world. Still others are designed to appeal to topical collectors who specialize in collecting stamps from any country that features their favorite topic (birds, ships, butterflies, etc.). The countries offering these stamps range from Caribbean ministates to the smaller nations of the Middle East and Africa. One obvious giveaway is that the semiotic icon or symbol featured has no relation to the country issuing the stamp, or that the stamp is not being issued for some important anniversary. It also turns out that the design and production of these stamps is not accomplished in the country supposedly issuing the stamp, but rather in New York under the aegis of a middleman corporation that proposes the stamp, produces it, and then markets it via the livelier journals of the philatelic press.[89]

Some examples of this process illustrate how philatelic legitimacy has been violated: Guyana: O. J. Simpson (after his trial);[90] Antigua and Barbuda: Elvis Presley (tenth anniversary of his death); St. Vincent and the Grenadines: *Star Trek* characters; Nicaragua: space aliens and UFOs; and an all-time favorite: Liberia's two separate sets of stamps commemorating the presidential victory of Al Gore as well as that of George W. Bush. Apparently what happened was that to cover their bets in a close election the issuing corporation prepared two separate sets, and intended to destroy the set featuring the loser. However, due to conflicting election return reports from Florida in November 2000, both sets were prematurely released for sale. The President Gore stamps were eventually withdrawn and destroyed, but not before significant numbers were sold.[91]

2 AN OVERVIEW OF LATIN AMERICAN POSTAGE STAMPS

The first postage stamp was issued by England in 1840 and did not include the name of the country; Great Britain has continued the practice of not putting the country name on its postage stamps ever since, in tacit recognition of its primacy of issue. Few other countries have followed this lead, although the United States has had two twentieth-century stamps without a country designation. In both cases the icon and symbols involved (U.S. flag and the White House) have been obvious indexes leading back to the issuing nation. One other indicator of the impact of the first British stamps is that the size and vertical format selected for the original "Penny Black" 1840 stamp is approximately the same size used by most definitive (i.e., noncommemorative) stamps ever since. In effect, the designers of this first stamp had hit upon an excellent balance between the economy of small scale, and the minimal size for the required information: index, icon, and symbol, as well as the monetary value of the stamp.

Mail systems had obviously existed for many centuries previous to the first stamp in 1840. But they were a problem for the governments involved since the postage had to be paid by the recipient. If the recipients could not be found, or if they refused to accept the letter, the postal administration had to return the letter to the sender (at government cost) or simply discard the letter. The British approach in 1840 not only eliminated this problem, but also standardized rates on a per-ounce basis, and soon led to international agreements that established common rates for international mail.

The first Latin American stamps were the so-called bull's-eyes issued by Brazil in July 1843 (figure 1.1), soon followed by portraits of the progressive emperor Dom Pedro (Scott Brazil 23).[1] The United States weighed in with its first stamp in July 1847. Shortly afterward came Mexico and Uruguay (1856) and Peru (1857). The Argentine case is especially interesting in that it reflected the fragmented nature of the political system in those years (centralist Unitarians versus the Federals). The province of Corrientes (figure 1.2, Scott Argentina, Corrientes 1) issued the first stamp in what is today Argentine territory in 1856, followed by Córdoba and Buenos Aires province in 1858. The first Argentine Confederation stamps were also issued in 1858, and the first "Argentine Republic" stamps in 1862, by which time the nation had consolidated under the leadership of Buenos Aires.

As can be seen from the illustrations in plate 1, the first Latin American stamps were rather crudely printed, using local presses designed for newspapers and official government journals and records. The early ones were imperforated, and had to be cut apart, resulting in a large number of varieties. Reprints using different inks and types and thicknesses of papers were common, as were forgeries. Toward the end of the nineteenth century Latin American postage stamps had begun to acquire the main features of the so-called classic stamps issued by most countries of the world by then (e.g., figure 1.3). These features included a high-quality engraving printing process and a simple national graphic icon or symbol such as an independence hero, a president or monarch, or a flag and crest. By 1866 Brazil had given up the austere "bull's-eye" design (with no national index feature) and had moved on to the classical pattern of chief of state, with the index function reinforced by the word "Brazil," later changed to "Brasil," and the stamp's denomination spelled out (e.g., "cem reis").

Although these classical late nineteenth-century stamps were appealing in their simplicity, austerity, and high quality of engravings (in most cases), they suffered from a certain drabness and uniformity of appearance, in part because many of them were printed by a small number of reputable banknote houses in England and the United States. Furthermore, in many cases the face of the chief of state would not be recognized in other countries, and in some cases not even in his or her own country. National symbols probably fared a little better, but in this classical period postage stamps served mainly the pragmatic purpose of ensuring that the postage was prepaid by the sender. Apparently it did not occur to anyone that the postage stamp could also serve the purposes it was later assigned: propaganda, icon of nationalism, economic and commercial advertising, international relations, and the honoring of major cultural and sports figures of each country. Nor did governments recognize the financial implications of issuing significant numbers of stamps that would be bought (and kept) by collectors in unused mint condition and thus never be placed on a letter and employed for postage.

The first serious interest in studying and collecting postage stamps in Latin America began with the wave of European immigration in the late 1800s, especially from Germany, Italy, and England. Many of these immigrants were literate representatives of the middle class, and they focused attention on the varieties, errors, and types of postage stamps up to that time. They were, in effect, reflecting the increasing interest in postage stamps in their European home countries. A number of stamp clubs and societies were founded, dealers set up shop, exhibitions were organized, and philatelic journals were published, especially in those countries with high numbers of recent middle-class immigrants, such as Argentina and Chile.[2] An examination of the mastheads of these journals and the publicity materials of the dealers reveals a disproportionate number of names of English, Italian, or Germanic origin.

THE "SEEBECKS"

The late nineteenth century witnessed one of the more controversial episodes of Latin American philately: the issuing of large numbers of so-called Seebeck stamps in the 1890–1898 years. Nicholas Seebeck was an officer of the Hamilton Bank Note Company of New York, and offered the governments of four Latin American countries a seemingly irresistible deal: his firm would print their stamps for free and provide them with as many stamps as they needed for postal use over relatively short periods of time, after which they would be demonetized (i.e., lose their ability to carry the mail) and be replaced by new issues of stamps. However, as part of the deal Seebeck's firm would retain the original plates and the right to print as many of the stamps as they wanted for sale to collectors once the period of official use expired. The result was to flood the stamp collectors' market with thousands of stamps, many of which were quite similar in general design and appearance since they had been turned out quickly by the New York firm.

Nicholas Seebeck was born in Germany in 1857 and in his youth emigrated to New York, where he became involved in a stationery business and then the stamp trade.[3] He later became an officer of the newly formed Hamilton Bank Note Company, and eventually rose to become secretary and president. He had made several stamp purchasing trips to Latin America, and in 1889 undertook the fateful trip that resulted in the first of several contracts with the nations of El Salvador, Nicaragua, and Honduras (Ecuador also later signed a Seebeck contract). Under the terms of the contract a date would be placed on the stamps printed by Seebeck, and the stamps would be postally invalid after that date, which then permitted Seebeck to reprint and sell to dealers and collectors. It should be noted that these were not "counterfeit" stamps since they were "reprints" made from the original plates by the same printing firm using the same materials.

The Seebeck stamps were of uniformly high quality and featured themes such as allegories, national crests and flags, presidents, and the Columbus anniversary (figure 1.3). The scope of the Seebeck operation can be seen from the figures given by Danilo A. Mueses: for the four countries (El Salvador, Nicaragua, Honduras, and Ecuador) in the Seebeck years 1889–1898 a total of 1,302 different items (postage and telegraph stamps, stamped envelopes, etc.) were printed and sold.[4] In some years the quantity of stamps printed was several dozen times as large as the total population of these countries, whose literacy rates (and thus interest in letter writing) were relatively low. After Seebeck's death in 1899 a second speculator bought up the remaining stamps, which amounted to the astonishing number of about 90 million unused Seebeck reprints. Many of these were given away in small packets as promotions for a variety of products designed to appeal to young people, and presumably were a stimulus to get these children involved in collecting stamps. Over the past century these stamps have trickled into many collections, and catalogue prices have consistently remained low for unused Seebecks that have never carried mail or entered the postal system.

The reaction to the Seebeck reprints was outrage among serious collectors, the generally conservative philatelic press, organized philatelic societies, and dealers who were not part of the operation. In his defense, Seebeck noted that he had done nothing illegal, that there were ample precedents for reprinting outdated issues, and that he was benefiting the hobby by making a wide range of colorful and attractive stamps available to new (and especially young) collectors. Furthermore, although the mint (unused) Seebecks were cheap and roundly condemned by serious collectors, stamps from these countries which had been legitimately used in the mails were relatively rare and prized, especially if still "tied" (attached) to the original envelopes with legitimate cancellations. The final judgment on the Seebeck reprints remains mixed. A permanent stigma is still attached to the issues of the four Latin American countries in this period, and to some extent this stigma has unfairly extended itself to the collection of stamps of all Latin American countries of all periods. On the plus side, Seebeck's defense has some validity, and his stamps opened up the hobby of collecting Latin American stamps to many new and younger hobbyists.

THE COMING OF THE COMMEMORATIVES

In 1871 Peru issued one of the earliest commemoratives in the history of global philately. As opposed to definitive stamps, which carry general themes and remain in circulation for many years, commemorative stamps are issued for short periods and are intended to celebrate specific events or anniversaries. The 1871 so-called Callao Peruvian stamps (Scott Peru 19) commemorated the twentieth anniversary of the first railway in South America, which linked the port city of Callao with the capital city of Lima. It featured a silhouette of the train, along with the national coat of arms and the words "Chorrillos/Lima/Callao" (three stations on the line). The celebration in 1892 of the four-hundredth anniversary of Columbus's landing in the Western Hemisphere produced a number of commemorative stamps, and marks the real birth of the realization that stamps could be more than just indicators of postage prepayment. The United States organized a major international fair in Chicago to celebrate the event, and the celebration included an important set of U.S. commemorative stamps. In some cases Latin American countries participating in the fair, such as Venezuela, issued similar (and indeed, almost identical) stamps, which should not be surprising considering the fact that they were prepared by some of the same U.S. banknote companies. The 1892 celebration produced an oddity: the only Puerto Rican commemorative stamp, issued while the Spanish were still in control of the island.[5] After 1898, only U.S. stamps were used, sometimes with an overprinted "Porto Rico" legend, indicating semiotically, and not too subtly, the limited sovereignty of the island.

The increase in Latin American commemorative stamps was sharply accelerated in the 1910–1924 period with a series of issues celebrating the centennial of independence of many of the Latin American nations. These were generally of high quality, and provided an opportunity to feature national heroes and symbols. The celebration of independence using postage stamps was also a major feature of U.S. postage stamps, especially the bicentennial in 1976, when many U.S. (and quite a few foreign) stamps were issued. An echo of the Latin American 1910–1924 series of independence centennial stamps was seen in 1960–1974, on the 150th anniversary of the events and battles. By the late 1920s Latin American postage stamps had begun to distance themselves from the excesses of the Seebeck period, and, stimulated by the successes of the 1892 and 1910–1924 commemoratives, entered into a period in which many high-quality commemoratives were issued, providing us with an opportunity to apply semiotic analysis to the message delivered by these stamps.

The World War II years saw postage stamps used in support of the Allied war effort, especially in those countries (Cuba, Brazil, Costa Rica) with close ties to the United States. The Pan American Union, working with the U.S. Department of Education and the State Department (Nelson Rockefeller's Office of Inter-American Cooperation), made a conscious effort in the 1940s to use postage stamps as a vehicle for forging closer ties between the hemisphere nations.[6] One such example comes from Cuba (Scott Cuba 375–379), where stamps urged citizens to fulfill their patriotic duty by destroying the "fifth column," a reference to spies. A second example, from Brazil, shows the insigne of the Brazilian Expeditionary Force, which fought in World War II under the command of the U.S. Fifth Army, whose patch is also shown against the background of a large American flag (figure 1.4, Scott 637).

The postwar years saw a continued growth in the issuing of commemoratives and the full realization of the political, international, and financial aspects of such stamps. There were some excesses that diminished collectors' interest in certain countries, as it became obvious that some series were being issued not for internal postal use, but mainly for sale to collectors. Paraguay, Panama, and Nicaragua were especially brazen in their issuing of stamps with no logical connection to their countries' history, geography, or culture. These stamps were frequently large in format, garish in appearance, and stressed themes that seemed obviously intended to appeal to young or topical collectors (space accomplishments, flowers, animals, European art classics, trains, airplanes, etc.).

Contemporary trends include much greater attention to the messages stamps convey as symbols of the nation and its achievements. In some countries (Mexico, Bolivia, Peru, Guatemala), where there is a conscious effort to honor the pre-Columbian past, there have been stamp issues specifically focused on these themes (figure 1.6, Scott Guatemala 399; figure 1.8, Scott Mexico 1201). The partial privatization of the postal system in Argentina, and the growth of private mail and courier services in the face of the inefficiencies of government postal systems, have produced unofficial nongovernmental postage stamps to indicate prepayment of these private postal charges.[7] In the Argentine case (see chapter 5), the partial privatization of the postal service in 1998 and the issuing of private stamp labels has not prevented the government from continuing to issue stamps identified as "Correo Oficial," which are not "official" stamps (i.e., for government use only), but rather are called "Correo Oficial" to distinguish them from the private posts. They are also clearly intended to appeal to collectors, and continue to deliver the semiotic messages we have identified previously.

Oddities and unique stamps continue to be issued. Brazil, for example, in November 2000 issued a stamp advertising Brazilian coffee that carried the scent of coffee, if one bothered to smell the stamp. Other innovative Brazilian philatelic plans included a "thermochromic" stamp, which would reveal brilliant colors through a holographic process when it was exposed to the heat of the sun or the hand of a curious observer.[8]

The number of issues in the mid-twentieth century can be seen from some comparative data. In 1938, there were 2,634 issues of postage stamps worldwide; in 1941, the number was 2,612. Issues dropped to 1,765 in 1944, and rose in 1946 to 2,313.[9] Of these totals, Latin America issued anywhere between 15 percent and 20 percent. In contrast, the year 2000 saw a record total of over 15,000 different items (13,879 stamps and 1,595 souvenir sheets) issued worldwide by some 260 postal "entities," for a face value of approximately $8,900. For 2002 the total number was 12,531 items (11,319 stamps and 1,212 souvenir sheets), for a total face value of $8,047.[10]

Table 1 provides data for recent years on new issues of different stamps, as well as the total number of stamps since the first issue.[11]

In contrast, for the year 2002 the United States issued 264 stamps of various types, while the United Nations at New York issued 25, and the United Nations at Geneva another 26.

PROBLEMS AND ERRORS

I noted earlier some features of Latin American postage stamps that created problems, indicated fraud or exploitation, or involved errors. In this section I will briefly explore some of these categories. Additional examples will be provided for different countries in chapter 8.

In the first category of stamp issues to have caused problems we have the exploitative ones, such as works of art with no connection to the country producing the stamps. These generally become obvious when the amounts printed, the themes, or the high face values cannot be justified by the legiti-

Table 1: Number of stamps issued in selected years

	1994	1998	2000	2002	Average per year since first issue	Total
Argentina	34	67	73	90	66.0	3,047
Bolivia	46	28	37	52	40.8	1,523
Brazil	75	146	131	90	110.5	3,079
Chile	50	47	69	32	49.5	1,824
Colombia	25	29	9	43	26.5	2,677
Costa Rica	16	25	28	20	22.2	1,798
Cuba	78	98	69	96	85.2	4,566
Dom. Rep.*	49	62	35	8	38.5	2,092
Ecuador	30	32	79	99	60.0	2,609
El Salvador	28	39	58	34	39.8	2,561
Guatemala	8	1	0	14	5.8	1,432
Haiti	0	22	0	7	7.2	1,659
Honduras	6	41	70	35	38.0	1,718
Mexico	89	80	56	59	71.0	3,327
Nicaragua	271	35	171	11	122.0	4,359
Panama	1	8	0	17	6.5	1,525
Paraguay	39	32	29	24	31.0	3,646
Peru	21	36	49	57	40.8	2,128
Uruguay	43	95	66	60	66.0	2,654
Venezuela	34	189	33	5	65.2	2,748
BAT**	17	22	12	18	17.3	370
Falkland Is.	26	30	21	30	26.8	990
S. Georgia	20	11	12	16	14.8	277

* Dominican Republic

** British Antarctic Territory

Notes: Average per country in Latin America: 2,549; in the British territories: 546.

Average for Latin America from these years: 49.6; for the British territories: 19.6.

Total stamps for Latin America since the first issues: 50,972; for the British territories: 1,637.

mate postal needs of the country involved. Another clue is when announcements of the issues appear prominently in some of the widely circulating stamp journals, showing colorful and large-format stamps with certain themes designed to appeal to foreign topical collectors. Two such exploitative issues involved stamps from Panama and Haiti that would feature the more than 260 identifiable popes of the Catholic Church. Each pope would merit a stamp, and the postal administrations of both countries explained that part of the profits would go to Catholic charities, and that the Vatican was cooperating in the project.[12] An American artist was commissioned to begin painting the Panamanian pope series, and a California firm was contracted to begin the printing. Criticism of both the Panamanian and later the Haitian schemes was quite strong in the philatelic press of the United States and several European countries, and eventually the project was dropped, but not before Panama had issued twelve stamps bearing the portraits of all the popes named Pius (e.g., Scott C210), arguing that this was a legitimate homage to Pope Pius XII on his birthday.

A notorious exploitative series of stamps, also associated with manipulation and fraud, was the Dominican Republic's Olympic stamps of the late 1950s. The stamps portrayed a large number of Olympic champions and competitors, none of whom was from the Dominican Republic. They were large-format stamps, colorful, and with varied designs. The total number of Olympic stamps and souvenir sheets for the five-year period they covered was 170, divided up as follows: 88 perforated stamps, 48 imperforated stamps, 17 imperforated souvenir sheets, and 17 other souvenirs.[13] Beyond the sheer numbers, there were accusations that the New York firm that was given the printing contract (J. & H. Stolow) had printed many more stamps than requested and delivered to the Dominicans; these stamps were sold for years afterward by the firm at prices well below the face value. Equally disturbing was manipulation carried out by the stamp agency in Santo Domingo, which released a small number of the stamps at face value, then declared that the stamps and sheets had been sold out. However, the agency later released additional copies, which made their way onto the market at considerably higher prices. The dean of Dominican Republic philatelic writers lamented the way in which these abuses were resulting in a lack of confidence and interest in all Dominican stamps by collectors.[14]

Speculative issues that are more clearly in the category of fraud have been reported numerous times. Occasionally this happens in developing countries when private printing firms in developed countries contact postal administrators offering a deal similar to the Seebeck one mentioned above. In other cases corrupt postal officials have approached printing firms or philatelic organizations with a similar offer to issue stamps for speculative purposes, with the proceeds being split between the various players. A variant of the fraud scheme consists of selling a very small number of stamps of a given issue legitimately, and then holding the remainders and cornering the market until the scarcity of the legitimate issue drives up the price for the remainders, as was done in the case of the Dominican Republic's Olympic series.[15]

Another category of philatelic fraud that is unfortunately not unknown in Latin America is the issuing of labels or souvenir sheets that look all too much like legitimate issues, to include the name of the country that supposedly issues them. Few countries have laws against printing and selling such items as long as there is no intent to actually use them in lieu of regular postage in the mails. Frequently these fraudulent issues are timed to appear at major sports events such as the Olympic Games or World Cup soccer tournaments. There are many collectors who specialize in these specific topics, and they represent an attractive market for these items. The Universal Postal Union has a service (now available on the Web) by which legitimate postal administrations can denounce these issues and warn that any attempt to use them in the mails or claim that they are legitimate postal items will be prosecuted under the law. One example of this type of activity (and its denunciation) is the notice on the UPU Web site dated 10 January 2000 passing on the information provided by the postal administration of Ukraine to the effect that stamps issued from 1992 to 1999 by something called the "Ukrainian Antarctic Post" are invalid and cannot be accepted as means of postal prepayment. Ukraine does have an Antarctic presence, at the Vernadsky scientific station it received from the United Kingdom (the old Faraday Station). Further, Ukraine did issue a legitimate stamp (Scott Ukraine 248, November 1996) commemorating Ukrainian Antarctic activities. The Ukrainians should not be surprised that speculators are attempting to imitate their legitimate stamps, inasmuch as these have been issued in considerable numbers, and in colorful thematic groups aimed at collectors.[16]

The Argentine case is somewhat different. A UPU bulletin of 18 August 1997 passed on the information that two souvenir sheets, issued by the Círculo Filatélico Argentino (Argentine Philatelic Society), were being sold, but the postal administration was not aware of this organization, and the stamps on the souvenir sheet were not valid for postal use.[17] The situation here may have been that a little-known philatelic club had issued the sheet as a promotional device without intentions of fraud.

Errors abound in postal issues of all countries, sometimes producing rare stamps of great value, such as the U.S. inverted Curtis Jenny aircraft stamp of 1918, valued at $170,000.[18] The inversion of one part of the design was the result of a printing error, caused by the need to run the sheets through the printing press more than once (the center vignette is of a different color than the surrounding frame). Inverts and a wide range of printing errors exist among Latin American stamps, although their scarcity and demand do not rise to the level of the inverted Jenny. Minor errors involving typos or errors in dates and names are also abundant.[19] Other errors are introduced by the need to accommodate a given icon or symbol on the small surface area of a commemorative stamp. Mexico provides two examples.[20] The first is the 1969 stamp intended to celebrate the colonizing efforts of Father Junípero Serra, who founded San Diego, California. The icon in the stamp (Scott Mexico C346) was based on a 1785 painting of Father Serra and a fellow priest, Father Francisco Palóu. The designer of the stamp mistakenly featured the wrong priest: the single portrait on the Serra stamp is of Palóu, not Serra. The second Mexican example (Scott Mexico 1056) consists of an error in a symbol, not an icon. This 1973 stamp was to honor the twenty-fifth anniversary of the Higher School of Chemical Engineering, and shows a molecule of methane gas, which consists of one atom of carbon and four of hydrogen. However, because of the layout of the stamp (again, a function of the small size), the designer dropped one of the hydrogen atoms and the resulting methane molecule has only three hydrogen atoms instead of four.

One last type of error I will consider here is that deliberately introduced by the printing company in the design stage to save time and money. To understand the causes of this type of error one must appreciate that, in the case of many Latin American stamps produced in the United States by U.S. banknote companies in the nineteenth and early twentieth centuries, there is a considerable cultural gap between the Latin American postal service and the U.S. banknote company. The request for a given theme on a stamp is sent from the Latin American country to the U.S. firm (frequently in New York), which prepares a vignette, or proposed final test printing, usually based on a photograph or design forwarded by the issuing country. The particular example presented here concerns the fact that two presidents of Haiti appeared on two different stamps with exactly the same uniform. The first was

President Nord Alexis, who was removed from office by his political enemies shortly before his term was due to expire in 1908.[21] His effigy had appeared on a series of Haitian stamps during his term, usually showing him wearing a formal military uniform. With a new, civilian president (Antoine Simon), it was clear that the old stamps would have to be replaced by new ones featuring the current president. The American Bank Note Company of New York received the appropriate photograph, accompanied by the request that the new stamp be issued as soon as possible. The photograph of President Antoine Simon showed him wearing civilian clothes, but in its haste to put out the new stamp the American Bank Note Company simply replaced the head of President Alexis with that of President Simon, who thus appeared in military uniform (not his own), instead of civilian clothes. The company apparently did not understand (or did not care about) the implications of portraying a civilian president in a military uniform.

A classic example of some of the problems encountered by Latin American postage stamps is provided by the striking and notorious "Gate of the Sun" stamp issue of Bolivia.[22] The story is long and complicated, and is tinged with Bolivian prehistory and philatelic irregularities, as well as the impact of Bolivian inflation. The object in question is one of Bolivia's principal archeological jewels, the Gate of the Sun monolith at Tiwanaku (Tiahuanaco), close to Lake Titicaca on the border with Peru. The monolith is essentially a doorway weighing approximately ten tons, decorated with a frieze along the upper part, believed to be a calendar. The frieze is dominated by a central figure, the god Viracocha, who holds a condor in each hand, and is decorated with stylized pumas, birds, and sea shells. The Tiwanaku culture flourished from about 100 to 1200 C.E. and had all but disappeared by the time of the rise of the Incas, although archeological remnants still can be found on the Bolivian altiplano. The philatelic story of the Sun Gate centers around a proposal made by an archeologist named Arturo Poznansky to the effect that to supplement the stamps commemorating Bolivia's independence in 1926, a spectacular series of stamps honoring the Tiwanaku Sun Gate should be issued to honor Bolivia's pre-Columbian past (he described his design concept as "una edición de gran lujo y única en el mundo" — "an issue of great elegance, and unique in the world").[23] His proposal involved a set of nineteen stamps that would reproduce the major icons of the Sun Gate's frieze; the large stamp honoring the central god Viracocha would dominate the lesser icons of the frieze.

Dr. Poznansky's proposal was accepted and a decree was issued authorizing him to undertake the project. The terms of the agreement were that he would bear the full cost of designing and printing the stamps, and in return would get 3 percent of the stamps for sale to collectors as his payment (his request for 10 percent was denied). Dr. Poznansky proceeded to make a detailed cast of the frieze and take it to Germany, where he worked with engravers to create the nineteen stamps. To increase the attractiveness and impact of the stamps, they were printed on special paper that had first been coated with gilded ink. The overall effect was striking and unusual, although it was noted that the typography (especially the face value denomination) was very hard to read because of the dark gilded paper (figure 1.9).

The stamps were printed, but before they could be shipped to Bolivia and released, the government learned that sets were being sold without authorization in Europe. Subsequent investigations never definitively determined if these were from Dr. Poznansky's 3 percent share of the stamps, or were unauthorized extra reprints. In any case, the Bolivian government reacted swiftly, prohibiting the sale of the stamps in Bolivia and locking them up in government bank vaults. The stamps were recognized by some catalogues, which listed them as "authorized but not issued"; the current *Scott Standard Postage Catalogue* prices the set at over ninety-two dollars.

The stamps languished in the vaults for thirty-five years until they were rediscovered by a government official searching for other documents. Although some of the stamps had been damaged by humidity, the government felt that enough time had passed since the 1926 irregularities to permit the reissuing of the stamps. A not-so-small problem of inflation remained, however. The value of the national currency (the boliviano) had declined to a fraction of its 1926 value, so the 1960 version of the stamps carried surcharges that in effect raised some of the stamps' face value close to ten thousand times. The highest value five-boliviano stamp of the series (Viracocha) was surcharged to a value of five thousand bolivianos.

Despite these setbacks and irregularities, interest in Latin American postage stamps remains strong. However, this interest has suffered (as has interest in stamps generally), due to the inroads made by email and the fact that young people today are more interested in computers and video games than collecting things generally, and postage stamps in particular. This decline in interest on the part of the five-to-twelve-year-old cohort has caused some alarm among collectors, and a visit to any major philatelic exhibition makes it clear that the hobby is dominated by apparently affluent middle-aged (and older) males. Nevertheless, a number of stamp collecting clubs and study groups exist, many of which publish newsletters containing a deluge of information focusing on technical details, and sometimes with analysis of political or semiotic material.[24]

One sad commentary on the declining appeal of stamps to the five-to-twelve-year-old cohort was conveyed by a *Dennis the Menace* comic strip in July 2005. In the strip Dennis is visiting his neighbor Mr. Wilson, who does not appreciate such visits, and uses a detailed explanation of his stamp collection to get rid of a bored Dennis, who wanders off in pursuit of more exciting activities.[25]

3

INTERNAL POLITICS AND LATIN AMERICAN STAMPS

In chapter 1 I examined, among other topics, the politics and propaganda aspects of postage stamps in general terms. In this chapter I will focus this approach on Latin American stamps, giving selected examples. As might be expected, totalitarian and authoritarian regimes, with their tight control over the political process and its propaganda efforts, have made ample use of their postage stamps for this purpose.[1]

The long dictatorships of the Somoza family in Nicaragua and of Stroessner in Paraguay were accompanied by numerous series of stamps, twelve in the Somoza case and sixteen in Stroessner's (figure 2.1). Guatemala provides an excellent example of how two authoritarian regimes (sandwiching a democratically elected reform government) accomplished this. We start with the long dictatorship of General Jorge Ubico (1931–1944). As his second presidential term began in 1937 the government issued an extended set of stamps (Scott 280–291) celebrating the accomplishments of the regime, and featuring as its highest values a one-quetzal stamp of Ubico in uniform on horseback and a one-and-a-half-quetzal stamp formal portrait of Ubico. The following year, on the occasion of a philatelic exhibit in Guatemala, another set of stamps (Scott C93–C99) showed the Central American presidents, portraying President Ubico on the highest value stamps; other stamps in the series featured president-generals Anastasio Somoza of Nicaragua and Maximiliano Hernández Martínez of El Salvador. After Ubico resigned, two elected reformist presidents (Juan José Arévalo and Jacobo Arbenz) led the so-called Guatemalan Revolution of 1945–1955. Their governments issued stamps (Scott 312, 320–323, C128–131, C136, C185–187) with allegories of the October 1944 Revolution, and honoring democracy and labor. The transfer of power from Arévalo to Arbenz by free elections in 1950 gave rise to a stamp (figure 2.2, Scott C185) with the icons of a national flag and the constitution being passed from the hand of Arévalo to the hand of Arbenz.

The Arbenz regime was brought down by a coalition of right-wing forces led by Colonel Carlos Castillo Armas, with support from the CIA, in 1954. The Castillo Armas regime promptly issued stamps (Scott 363–364 and C210–218) with a Mayan warrior holding the dagger–cross symbol of the "liberation movement" of 1954, and a hammer destroying the hammer and sickle symbols of Communism. The stamps also carried the liberating revolution's slogan of "Dios Patria Libertad." Castillo Armas himself was assassinated in 1957, and the event was commemorated with a stamp showing his portrait framed in black (Scott C223).

The most extreme case of the use of stamps for political purposes over an extended period of time is that of the Trujillo regime in the Dominican Republic. If it were not for its violent and tragic aspects, the regime's stamps over these years (1930–1961) would be almost comical in their exaggerated tributes to the dictator and to so many members of his family. Placing Trujillo and his relatives on Dominican stamps violated a 1930 law (similar to the U.S. and Argentine approaches) that prohibited such portrayals until the individual concerned had been dead for at least ten years. The first stamps showing Trujillo are from a 1933 set of three that violated this prior law, and thus it was felt necessary to authorize their emission using a second law, which would trump the earlier one prohibiting this tribute to a living person.[2] The stamps honored him on his forty-second birthday and show Trujillo in both civilian clothes and his general's uniform; even in civilian clothes he wears a medal on his lapel (Scott 286–288).

A year later a stamp commemorating the opening of the Generalisimo Trujillo Bridge over the River Yuna appeared (Scott 292–294), and a year after that a similar one (Scott 295–298) celebrating the Ramfís Bridge (Ramfís was the name of Trujillo's son). Neither stamp carried a Trujillo portrait. Numerous other stamps issued between 1935 and 1939 did carry Trujillo portraits, as they commemorated events as varied as a peace treaty with Haiti, the dedication of George Washington Avenue in the capital, and the change of the city's name from Santo Domingo to Ciudad Trujillo (figure 2.3). Other Trujillo portraits included his father on the fourth anniversary of his death, and his mother, featured on four stamps for Mother's Day in 1940. The Trujillo-Hull Treaty of 1941 was noted with the portraits of three "Padres de la Patria" ("Fathers of the Nation") accompanied by one of Trujillo himself (Scott 369); U.S. Secretary of State Cordell Hull was not shown. The 1955 twenty-fifth anniversary of the Trujillo era was commemorated with a high-quality set featuring the dictator (in an equestrian statue as well as in portraits in civilian clothes and military uniform, complete with plumed cocked hat), his brother, who was president at the time, symbols of the culture and progress of the Trujillo era, and the joined flags of the republic and the army (Scott 462–465 and C91–93).

In 1955 the Dominican Republic hosted an expensive and sparsely attended International Fair of Peace and Brotherhood, which was noted with another high-quality portrait of Trujillo (Scott 466–467), and also with a stamp honoring his daughter Angelita, queen of the fair, but she merited only a poor-quality lithographed stamp (Scott 468). His son Leonidas Rhadamés fared little better, in another blurry lithographed stamp, which honored him for leading the national polo team (Scott 509). The Trujillo era came to a violent end with his assassination ("ajusticiamiento" — "bringing to justice" in the Dominican parlance) in May 1962; the commemorative stamps (Scott 561–63, C122) show the date of his death and a set of broken chains. During the thirty-one years of the dictatorship citizens had to be careful with any stamps bearing the image of the "Benefactor of the Patria." Mueses tells the story of a Trujillo opponent who once complained loudly about the Trujillo stamps at a local post office. According to Mueses there was an informant present, and the protesting individual disappeared shortly afterward, never to be heard from again.

During the presidency of the Marxist Salvador Allende in Chile, stamps were issued to mark major events with political implications, including those celebrating Chile's new mastery of its own destiny (Scott 418) and the nationalization of copper (figure 2.4). The many years of the Pinochet regime in Chile produced numerous examples of postage stamps supporting the military and celebrating the violent removal of Allende from power on 11 September 1973, an event that has frequently been commemorated by a stamp issue. Typical of these was the 1984 stamp (Scott 677), in large format, and featuring the flame of liberty and the icon of Chilean independence, General Bernardo O'Higgins, in a heroic equestrian pose. The notation on the stamps read simply "11.IX.84, 11 Anõs de Libertad"; there was apparently no need to mention General Augusto Pinochet or the events of September 1973. The stamp issued on the third anniversary (figure 2.5) showed a winged angel breaking free from the chains of Marxism over the legend "Renace la Patria" ("The Fatherland is reborn").

As we noted above in the example of the Guatemalan democratic revolution, authoritarian regimes are not the only ones using stamps for political purposes. When the military regime that ousted Perón in Argentina in 1955 turned power over to an elected civilian regime in 1958, stamps were issued to celebrate the occasion. The decree authorizing the stamps noted that the incoming civilian president was the result of "an absolutely democratic and exemplary election," and that for this reason it was appropriate to "issue commemorative postage stamps that would remember and perpetuate the event."[3]

In Nicaragua, soon after taking power from the Sandinistas, the elected government of Violeta Chamorro (1990–1996) issued a stamp commemorating the president's late husband, the journalist Pedro Joaquín Chamorro, who had been assassinated by the Somoza regime in 1978. The stamp (Scott 1844) featured a portrait of the murdered Chamorro, with the notation "Martyr of public liberty." More recently, the government of the Colombian president Alvaro Uribe authorized a stamp (Scott 1196) to commemorate the assassination of Consuelo Araujo-Noguera, Colombia's minister of culture in the prior regime of Andrés Pastrana, by the Fuerzas Armadas Revolucionarias de Colombia guerrilla group (FARC, Revolutionary Armed Forces of Columbia). The decision to issue the stamp, along with other commemorative acts, was interpreted as a sign that the Uribe regime would be a lot tougher on the guerrillas than the Pastrana regime, which was characterized by fruitless attempts to negotiate with the guerrillas to find a peaceful solution to their insurgency. Reactions to some of the more politicized stamp issues also provide an insight into their political impact. In 1985, for example, Vice President George H. W. Bush cited Nicaraguan postage stamps honoring Karl Marx (figure 2.7, Scott 1182) as an indicator of the Marxist nature of the Sandinista regime. The *New York Times* pointed out, however, that the Nicaraguans had issued many stamps honoring world leaders, including George Washington and Pope John Paul II.[4]

Another example of the reaction postage stamps can sometimes produce is the response to an Argentine stamp honoring Ernesto "Che" Guevara (who himself was Argentine) on the thirtieth anniversary of his death in 1997 (figure 2.6). A number of countries commemorated this anniversary in a variety of ways, to the point that a Spanish news source spoke of the prevailing fever of "Chemania" that was playing a special role in the arts to recreate a human being now converted into a myth.[5] President Menem justified the decision to issue the stamp on the basis that Che was a universal figure, and that the stamp was "a way of moving forward toward peace and understanding among Argentines." The official decree expressed the wish that "this stamp would show an Argentina that excluded no one for ideological reasons," and that it represented the "philosophy of concord" inspired by such events as the repatriation of the remains of Juan Manuel de Rosas and the social revindication of Eva Perón and Domingo Faustino Sarmiento. Other sources were not as charitable: the Buenos Aires newspaper *Clarín* quoted the Radical Party politician Juan Manuel Casella: "This is an election maneuver by President Carlos Menem, which appeals to the commercial fetishism of the image of Che to compensate for the lack of support from the right."[6] *Clarín* also quoted the conservative Tradition, Family, and Property group as saying that this official homage "favors the revolutionary dynamism which already had bloodied the country in the decade of the 1970s."

STAMPS AS INSTRUMENTS OF GOOD CITIZENSHIP

Governments can (and in Latin America frequently do) use postage stamps and their cancellation messages as vehicles for promoting good citizenship; such stamps urge the population to adopt healthy lifestyles by exercising, observing safe sex, and quitting smoking. Sometimes good citizenship stamps take the form of support of a worthy organization, such as the Red Cross, Boy Scouts, Lions, Rotary, hospital "beneficencias," and so on. These stamps are also sometimes issued with a face value plus a surcharge, which is then presumably passed on to the organization involved. In the United States we have had only a very limited number of such surcharge issues, breast cancer research being a recent example. In Mexico, long plagued by corruption among officials ranging from the policeman on the corner to the highest levels of government, a campaign launched by the new Vicente Fox administration in 2002 included a postage stamp (figure 2.8, Scott 2291) calling for a more honest administration, with no more "mordidas" (the petty bribes demanded by police and other low-level bureaucrats). Another stamp (Scott 2292) laid out a "Code of Ethics for Public Services of the Federal Administration."[7]

Another postal mechanism for promoting good citizenship is the message that can accompany the cancellation marking on an envelope. These can be quickly and easily changed, and do not have to go through the lengthy design process that a stamp does. Some Argentine examples are "A peso saved is a peso won"; "World campaign against hunger. Support it"; "Lions Club—peace is possible"; "Don't waste potable water"; "Save a life. Give blood"; "We need to make the whole Republic a school"; "Rehabilitated persons place their faith in the future"; "Help epileptics by collaborating with the Anti-epilepsy Association"; "Contribute to the country—pay your taxes on time"; "Water and energy—factors for progress"; "14 September—mail carrier's day"; and "People's Library Week."[8]

STAMPS AS INSTRUMENTS OF NATIONAL IDENTITY

Well-designed postage stamps are a natural vehicle for circulating symbols and icons of national unity. Because they are so ubiquitous, they are seen and handled by the general population more than any other instrument of government, except coins and bills. But the design of postage stamps, in contrast with the design of coins and paper money, is constantly changing, and this permits a variety of images and messages, although frequently focusing on the same general theme of consolidating national unity. Moreover, the repetitive nature of the citizen's contact with a given postage stamp reinforces the impact of the semiotic message.

The simplest icon of national identity is the country's flag, which appears on many stamps of all countries. Sometimes the appearance is subtle, simply using the national colors instead of the flag itself (e.g., Scott Brazil 1974). An example of the significance of the national flag on a stamp comes from the period of transition from empire to republic in Brazil. With the departure of the last emperor in 1889 the newly formed republic had to design new symbols of national identity that linked to the past without too overt a relationship to the symbols of empire. Obviously the stamps of the new republic could no longer bear the image of Dom Pedro II. But the national colors of Brazil (green and yellow) did carry over, with this official explanation: "[The colors] commemorate the victories and achievements of our army and navy, in the defense of our fatherland, and these colors, independently of the form of our government, represent the perpetuity of our fatherland among the other nations."[9] The stamps of the new republic would thus carry these old colors, but with the addition of the positivist slogan "Ordem e Progresso," the Southern Cross, and twenty-one stars representing the twenty states of the republic and the special municipality of Rio de Janeiro. The decree setting out the guidelines for these designs specified that all previous stamps (i.e., of the emperor), and stamps that did not conform to these norms, were illegal and could not be used for postage.

Related symbols used on stamps to assist in the forging of national identity included national crests (which frequently involved complex combinations of icons and symbols), "escarapelas" (rosettes with the national colors), or simply the colors of the flags themselves. More subtle themes of national unity to be found on the postage stamps of Latin America include national flowers (e.g., the orchids of Colombia); other flora and fauna typical of the country; folk dances; patron saints (such as Santa Rosa de Lima, and the Virgin of Luján in Argentina); art, most notably of the Mexican muralists (Scott C554); and literature. In this last category Colombia issued a stamp (Scott C245) honoring not so much Jorge Isaacs, the author of the famous nineteenth-century romantic novel *María*, as the main character herself, as portrayed in a spectacular monument in Cali, near the site of the principal episodes of the novel. Nicaragua's principal poet, Rubén Darío, is also seen as a contributor to the self-image of Nicaragua as a land of poets, and several stamp series have honored the poet, including one that carried allegorical scenes from some of his most famous poems (Scott C602). The swan, icon of the modernist literary movement that Darío led, figures prominently in these series.

Heroic feats, usually of the independence period, but sometimes from later epic events, provide another theme for national unity. Since these are events that every schoolchild learns about, and that are also usually commemorated with public statuary and art, the postage stamp serves to reinforce the value of the icon. As an illustration, the official decree authorizing stamps commemorating the centennial of the death of Argentine independence hero Admiral Guillermo Brown carried this explanation: "It is the inescapable duty of the people to exalt the personality of the men who have forged their nationality, selflessly, and with disinterest and sacrifice. . . . In that sense, the figure of Admiral Guillermo Brown, the creator of our navy, projects itself through time in the memory of Argentine generations, and constitutes a true symbol which must be remembered as an example and stimulus for all of us who bask in the warmth of the Motherland."[10]

Latin American nations that have undergone a violent and profound revolution, such as Mexico, Cuba, and Nicaragua, incorporate themes from their struggles and key events into their postrevolutionary postage stamps. The portrayals of revolutionary heroes in the murals of Diego Rivera, David Alfaro Siqueiros, and José Clemente Orozco have provided many graphics for Mexican stamps. Cuba's stamps after the 1959 victory of Castro's forces portrayed triumphant scenes from the 1956–1958 fighting (figure 2.9, Scott C200). In Nicaragua a Somoza-era stamp (Scott C885) proclaimed Anastasio Somoza president from 1974 to 1981, a tenure that was cut short by the Sandinista revolution. The Sandinistas followed much the same pattern as

Cuba, issuing a commemorative stamp each year, as well as many others in between extolling the achievements of the revolution (Scott 1111). In both Mexico and Bolivia revolutions in the twentieth century included a deliberate search for pre-Columbian roots after many years of slavish nineteenth-century imitation of European cultural models. The significance of this homage was underlined by a special set of United Nations stamps in early 2003 that featured eighteen stamps portraying Latin American and Caribbean indigenous art, in three souvenir sheets.[11]

Peru presents a special case. The inland city of Cuzco was the center of the Inca empire, but for the colonial years it was the Spanish coastal city of Lima that predominated. The nation's cultural identity was fostered by the white elites of Lima, who looked down on the indigenous and mestizo middle and lower classes. And so when a mestizo middle-class revolutionary government (led by a unique group of reformist military officers) took power in 1968, there was a determined effort to reach back to pre-Columbian roots in search of icons of national identity. An original if complicated design appears in a 1970 stamp (figure 3.1, Scott 534), whose theme is "The people and the armed forces forging a new Peru." The central iconic figure is a man, but the design is split down the middle. The right side of the man is dressed in Inca clothes, and features a sprig of wheat as a symbol of agriculture. The left side of the man wears a military helmet and uniform, and the background shows oil wells, symbols of the Peruvian revolution's search for economic independence.

The oil well theme is repeated in another Peruvian stamp of the period (figure 3.2, Scott 513), which shows a bare-chested worker holding an oil well and a giant Peruvian flag. The stamp is titled "Day of National Dignity" and celebrates the nationalization of the La Brea oilfields, which were taken from foreign investors in 1968.[12] The bare-chested figure is perhaps an echo of the Peronista *descamisados* of Argentina, workers who were too poor to own a shirt. Another Peruvian stamp of the period (Scott 519) celebrates the Agrarian Reform Law, and shows a campesino wearing an Inca-style hat and breaking loose the chains of economic oppression; the legend is "Land for he who tills it." There was also a conscious effort to associate the 1968 revolution with Túpac Amaru, who rebelled against the Spanish colonial regime in the late eighteenth century. Stamps were part of this process (Scott 631, 734), and featured both Túpac Amaru and his wife Micaela, who was executed with him after the Spanish crushed his rebellion.

Another common theme that involves national icons on postage stamps is the recognition of famous citizens with accomplishments in a number of fields: literature, art, science, medicine, technology, and diplomacy. These are frequently honored on special anniversaries, but at times there seems to be no special occasion. Some countries (Argentina, for example) issue such series every year or so, and the figures involved are sometimes rather obscure citizens whose accomplishments are little known, even within their own country.

Portrayals of symbols of national unity can sometimes be controversial. In 1932 the Brazilian government held a contest to select three images to represent Brazil on stamps to be issued the following year. The selection committee, headed by the director general of the Postal and Telegraph Service, picked three images of Indians. These were widely denounced as not being representative of the nation. The stamps were never issued and the contest was canceled.

David Bushnell notes that there is one category of person severely underrepresented in the postage stamps of Latin America: women.[13] This is curious in light of the fact that the icon personifying many nations is a female figure, such as Britannia for England and Ceres and Marianne for France. No Latin American country has developed a female icon that personifies the nation in this same way; machismo is perhaps a factor. Bushnell has made a detailed study of the phenomenon as of 1997, and provides statistical data showing that the percentage of female figures on the stamps of the United States (11 percent) exceeds that of all the Latin American countries, although Argentina during the Perón years, Colombia since 1960, and revolutionary Cuba come close. Evita Perón is by far the woman most frequently appearing, thanks to the Argentine issues shortly after her death, and again when Peronismo was restored in Argentina in 1973. In the Colombian case the honor goes to the independence heroine Policarpa Salvarrieta, and in Cuba the Soviet cosmonaut Valentina Tereshkova. Curiously, in the United States stamp output the most honored woman has been the Spanish queen Isabella I (seven times), followed by Martha Washington (five times).

ECONOMICS (EXPORTS, TOURISM, INFLATION, SPORTS)

Complementing the theme of politics on Latin American postage stamps is the economic one, especially as it relates to stamps intended for circulation abroad (which are usually the higher values, especially airmail ones). A 1932 letter from the Argentine postal director to the minister of the interior expressed policy guidelines concerning postage stamps, "arguing that economic themes should be stressed because this would be free propaganda of unquestioned value, inasmuch as the postage stamp, circulating throughout all the countries of the world, will bring to mind the country of origin and its products and will thus awaken new markets." The same letter goes on to explain that the lower values of a new definitive series that would be used for over fifteen years (Scott 418–450) would carry nationalistic and patriotic themes, while the higher values (most likely to be used on international mail) would carry economic ones.[14] Chilean stamps have also shown a wide range of exports (figure 3.3, Scott 728).

Carlos Stoetzer notes that relatively underdeveloped nations whose exports consist of few primary materials or agricultural and mineral products display these on their international postage stamps, while European and other developed countries tend to publicize their industrial fairs and exhibitions.[15] Thus we have the examples of Argentine agricultural products (Scott 441), Bolivian and Chilean mineral wealth (Scott 292, 728), Venezuelan oil (Scott 847, C88), and coffee. Stamps featuring this final category come from the major producers such as Brazil (Scott 452), Colombia (Scott 595), Ecuador (Scott 305), and several Central American nations. The national coffee stamps are unusually competitive, frequently stressing that "our coffee is the best."[16]

Economic postal themes stressing industrialization and modernization can also carry a message of the pride a country has in its status as an emerging developed country. And so, along with stamps showing raw materials and commodities for export we also see themes of factories (especially steel mills), airports, and national airlines. The years of the first Perón administration in Argentina (1945–1955) are notable for the replacement of traditional agricultural themes by themes stressing industrial exhibits, shipping, communications, and the state-owned Aerolíneas Argentinas. Nationalization of key economic resources that had previously been under foreign control is frequently the object of postal issues and cancellations, such as when the Perón administration nationalized the rails in 1948: "The railroads are now Argentine! They now form part of the national patrimony." Other examples of nationalizations that were celebrated with postage stamps include Salvador Allende's nationalization of the Chilean copper industry, and nationalization of oil holdings in Peru, Venezuela, and Brazil. Stamps have also frequently been used internally to stimulate economic production. The Peronista five-year plans were the subject of a series of attractive and well-designed stamps, as well as cancellation slogans such as this item: "An Argentine who knows the Second Five Year Plan can carry it out under all circumstances—Perón."[17]

At times postage stamps can get caught up with rather unusual attempts to promote certain products. In 1998 Brazil issued a stamp (Scott 2693) that promoted a mango juice drink produced under the brand name Frisco. The iconography of the stamp shows both raw mangoes and the Frisco drink in a glass. The stamp is labeled "Promoção Frisco," and involved a raffle described in a popular television program. To enter the raffle, entrants were to send a letter (using the mango stamp), and the winners would be drawn from those received in a given time period. We noted earlier that Brazil also had a unique entry in the philatelic competition to advertise their coffee internationally: a stamp that smelled like coffee, and timed to mark the one-hundredth anniversary of the Rio de Janeiro Coffee Chamber of Commerce.[18] This was not the first time a Brazilian stamp featured an aroma: in 1999 a series of four stamps (Scott 2717a–d) featuring animals and a burnt tree trunk were released to draw attention to the importance of preventing forest fires. The aroma used in this series was burnt wood.

Also unusual was the Colombian experience with a United Nations stamp and first-day cover envelope in 1986. The project involved honoring each member state of the United Nations with a stamp and commemorative envelope noting the principal exports of that nation. The envelope's notation stated that Colombia's main industry was agriculture, "with coffee, cocaine and marijuana being the principal crops."[19] The Colombian U.N. delegation protested vigorously, and the envelope was canceled. It had been prepared by a commercial first-day cover cachet company by someone with a peculiar sense of humor, and the United Nations disavowed responsibility for the offending item.

A series of six Argentine postage stamps in 1998 had a clear international political message as well as an economic one (figure 3.4, Scott 2008; Scott 2006–2011). The six stamps featured the principal Argentine beef cattle breeds, and all carried the slogan "A country free of hoof-and-mouth disease [*aftosa* in Spanish] and BSE [bovine spongiform encephalopathy, i.e., mad cow disease]." The significance was that for many years Argentine beef, claimed to be the best in the world, could not enter U.S. and other markets because the U.S. Department of Agriculture (with some lobbying from the U.S. cattle industry) argued that it was contaminated with the highly infectious hoof-and mouth-disease. By 1998 Argentina had finally managed to convince U.S. authorities that the country was free of the disease and its importation was ultimately authorized.

Probably the most prolific category of economic stamps are those involving tourism. These stamps have multiple purposes.[20] The most obvious is to advertise tourist attractions nationally and abroad in the hopes of stimulating that industry. But they also serve to strengthen national pride in the natural beauties of one's country, and presumably create a positive image of the nation abroad. In the philatelic collectors' market they are also a source of income for the producing nation since they are usually well-designed, attractive, and with higher face value. The U.S. Postal Service used the theme of "National Parks" in a well-known series in 1934, which served to advertise the parks and became a highly prized classical set among collectors. At times tourism stamps border on the commercial, and one must wonder about the motives and lobbying behind a particular issue, such as the Dominican, Venezuelan, or Colombian hotel issues, which featured the top tourist hotels of the country (e.g., Scott Venezuela C1007), readily identifiable by location and chain.[21] Other stamps have shown specific and identifiable commercial tourist attractions and cruise ships, such as the Falkland Islands set of 1993 (Scott 584–587).[22]

The designation of 1973 as the "Year of Tourism in the Americas" gave rise to a number of postal issues on this theme, including Iguazú Falls, Machu Picchu, folklore icons, and many maps. Peru's Machu Picchu stamps over the years are especially detailed and attractive, showing many of the elements of that unique archeological site as well as icons of Inca culture (figure 3.7, Scott 726; Scott 464). The visit of the king and queen of Spain to the site in 1978 produced a panoramic stamp of the ruins, with the profiles of the royal visitors off to one side.[23] Tourist stamps, of course, always stress the positive, respectable, and beautiful side of the industry, becoming something like miniature, idealized posters promoting the nation's principal attractions. As Denis Altman points out, however, tourist stamps never show some of the seamier aspects (such as the sex tourism industry), and rarely gambling.[24] Monaco is an exception to the latter, and so was Argentina, when it featured one of the world's major casinos in Mar del Plata.

The somewhat unrealistic emphasis on only the positive aspects of tourism has occasionally backfired. A travel article on the Cayman Islands in a recent Scottish newspaper begins with the words "Never trust philately."[25] The author's point is that his impressions of the Cayman Islands were based mainly on the stamps he had collected as a boy: "The images on those postage stamps not only enhanced my fascination with all that overseas exotica, but educated me as to the nature of the culture and history of those far-off places. Or so I always believed." He goes on to tell of his trip to the islands, whose natural beauty he found quite attractive, but somewhat marred by the commercial aspects of the tourist areas, complete with numerous American fast-food outlets.

An important subcategory of tourism philately is that involved in major sporting events such as the Olympics and World Cup soccer. As one might expect, the host country for any such event places major philatelic emphasis on the occasion for some time before the date in order to publicize it and hopefully draw attention both nationally and internationally to its significance. Frequently countries that produce medal-winning teams or individuals honor them with stamps. Jumping on the bandwagon, states with no special connection to the event, and no hopes of winning medals, produce numbers of these stamps with the hope (frequently realized) that topical collectors of sports philately will purchase them. There are a number of specialized journals devoted to various sports on Olympic stamps, and several doctoral dissertations have been written on the subject. Myrtis Herndon's dissertation, for example, traces the economics of sports philately from the revival of the modern Olympics in 1896 to what she notes was the dramatic growth in such stamps in the last few decades.[26] The stamps issued by Mexico for the 1968 summer Olympics and the 1970 World Cup soccer games in Mexico City are now considered classic issues because of the historic nature of the events, and the original and highly stylized designs of the stamps (figure 3.8, Scott 983; figure 3.10, Scott C329).[27] The images portrayed in these stamps are attractive to many collectors and sports enthusiasts because they tend to use action-filled graphics showing the sports, the athletes, their attire, sport facilities, awards, and tourist attractions. There is a considerable market for these stamps, most of which are never used in the mails and thus represent an important source of revenue for the issuing nation.

Stamps celebrating soccer, and especially the World Cup, account for many stamps among those Latin American nations with some hope of reaching the end stages of the competition, such as Brazil and Argentina. And when a country hosts the World Cup, and wins it, the output is multiplied (figure 3.5, Scott Brazil 2848), and their great players, such as Pelé of Brazil, are honored (figure 3.6, Scott 1144). Other nations with less or no chance of winning still issue stamps celebrating their participation (Scott Bolivia 906).

One final economic phenomenon with political implications concerns the way postage stamps reflect inflation, both to a national and international audience.[28] The postage required to move a letter from one country to another is usually a fairly accurate and up-to-date indicator of inflation because these postal rates are set by international agreements, and are measured against a stable currency such as the dollar, pound, or (in pre-euro days) mark. A country that is suffering from inflation must raise the face value of stamps or lose money in the international postal system (e.g., see Scott Argentina 1198). Because postage stamps can be easily surcharged to reflect new values, they can quickly reflect such inflationary pressures. Sometimes the inflationary trend is disguised by changing the monetary unit or simply dropping zeroes, as occurred in Nicaragua in 1990, when one million "old" córdobas became worth one córdoba "oro."

Some of the rates of inflation suffered by Latin American nations are astounding: Nicaragua, 36,000 percent in 1988; and for the same year Argentina 4,500 percent, Peru 2,800 percent, and Brazil 1,800 percent. Michael Laurence describes how hyperinflation affected the Peruvian postage rate for a small newsletter: in late 1988, 75 intis; October 1989, 1,200 intis; February 1990, 7,000 intis; June 1990, 13,500 intis; August 1990, 230,000 intis.[29] By this time the inflation rate had outpaced the surcharges, and metered postage was used instead, with the newsletter requiring several passes through the meter because the metering system had only five digits, for a maximum of 99,999 intis. The impact of hyperinflation has many aspects, including the virtual wiping out of savings accounts, constant changes in prices of retail items in stores, and speculative investment in those items that tend to hold their true value, such as real estate. Internally, there is a demoralizing effect, with a corresponding mistrust of government and national institutions. One international phenomenon reflected in postage stamps is the creation of an image of national irresponsibility and economic instability, sometimes with political implications. We can illustrate this with an Argentine stamp issued on the first anniversary (April 1983) of the disastrous invasion of the Malvinas/Falklands. The large-format stamp features a map of southern Argentina and the South Atlantic Ocean, to include the Falklands/Malvinas, South Georgia, and South Sandwich Islands (figure 8.9). In the center of the stamp there is an Argentine flag with the inscription "1982—2 April—1983. First recovery of the Malvinas, Georgias and South Sandwich islands." The implication of the "first recovery" comment was that a second (and presumably more successful) recovery would be forthcoming at some future date. The slogan was the object of some sarcastic commentaries,[30] and it was noted that the face value of the stamp (20,000 pesos) was an indicator that Argentina had some grave economic as well as political and military problems to resolve before it would be taken seriously on the world scene again. A few months later the old peso was replaced by a new monetary unit, and the postage rate was down to single-digit pesos.

HOW THEMES ARE SELECTED

I noted in chapter 1 the politicized nature of the process of selecting stamp themes in the United States, and the pressures that the Citizens' Stamp Advisory Committee is subjected to by various groups and individuals with their favorite causes. With the exception of the larger countries (Argentina, Brazil, Mexico), little information is available regarding the stamp selection process in Latin America. Even in those countries in which stamp selection committees exist, it is clear that the administration in office has strong representation on the committee, and that the final decision on themes is probably made by the highest officials in the postal administration, with the strong likelihood that the political wishes of the chief executive or his representative carry a great deal of weight.

The greatest body of information is on the Argentine case, where an active philatelic press follows the process closely, and indeed has a representative on the Comisión Asesora de Filatelia (Philatelic Advisory Commission). The Argentine commission was created in 1970 by presidential decree, which gave it the mission of "preserving the fundamental historic values that in the various fields of human activity establish the essence of philately and the interests of the community."[31] The commission reports to the secretary of state for communications, and is composed of representatives from the National Academy of History, the Association of Philatelic Journals, the National Foundation for the Arts, the Argentine Federation of Philatelic Entities, and ENCOTEL, the country's philatelic enterprise dedicated to selling stamps to collectors. The commission meets twice a year to consider the themes of Argentina's commemorative stamps and make recommendations for the approximately twenty-four commemorative stamps issued yearly. Suggestions are received from various government and private organizations as well as individuals. The privatization of the Argentine mail system in 1997 changed the structure of the commission somewhat, and placed it under the jurisdiction of the Secretariat of State Communications.

The scope of the Argentine commission's work can be seen by the 319 requests for stamp issues it received in 1998,[32] organized in the following categories (the numbers in parentheses indicate the quantity of requests):

1. Arts and letters (125)
2. Postal and universal commemoratives (16). These support such national and international postal activities as philatelic exhibitions, joint binational issues, and coordinated international campaigns on themes such as combating AIDS.
3. Sports and hobbies (9)
4. Ethnography, geography, and history (103)
5. Youth, family, and celebrities (7)
6. Medicine and welfare (7)
7. Nature (20)
8. Religion, sects, and mythology (16)
9. Technology and transportation (16)

This commission recommended nineteen themes, and a check of the *Scott's Catalogue* for the corresponding year indicates that all nineteen of these themes were adopted. Additions that had not been recommended by the commission included issues commemorating historic chapels, journalists' day, MERCOSUR (the South American Common Market), the fiftieth anniversary of the state of Israel, a children's hospital, Raoul Wallenberg, and a Spanish philatelic exhibition.

Brazil's National Communications Code prescribes the formation of an eleven-person "Philatelic Commission" made up of representatives of the Ministries of Foreign Relations, Communications, Education, and Culture, as well as several museums and the philatelic clubs of Rio and São Paulo. The commission is presided over by the postmaster general, who is assisted by the head of the Philatelic Bureau of the Post Office. It meets twice a year and makes recommendations for the approximately forty-five new stamps issued each year. Once the themes are selected, the commission selects private or government artists to produce the stamp designs.[33]

The Mexican process is similar, with a five-person advisory commission consisting of four government officials and a representative from the National Autonomous University of Mexico. The commission is presided over by the postmaster general, who makes the final recommendations, which must be approved by the Office of the President before production can begin. Decrees require that 70 percent of the stamps produced be provided for actual mail use, and 30 percent be forwarded to the Post Office's Philatelic Department for sale to collectors.[34]

Guatemala also has a five-person National Philatelic Council, established in 1975. Its members include a representative of the Ministry of Communications (who presides), one from the Ministry of Finance, one from the Geography and History Society of Guatemala, a representative of the Philatelic Association of Guatemala, and a prominent philatelist. In making decisions on stamp themes, the Ministry of Communications is instructed to give preference to the opinion of the council. A Guatemalan philatelic organization notes dryly that Guatemalan commemoratives are frequently issued a year or more late due to bureaucratic delays and the need to get the approval of two ministries and the Office of the President of Guatemala.[35]

CENSORSHIP AND THE READING OF MAILS

For as long as there have been mail systems (and long before the 1840 arrival of the first postage stamp) governments have been tempted to interfere with the mails, either by secretly reading correspondence, or (especially in wartime) by ensuring that the international mails contained no information that would help the enemy.

A well-documented effort at state censorship of mails dates to the Cromwell regime in England when the lord protector asked Secretary of State John Thurloe in 1655 to set up a system by which suspicious mail could be opened, read, and resealed without the recipient being aware of it. Thurloe was an effective collector and analyst of intelligence who set up a room in the Foreign Office, where every evening his censors examined all suspect mail and resealed the letters after Thurloe had seen them.[36]

The first organized censorship during wartime occurred during the 1899–1900 Boer War, and was greatly expanded during World War I, including in the U.S. postal system. Censorship was extensive in the Spanish Civil War (1936–1939) and World War II. Mail opened by U.S. and British censors was required to carry a notation that it had been opened, and a censor identified by number (figure 3.9). Mail that did not pass the censor would be returned to the sender with a sometimes vague explanation as to the reason. Latin American mails were involved when they entered or left the United States, since there were suspicions of pro-Axis groups in a number of hemisphere countries. It also appears that the FBI operated a censorship bureau in Mexico City.[37]

One example of acknowledged censorship by a Latin American government occurred as part of the Argentine military coup of September 1930, which brought down the Radical government of Hipólito Yrigoyen. As reported in a Uruguayan philatelic journal, it involved only a small number of pieces of mail opened by Argentine army officers who took over the main post office as part of the coup.[38] The censored letters carry the rubber stamp "CENSURA MILITAR" and the signature of the person opening the envelope, which would then be resealed. The censorship activities apparently lasted only a few days, and the Argentine philatelist writing the article, noting that such activities were contrary to the Argentine constitution, concluded that these censorship activities were the result of a political reality based on the extraordinary circumstances of the moment.[39] As we shall see in the Argentine case, during the 1982 war the navy censored mail going through its postal system, which operated independently from the official Argentine one. Other examples of censorship occurred in Colombia's War of the Thousand Days and with the World War II Brazilian Expeditionary Force, where the censorship system was modeled after the one in the United States during that conflict.[40]

4 INTERNATIONAL RELATIONS AND LATIN AMERICAN STAMPS

Latin American postage stamps have played a part in a series of international relations issues.[1] Some of these (discussed toward the end of the chapter) are uncontroversial and usually involve a nation's support of an international organization, or are issued to commemorate the visit of a friendly head of state. Others, however, are linked to interstate strains, usually over border and sovereignty issues. In these far more interesting cases the postage stamp frequently plays a political or propaganda role in favor of the country's position on the issue. The most dramatic and effective of these postage stamps involve maps showing the issuing country's claim and demonstrate the impact of a well-designed postage stamp using a map as the iconographic sign illustrating the country's views, and the semiotic use of a powerful national symbol (the map of a country). Sometimes the problem arises through mistakes in the drawing of maps, but the injured country in such circumstances is still likely to be suspicious and react accordingly. The topic of maps on stamps, and the problems caused by errors—deliberate or accidental, has led to a philatelic subspecialty, complete with its organization (CartoPhilatelic Society) and journal (*New CartoPhilatelist*).

The Argentine stamp showing the South American continent, first issued as part of the definitive set of 1935 (figure 4.1), is an illustrative example. This is the "with borders" stamp, which included the frontier demarcations of all the South American nations, and shaded the Malvinas/Falkland Islands the same color as the Argentine mainland, although it did not name or label the islands as Argentine. Predictably, there were a number of protests over the boundaries and shadings. Peru objected because its border with Ecuador favored the latter in the age-old dispute over the Amazon area. Chile noted that the geography around the southern tip of the continent (Tierra del Fuego and the Magellan Strait area) seemed to favor Argentina at Chile's expense. And the British were not happy at seeing the Falkland

Islands shaded the same color as mainland Argentina. The British Foreign Office was not eager to get into a diplomatic spat with Argentina over the matter, and attempted to resolve it by informal conversations at a lower level between embassy staff and junior Argentine authorities. In light of the various protests the Argentine Dirección General de Correos acknowledged that the stamp contained errors, especially on the matter of the southern boundaries with Chile, and that it was willing to withdraw the stamp and redraw it to correct the errors. However, it was not willing to disown the stamp, or redraw the shading of the Malvinas Islands, because to do so might imply that it was retreating on Argentina's Malvinas claim.[2] As the director of the Postal Office put it in a 22 April 1936 memo to the Ministry of the Interior: "The withdrawal of the stamp could lead to the belief that the Argentine Republic was backing off from its rights to the Malvinas Islands."[3]

The stamp was indeed redrawn and reissued without the borders that had caused problems (figure 4.2, Scott 446). To assuage the Chileans, the stamp showed a greatly exaggerated piece of Chilean territory in the south, so exaggerated that one must wonder if this was a deliberate attempt to make the Chileans look foolish. There was no attempt to satisfy the British concern, and the Malvinas continued to be shaded in the same color as mainland Argentina. To add insult to injury, several propaganda postcards showing the Malvinas Islands as Argentine and featuring the Argentine flag were also issued in the 1936–1937 period.[4]

The British were reluctant to raise the level of diplomatic tension over the stamps, and in answer to a question in the House of Commons Foreign Minister Anthony Eden noted that there was little Great Britain could do to stop Argentina from issuing stamps labeling the islands as Argentine.[5] A sequel came in 1951 during the Perón era, when the Argentine Antarctic claim was added to the basic design (figure 4.3, Scott 594).

CARIBBEAN

Dominican Republic and Haiti

Relations have never been particularly good between these two Caribbean countries that share the island of Hispaniola, for a variety of historical and ethnic reasons. There had also been some historic confusion regarding the exact demarcation of the border between the two countries. And so, when the Dominican Republic issued a map stamp of Hispaniola in 1900 (figure 4.4, Scott 111–119) the Haitians were quick to notice that the boundary ran quite a bit farther west across the island than they believed should be the case.[6] The Haitian government protested via diplomatic channels, but the Dominican reaction was to send troops to the border area to push out any Haitian citizens in the disputed zone. Diplomatic pressure resulted in the Dominican Republic's withdrawal of the stamp, but large numbers of the stamp had already circulated, and many counterfeits were also produced. However, a few years later in 1928 the Dominican Republic's first airmail stamp (Scott C1) also raised questions about the border shown on the map. The borders of the 1900 Dominican map did have a historical basis: they roughly follow the line set by the Treaty of Aranjuez between Spain and France in 1777.[7] But later agreements moved the border to the east, and Haiti had legitimate reason to be concerned that the map stamp could be an attempt to reopen the issue. After the controversial stamps appeared a prominent stamp expert asked the American Bank Note Company, which printed many of these issues, about the cartographic problems and was told that the company used maps supplied by the countries involved and took no position on controversial issues such as border disputes.[8]

Haiti's response was a 1924 stamp that shows no boundary at all between Haiti and its neighbor (Scott 317), and this could be interpreted as an attempt to avoid further controversy. The border issue was resolved in a 1929 treaty after arbitration by Brazil, Venezuela, and the United States (which had occupying troops in both countries at various periods in the early part of the twentieth century). Both countries promptly issued stamps commemorating the signing (Scott DR 249–253; Scott Haiti 321), but used portraits of their presidents as the stamp icons, and avoided including maps showing the demarcation of the border. Haitian-Dominican relations remained strained, however, and were worsened by the frequent harassment and murders of Haitians crossing the border as they looked for work in the sugar cane fields of the area. A more definitive border treaty was signed in 1935, and the Dominicans marked the occasion with a stamp set featuring President Rafael Leonidas Trujillo (Scott 299–302).

Mexico, France, the United States, and Clipperton Island (Isla de la Pasión)

This flyspeck of an island in the Pacific would be of no importance except for the guano that covers it in thick layers, and an unusual attempt to issue postage stamps for use by the guano workers. The island has been uninhabited for most of the time since its 1704 discovery by the pirate John Clipperton, who used it as his lair. It is about two square miles in area, located approximately eight hundred miles southwest of Acapulco, Mexico, in the Pacific Ocean. Its location would seem to make it part of Mexico, but the French claim that it is the easternmost island of French Polynesia.

Under the Guano Act of 1856 the United States claimed it as a temporary possession for the purpose of exploiting the bird droppings but did not occupy it before the French took possession of it in 1858. Shortly before the Spanish-American War a group of Americans raised the U.S. flag on the island, but they were disowned by Washington, which recognized the French claim. In 1897 the Mexican government sent a small garrison, which stayed until 1917. The sovereignty dispute between France and Mexico was turned over to the king of Italy for arbitration in 1908; he decided in favor of France in 1931, and Mexico withdrew its presence in 1932.[9]

The philatelic history of the islands stems from a group of some two hundred employees of the San Francisco–based Oceanic Phosphate Company, who worked the guano deposits from 1895 to 1917. In 1895 the company's agents were authorized to issue a set of ten stamps featuring a map of the island and its fauna, and some of these were apparently used legitimately to carry letters from the workers on the island to San Francisco. However, several philatelic groups and journal publishers denounced thc stamps as fraudulent since no national government had authorized their printing. There also exist Mexican stamps overprinted "Clipperton," and it is possible that these were used to carry mail from the island to Acapulco, although most experts doubt their legitimacy.

Despite its remoteness and lack of resources (except for guano) the island has had periodic visits from French and U.S. military vessels, including one carrying President Franklin Roosevelt in 1938. The United States was apparently interested in using the island as an outpost for the defense of the Panama Canal, and kept a small garrison there in the World War II years. The significance of the Clipperton Island postage stamps is that their use, had they been officially sanctioned by the U.S. government, could have been the basis for strengthening the U.S. claim on the island, since it would have been an act of sovereignty demonstrating actual possession under international law. However, the decline in the economic value of guano, and the subsequent abandonment of the island, meant that it once more sank into obscurity in the vastness of the eastern Pacific.

Clipperton Island also figures in a bizarre scheme under which it is part of the territory of the nonexistent "Dominion of Melchizedek" (which also includes a portion of Antarctica). This "Dominion" was proclaimed in 1990 and has served mainly to sell phony banking and incorporation papers employed by con men.[10]

The United States and Cuba

Although there were no sovereignty issues involved in Cuban stamps focusing on the United States, there are a number of Cuban stamps that have been used for anti-American political and propaganda purposes. These should be set in the context of the fact that revolutionary Cuba, following the example of the Soviet Union/Russia, has issued a great many stamps (some 3,500 from January 1959 to late 2000, compared with some 600 from 1855 to the coming to power of Castro in 1959). Although many, if not most, of these stamps were issued primarily for collectors, it is also true that they present a many-faceted visual compendium of the things the revolutionary government felt were important.

One fundamental and consistent anti-American theme has been the defeat of U.S.-supported forces at the Bay of Pigs in April 1961, known to the Cubans as the "Victory of Playa Girón." For the first few years after the event a new set of stamps was issued each April (for example, figure 4.9, Scott 3308), some of them with quite striking icons. On the first anniversary, two Cuban soldiers were shown against the background of a burning plane supporting the invading forces (Scott 706–708). One of the soldiers brandishes a rifle, and the second holds a large Cuban flag. On the third anniversary, the icon shows a falling eagle caught in the gun sight of a Cuban antiaircraft weapon (Scott 825–827). After the fifth anniversary in 1966, the event was commemorated on the tenth and fifteenth anniversaries.

A second theme is support of guerrilla movements and the "anti-imperialist movement" worldwide. Issues in this category have included those celebrating meetings or the hero Che Guevara. Meetings of the Organization of Latin American Solidarity (Scott 1245–1248 in 1967) have been featured, showing various guerrillas in Latin America. One particular meeting in 1964 produced the Declaration of Havana, in which the estimated 25,000 words of the text of the declaration were printed in miniature fonts on the series of nine stamps. According to some philatelists, this is the smallest printing ever successfully achieved on a postage stamp (Scott 931a–e and 932a–e).[11] Numerous issues celebrate Che Guevara (Scott 1318, 1347–1351), culminating in the 1998 ones commemorating the thirtieth anniversary of his death in Bolivia, and the return of his remains to Cuba.

Another consistent theme, especially in the 1960s and early 1970s, was support for Vietnam, and the National Liberation Front (Vietcong). Comparisons were made between Cuban independence hero José Martí and Ho Chi Minh (Scott 1696–1698), and there were frequent philatelic calls for the unification of Vietnam, to be achieved after the Americans left (Scott 846). Vietcong guerrillas were shown in heroic poses defeating well-equipped U.S. soldiers (Scott 846–849). Particularly virulent was a 1966 series of stamps titled "Genocide in Vietnam" (Scott 1163–1165). U.S. aircraft were depicted dropping bombs, followed by stamps showing the ensuing casualties (mainly women, children, cattle). Some victims were shown with gas masks, suggesting that the United States was using chemical or biological weapons.

CENTRAL AMERICA

The United States, Panama, and Nicaragua

One of the most enduring of philatelic myths (partially true) is how a postage stamp changed the course of the isthmus canal from a Nicaraguan location to a Panamanian one. After the disastrous French attempt to build a sea-level canal under the leadership of Ferdinand de Lesseps, two competing plans were considered by the U.S. Congress, and supporters of each mounted an intense lobbying effort: the Panama route would roughly parallel the old French canal, but with locks to avoid the engineering problems de Lesseps encountered. The Nicaraguan route, although longer, relied on using an existing river and Lake Nicaragua, and was thus technically easier. As the U.S. Senate and House neared a vote in mid-1902, it appeared the Nicaraguan lobby was going to win. One argument being used by the Panama advocates was the presence of active volcanoes in Nicaragua, in contrast to the more stable geology of Panama. Concern over volcanoes was heightened when Mount Pelée on Martinique erupted in May 1902, killing some thirty thousand inhabitants of the town of Saint-Pierre. The Nicaragua lobby argued that this was not relevant to their country, and that there were no active volcanoes that could endanger a possible canal. Unfortunately, a 1900 postage stamp of Nicaragua (figure 4.8 and Scott 121–133) showed the Momotombo volcano on Lake Nicaragua in eruption, and this was seized by the Panama lobbyist Philippe Bunau-Varilla as a powerful weapon to be used against the Nicaraguan lobbyists.[12]

Bunau-Varilla described the process by which he used the Nicaraguan postage stamp to influence the United States Congress:[13]

> We were reaching the end of the discussion. If the vote were to be taken under this impression Panama was done forever. Only six or seven days remained.
>
> The game, however, was won.
>
> Fortunately I had a sudden inspiration.
>
> The official documents, which I was looking for, I had under my very hand. They were the postage stamps of the Republic of Nicaragua, which I had mentioned in the pamphlet containing the substance of my lectures of 1901. I hastened to call on all the postage-stamp dealers of Washington. I was lucky enough to find there ninety stamps, that is, one for every Senator, showing a beautiful volcano belching forth in magnificent eruption. It was the up-to-date proof of the existence of these volcanoes in activity, which the officials of the Nicaraguan Government denied.

Bunau-Varilla goes on to tell how he mounted his volcano stamps on sheets of paper, writing at the top "Postage Stamps of the Republic of Nicaragua," and below the stamps, "An official witness of the volcanic activity of Nicaragua." He was pleased to note that the volcano was identified as Momotombo, and that the wharf pictured in the foreground was the one destroyed by Momotombo a month earlier. The stamps were distributed to the senators three days before the vote, and the effectiveness of Bunau-Varilla's bold stroke can be seen in the comment by one senator that it was unreasonable to put the canal "in a country which had taken as its emblem on its postage stamps a volcano in eruption."[14] The Senate vote was forty-two to thirty-four in favor of the Panama route. A few days later Bunau-Varilla repeated his postage stamp effort with the House of Representatives. He had to go to New York to obtain enough Nicaraguan volcano stamps, but eventually was able to round up five hundred of them and printed a brief pamphlet explaining the significance of the erupting Momotombo. Upon his return to Washington the stamps were distributed, and on the following day the Spooner Bill (favoring Panama) was adopted with only eight dissenting votes.[15]

It is difficult to assess the impact of Bunau-Varilla's stamp lobbying effort. He was not a modest man, and he claims that his effort was decisive. McCullough, in his authoritative history of the Panama Canal, has this to say: "How much the little postage stamp really mattered, whether it actually changed any votes, is impossible to say. Probably it did not, Bunau-Varilla's assertions notwithstanding. His diagrammatic pamphlet probably had a more telling effect. Still, the stamp was an inspired bit of propaganda."[16]

Postage stamps figured prominently in the end stages of the control of the Panama Canal and its zone under U.S. administration. With the coming to power of de facto head of state General Omar Torrijos in 1968, pressures to return control and sovereignty of the canal and the zone to Panama increased. Torrijos was successful in obtaining considerable Latin American and third world support in favor of new treaties, and one of his public relations triumphs was getting the U.N. Security Council to meet in Panama in March 1973 and focus on the canal issue; stamps were issued by Panama to celebrate the event (Scott 541–543; C433, issued after Torrijos's death in 1981, shows him at the U.N. meeting).

After many years of intense and sometimes bitter negotiations, President Jimmy Carter and General Omar Torrijos signed new canal treaties on 7 September 1977 at the OAS Headquarters in Washington. Panama noted the event with a spectacular set of stamps in which all of the major players in the negotiation and signing are identified (Scott 588–589).[17] This was followed shortly by stamps honoring Carter and Torrijos (Scott 594, 597). In the first of these the iconography is not subtle: General Torrijos in uniform is seen walking with children carrying a Panamanian flag against the background of canal locks; the legend reads: "One people, one flag." As the twenty-two-year process of turning the canal and zone over to Panama progressed, stamps were issued to note important steps in the transfer, leading up to the final full reversion of the canal to Panama in December 1999 (Scott Panama 875–878). The last day of operation of the old U.S. Canal Zone Postal Service was noted with a special cancellation.

Belize and Guatemala

Stamps were a factor in the long-simmering dispute involving Guatemala's claim to part (and sometimes all) of the former colony of British Honduras, independent since 1981 as the country of Belize. Documents available in the National Archives of the United States reflect concern by U.S. Embassy officials over the dispute, and the way Guatemalan postage stamps were being used for political purposes.[18] The principal architect behind this effort was the Guatemalan president Jorge Ubico, who during his presidency in 1931–1944 made several attempts to pressure Great Britain to give up her colony.

As part of this effort Ubico ordered the preparation of a map stamp that showed Belice (the Spanish form of "Belize") as part of Guatemala (Scott 292–324). British Foreign Office protests led to the withdrawal of the stamp within a month, but the stamp was to make a significant reappearance a decade later when it was reissued in 1948 as part of a renewed campaign to pressure the British.

A less subtle philatelic renewal of the dispute took the form of a 1967 Guatemalan stamp (figure 4.11, Scott 396; Scott 397–398) in which the icon is a map of Guatemala (including Belize) with the blue-white-blue colors of the Guatemalan flag emblazoned on the "greater Guatemala" that would include Belize; the legend on the stamps reads "Belice es de Guatemala" ("Belize is Guatemalan"). Shortly after independence in 1981 the new nation of Belize issued a map stamp whose color shading unfortunately (and apparently inadvertently) seemed to indicate that part of Belize belonged to Guatemala. Owing to concerns that this might seem to be a concession to Guatemala at a time when diplomatic and even military tensions were high, the stamp was quickly withdrawn from sale.[19] In the ensuing two decades the issue has been resolved peacefully, with Guatemala in effect giving up her long-standing claim and recognizing Belize's territorial integrity.

Costa Rica: Cocos Island

A minor but illustrative use of a postage stamp to assert sovereignty was the 1936 Costa Rican stamp showing a map of "Isla del Coco" and making it clear that it is part of Costa Rica. The island, not to be confused with the Cocos (Keeling) Islands in the Indian Ocean, lies about three hundred miles southwest of Costa Rica in the Pacific Ocean. The island is uninhabited, but pirates in the seventeenth century were reported to have buried their treasure there, and the island was visited twice by President Franklin D. Roosevelt during fishing trips, which might have been a cover for scouting out a strategic island suitable for bases to screen any Japanese attack coming from the Pacific.[20] In 1935 a British treasure-hunting group organized an expedition to search for the pirate gold. In their prospectus they included a statement to the effect that Costa Rica lacked sovereignty over Cocos Island.[21] The Costa Rican reaction was swift: the government arrested and ejected the fortune hunters and issued stamps (Scott 169–178) to make it clear that the island was part of Costa Rica. More recently, Cocos Island was the setting for Michael Crichton's novel *Jurassic Park* and the subsequent movie. Pendleton notes that the Costa Rican stamps featuring the island show few interior features, which he interprets as revealing a lack of knowledge of the island beyond the coast, adding an air of mystery to the setting of the book and movie.[22]

Nicaragua and Honduras

A more serious situation developed between neighboring states Honduras and Nicaragua involving a long-standing border dispute aggravated by map stamps showing the positions of the two countries on the issue.[23] There were attempts to resolve the disputed territorial claims between the two countries between 1839 and 1904, when the matter was submitted to Spain's king Alfonso XIII, who in 1906 ruled in favor of Honduras; Nicaragua rejected the award, and the issue remained as an irritant in the relations between the two countries. The dispute heated up in July of 1937 when Nicaragua issued a set of airmail stamps whose primary purpose would be foreign postage (Scott C186–192). They featured a map of Nicaragua along with portions of Costa Rica and Honduras. The area of the 1906 arbitration award was labeled "territorio en litigio" ("territory under litigation"), which was technically correct, but provocative since the award had been given to Honduras. It did not take long for the rather large number of Hondurans living in Nicaragua to notice the stamps, and one group of Honduran students in Managua stormed the Post Office in an attempt to destroy the stamps. The ensuing riots resulted in some deaths and several hundred injuries. The Honduran government formally protested and demanded that the stamps be withdrawn. Nicaragua refused, arguing that the stamp showed the official map of Nicaragua; rumors flew that both countries were mobilizing military forces along the border, and Honduran postal authorities rejected any Nicaraguan mail bearing the stamps. Nicaragua in turn refused any Honduras letter carrying an earlier map stamp showing the Spanish arbitration (Scott C79). Tensions were relaxed somewhat when neighboring nations offered their good offices, and the Nicaraguan Post Office issued a new set of stamps to replace the offending ones.

Ultimately the border dispute festered until it was submitted to the International Court of Justice in The Hague, which in November 1960 upheld King Alfonso's 1906 arbitration award, in effect deciding in favor of Honduras. Honduras promptly issued a set of seven stamps showing King Alfonso against the background of a map of the award, and several scenes of the International Court making the award. Nicaragua chose not to mark the occasion with a stamp.

Central American conflict, 1979–1991

The coming to power of the Sandinistas and the establishment of a revolutionary regime in Nicaragua set off a protracted conflict involving all the Central American nations as well as the United States and Cuba and the Soviet Union.[24] The resolution of the conflict was slow and painful, and in turn involved the Contadora Group, consisting of Mexico, Panama, Colombia, and Venezuela, the United Nations, and several other countries (chief among them Spain and Canada). Eventually the Central American nations themselves, under the leadership of Costa Rican president Oscar Arias (figure 4.5, Scott 395), forged the Esquipulas Peace Treaty (Scott Guatemala C825). After-effects of the conflict still resonate in the region, and perhaps the most poignant philatelic reminder of the thousands of land mines that remain is a Salvadorean stamp showing the 1989 Amputee Soccer Championship (figure 4.6, Scott C546), an event that El Salvador won.

NORTHERN SOUTH AMERICA

Venezuela and Guyana

The Venezuela-Guyana border crisis presents a situation somewhat analogous to that of Guatemala and Belize. The dispute goes back to differences between an independent Venezuela and the colony of British Guiana over the delimitation of the border in the so-called Essequibo Territory. The maximum Venezuelan claim is to all territory west of the Essequibo River, which Great Britain refused to accept. In 1896 Venezuela, to honor an independence hero, issued a set of stamps titled "Apotheosis of Miranda," which consisted of maps showing their Essequibo claim (Scott 137–141). These map stamps are believed to be the first use of map stamps for propaganda involving disputed territories.[25] A few years later both sides accepted arbitration, which generally favored the British. Venezuela objected to the award, based on a series of alleged irregularities, and the dispute continued.

As Britain moved toward granting Guyana independence in the mid-1960s, the Venezuelans intensified their diplomatic and philatelic efforts to make good their claim to the Essequibo region. In 1965 an impressively detailed and colorful set of six historic map stamps, accompanied by fancy souvenir sheets (Scott 886–888, C905–907), showed various boundary lines in the region that indicated how Great Britain had been expanding westward at the expense of first Spain and then Venezuela over the years. The stamps carried the legend "Venezuela. Claim to its Essequibo," using the Spanish possessive adjective. Later Venezuelan stamps (such as Scott 1056 in 1973) showed the Essequibo claim in striped shading to indicate that the territory was still being disputed. Guyana's independence in May 1966 was accompanied by a series (Scott 20–23) with the new flag set against a background map of the old maximum British claim, now converted into Guyana's. The Guyanese never attempted to match the details of the Venezuelan map stamps, limiting themselves to a silhouette of the nation's territory with the slogan "Essequibo is Ours" (Scott 336–341, 391).

Peru and Ecuador

This border dispute goes back to the colonial period, when the Spanish authorities were not particularly precise about the boundaries between the different administrative units (which eventually became separate independent countries), and in any case, laying out boundary markers on the ground was extremely difficult in a number of key areas where mountainous jungle terrain predominates.[26] The region in dispute is the vast Oriente Province, which would double the size of Ecuador if it were to make its claim good; it would also give it access to the Amazon River and the possible oil fields in the region. Peru and Ecuador fought a brief but bitter war in 1941–1942, in which Peru got the upper hand and was able to persuade a number of hemisphere nations to support its claim, which was formalized in the 1942 Protocol of Rio de Janeiro. Ecuador has long argued that the 1942 Rio Protocol was forced on it by the larger nations of the hemisphere (including the United States and Brazil) because they wanted to quickly resolve this distraction from the mounting crisis in Europe, which was soon to draw them into World War II. In 1960 Ecuador formally proclaimed the protocol null and void, and a year later issued stamps (figure 4.7, Scott C377; Scott C378–379) showing their maximum claim in the Oriente region, with the slogan "Ecuador ha sido, es y será país Amazónico" ("Ecuador has been, is, and will be, an Amazonian nation"); stamps honoring heroes killed in battle followed.[27] Peru promptly issued large-format map stamps (Scott C175–177) showing the disputed border region, with a similar slogan: "Estas tierras y estos ríos han sido, son y serán peruanos" ("These lands and these rivers have been, are, and will be, Peruvian"), and the added words: "Frontera fijada por el Protocolo de Rio de Janeiro de 1942" ("Border established by the Rio de Janeiro Protocol of 1942").

Each year around the time of the anniversary of the 1941 war, tensions increased between military units facing each other across the border, and fighting broke out in 1981 and more seriously in 1995. Both countries issued postage stamps honoring their courageous fighting men. Peru's was a large souvenir sheet featuring their heroes in the conflict (Scott 1194 in 1998). In 1981 Ecuador's "National Defense" stamp (Scott 1010–1011) shows a soldier charging against a background map of Ecuador's maximum territorial claim. After the 1995 fighting Ecuador issued a dramatic series of stamps showing a soldier at the front writing to children, a hand holding the flag of Ecuador, and a soldier on guard in the wilderness (Scott 1363–1365).

The Central Bank of Ecuador, in a commemorative postal album that included the 1981 stamps, described the situation this way: "National Defense. The border problem between Ecuador and its southern neighbor—Peru—comes from many years back. After the Peruvian invasion of 1941, the situation has grown more serious, and tension between the two countries has become a hot coal about to rekindle the fire. The most recent wound opened in January–February 1981 with very serious incidents in the region of Paquisha and Yantatza, and this was the reason for this (stamp) issue."[28] After the 1995 series of clashes an intense negotiation and peacekeeping effort was launched by the "guarantor countries," including the United States and Brazil. Their efforts reached fruition in a 1998 peace treaty, which appears to have settled the conflict. Both countries issued commemorative stamps, and the Ecuadorian Foreign Ministry's press release stated that "the issuing of these postage stamps attempts to let the world know of the fruits of peace and development that both countries are embarked on."[29] The Peruvian stamp (Scott 1202) also honored the guarantor countries by including their flags.

SOUTHERN SOUTH AMERICA

Bolivia, Peru, and Chile

These three countries were involved in the "War of the Pacific" (1879–1883) in which a Peruvian-Bolivian alliance was decisively defeated by a numerically inferior but highly motivated and well-organized Chilean military force. The conflict proved disastrous for Peru, which lost two provinces (one, Tacna, was later returned, while the second, Arica, passed into Chilean hands), and especially for Bolivia, which permanently lost Antofagasta Province and thus its outlet to the sea.[30] For the Chileans the disputes surrounding the war were resolved long ago through various treaties signed early in the twentieth century. For the Bolivians the matter will never be settled until they recover their outlet to the sea, and for the Peruvians the war was a bitter defeat that echoes to this day. At present Bolivia refuses to have diplomatic relations with Chile, and there is an ongoing dispute over maritime boundaries between Chile and Peru, which has threatened to take the matter to the International Court of Justice in The Hague.[31]

Many of the military events of the conflict have appeared on postage stamps of the three countries (e.g., Scott Chile 568), and even the losers in the war found solace in the heroic acts of their armies and navies as they went down in defeat (see, e.g., Peru's long series commemorating the centennial of the war, Scott 687–698). One of the most colorful episodes concerns the final words of the Bolivian colonel Eduardo Abaroa, who, when the Chileans demanded his surrender at the 23 March 1879 battle of Topáter, answered, "¿Rendirme? ¡Que se rinda tu abuela . . . !" ("Surrender? Your grandmother should surrender . . . !"). The ellipsis replaces a crude expletive, which has gone into Bolivian folklore (Scott Bolivia 365).

As the advancing Chilean forces moved into Bolivian and Peruvian territory, the conflict generated much postal history, that branch of philately that concerns itself with the letters and postmarks as well as the actual stamps. Whenever the Chileans captured a town they used Chilean stamps dated and canceled with the name of the captured town, and the progress of the Chilean forces up the coast to Lima can thus be documented by this postal history.[32] One special category of stamp issued some years later was the Peruvian plebiscite stamps.[33] At the end of the fighting stage of the conflict in 1883 the peace treaty of Tarapacá was signed, under which Antofagasta and Tarapacá were awarded outright to Chile, and the fate of Tacna and Arica would be determined by a plebiscite to be held in ten years. The plebiscite was delayed by squabbling among the three nations, and in 1925–1928 the Peruvians issued a series of obligatory "Tacna and Arica Plebiscite Stamps" (Scott RA6–13), which were to generate funds as surcharges on regular mails; the Peruvian stamps featured a military hero of the conflict and the promontory rock formation in the area, the Morro de Arica. The purpose of the funds was to finance the return of Peruvian citizens who had fled the provinces during the fighting and subsequent Chilean occupation. Initially the stamps were voluntary, although they were seen as an indicator of a Peruvian citizen's patriotism. In 1926 they were made mandatory ("obligatorio"), but this requirement was dropped when popular protests emerged as the plebiscite was postponed again. In 1929 a protocol signed in Washington settled the issue by awarding Tacna to Peru and Arica to Chile. Peru celebrated the return of Tacna with stamps such as the fiftieth anniversary issue (Scott 702).

Bolivia has made the most consistent use of postage stamps to press for a return of its lost territories, or at least for an outlet to the sea. In 1925 a Bolivian stamp (figure 5.2, Scott 155) shows a condor facing to the right (presumably to the west) and the legend "Hacia el Mar" ("To the Sea"). On the centennial of the war (1979) Bolivia issued a commemorative series labeled "Centennial of our captive sea-coast." One stamp featured Abaroa, one featured the coat of arms of the lost Littoral Province (with icons of a sailing ship, an anchor, and the sea), and in the third a woman dressed in a shirt with the colors of the Bolivian flag is chained to a wall map showing Bolivia's lost coast; she struggles to break the chains, but is not successful (figure 5.1, Scott 634).

Under the terms of the various peace treaties the Bolivians were supposedly given commercial rail and highway access to the sea via their own old territories (now in Chilean possession), but the Bolivians constantly complained of Chilean bureaucratic delays and petty harassment. In the search for alternate arrangements, the 1992 Bolivian-Peruvian Port Access Agreement gave Bolivia easier facilities to reach the coast (through Peruvian territory), and this agreement was celebrated by stamps in both Peru (Scott 1018) and Bolivia (Scott 842).

Chile and France: Easter Island (Rapa-Nui) stamps

The Chilean-French contretemps over stamps of Easter Island (or themes related to the islands) has something of a comic-opera tone, but nevertheless reflects the use of postage stamps to assert and defend sovereignty claims. Chile has always been somewhat defensive about its possession of Easter Island, in part because of the lack of real ethnic or cultural links between the native population (which is Polynesian) and South American Chile. The sensitivity is also compounded by the distance factor, since Easter Island (also known as Rapa-Nui) is about 2,300 miles from the Chilean coast and about the same distance from French Pacific possessions in Polynesia; the closest neighbor of Easter island is actually the British Pitcairn Island group, about 1,000 miles away.

As Chilean philatelic specialists have noted, Chile has issued an impressive number of stamps (over forty) with Easter Island themes (figure 5.3, Scott 720).[34] They can be interpreted as reflecting the sensitivity of Easter Island sovereignty issues, as well as a reminder to Chileans and foreigners alike that the islands are a Chilean possession. (For examples, see Scott 347, 413, 452, 587, 791–794.) The philatelic dispute with France began with a set of French Polynesia stamps (Scott 534–537) celebrating the Maohi people of the Pacific. One of the stamps shows a Maohi man on Easter Island (Scott 535). A press release from French Polynesia notes that it was the Maohi, not the Europeans, who settled the islands of the South Pacific; it then refers to "the famous Polynesian triangle, the corners of which are Easter Island, the Hawaiian Islands and the two large islands of New Zealand."[35] Apparently Chilean officials interpreted the stamps as a veiled challenge to Chilean sovereignty over Easter Island, protested vigorously through press and diplomatic channels, and sent three warships to the island. The stamps were withdrawn from sale by the French authorities. However, a year later French Polynesia issued another stamp (Scott 560) showing a woman on Easter Island with indisputably Easter Island moais in the background. Again the Chileans protested, and the French withdrew the stamp; the Chileans then issued a pair of stamps (Scott 1010–1011) labeled "Isla de Pascua. Territorio Insular Chileno."

Some observers were unable to take the incident very seriously. The London *Daily Telegraph*, for example, noted that the Chileans had sent warships to the area, "apparently fearing an invasion of its Pacific paradise by a force of French postmen."[36] The French were not spared ridicule either: a French consumer organization said that if the French postal administration ever did invade Easter Island, they would probably get there late and in damaged condition. Also suspiciously tongue in cheek was the sending to Santiago of letters bearing a fake stamp with a figure of a moai and the designation (in Spanish) "Republic of Rapa Nui. Independent Easter Island." Chilean authorities were not amused, and the postal service filed a lawsuit against whoever might be involved.[37] Recent Chilean stamps with Easter Island themes include designs showing the first flight to Easter Island in 1951 (Scott 1358d), carvings and a map of the island (Scott 1361a,b), a moai, map, and a native in traditional costume (Scott 1396–1398).

Brazil and Bolivia (Acre), and the "Amazonia" stamps

A short-lived rebellion in the Acre region on the border between Brazil and Bolivia led to a postage stamp that apparently actually circulated among the rebels and can be seen as an attempt to legitimize their rebellion. The Acre area was in the heartland of the Amazon rubber boom in the late nineteenth century. Although part of Bolivia, the area had been penetrated by large numbers of migrant (and fiercely independent) Brazilian rubber tappers. The Bolivian government attempted to gain control over the rubber tappers by setting up a customs house and taxing rubber that was being shipped to Brazil. The rubber tappers, with covert Brazilian support, revolted and were able to successfully resist Bolivian military attempts to crush them. The end result was the annexation of the Acre region by Brazil following the payment of two million pounds to the Bolivians.[38] In the period between the outbreak of the revolt in 1899 and the Brazilian annexation in 1902, there was an attempt by the rubber tappers to set up an independent nation-state of Acre, to include the issuance of stamps (not carried in the *Scott Standard Postage Stamp Catalogue*) denominated in Brazilian currency (reis), and labeled "Estado Independente do Acre" ("Independent State of Acre");[39] the stamp carried as its central icon a rubber tree, as well as a native turtle. The nation-state disappeared as an independent entity (along with the stamps) when Acre was transferred to Brazil in 1902; it was formally admitted into the Brazilian Union as a state in 1909.

Jose Joquim Marques Marinho identifies some even more dubious stamps linked to independent or semi-independent entities in part of the Amazon region. One of these was the "Free State of Counani," supposedly located somewhere around Manaus, on the Amazon River, around 1893. Another philatelic entity that apparently issued stamps was "Amazonia" (in 1901), but Marques Marinho feels this was probably originated by a projected railway operating from Brazilian Amazonia to the French Guiana port of Cayenne.[40]

Bolivia and Paraguay (the Chaco War)

The 1932–35 Chaco War was the bloodiest twentieth-century Latin American conflict, and involved the dispute between these two countries surrounding the border area of the Chaco.[41] The roots of the conflict, as is true for a number of others, lie in the ill-defined Spanish colonial boundaries, fueled by the perception that a valuable resource (oil) might be found in the region. The conflict is also linked to two devastating nineteenth-century wars: the War of the Pacific, which left Bolivia resentful over the loss of its Pacific outlet (and perhaps caused it to view the riparian system of Paraguay as an Atlantic Ocean outlet), and the War of the Triple Alliance, in which Paraguay was devastated in a conflict against a combined Argentine-Brazilian-Uruguayan army.

As the *New York Times* noted, "The war between Bolivia and Paraguay over the Chaco district was not caused by stamps, but stamps with maps did grievously aggravate the situation."[42] The first of these stamps was a Bolivian map in 1928 (figure 5.4, Scott 191), which clearly labeled the disputed area as "Chaco Boliviano." This was also done on stamps in 1931 (Scott 200–202) and 1935 (Scott 219–232). Paraguay's response was large-format map stamps in 1932 and 1935 (figure 5.5, Scott 323; 324), which showed the same area as "Chaco Paraguayo" and carried the slogan "El Chaco Boreal ha sido, es y será del Paraguay" ("The Northern Chaco has been, is, and will be Paraguayan"), wording similar to that used on stamps in the Peruvian-Ecuadorian dispute. As was the case with the War of the Pacific, there is a rich postal history derived from the conflict in terms of letters (official and personal) mailed by soldiers and officials as the battles moved across the disputed area. The work of A. Shepherd and Erwin Hershkowitz is especially significant in documenting the postal history.[43]

After the war ended, thanks to intensive negotiating efforts by a number of countries, including the United States, Argentina, and Brazil, both sides (but especially Paraguay) issued stamps commemorating the peace and honoring the mediating nations. Paraguay's long series was especially well done, and included portraits of the presidents and the crests of the nations involved (Scott 355–361). The high value of the series featured a map of the new boundaries, which generally favored Paraguay, and the slogan "An honorable peace is more valuable than all military triumphs." Bolivia, which was once again feeling the sting of military defeats and territorial losses, was apparently less anxious to celebrate with postage stamps, although some years later it commemorated the end of the war (Scott 820).

STAMPS FEATURING INTERNATIONAL THEMES

Previous sections of this chapter have emphasized how stamps can reflect, and indeed aggravate relations between nations. At the other end of the conflict-cooperation spectrum lie a number of stamps that encourage and celebrate cooperation and positive internationalism. A set of categories and examples will briefly be considered below.

Stamps featuring presidential visits and related themes frequently are timed to coincide with formal visits by a head of state; others celebrate extended periods of friendly bilateral relations. (For examples, see Scott Uruguay 1218, 1227.) At times the stamps have a political message, intended or unintended. As an example, Brazil issued stamps celebrating the 1933 visit of Argentine president Justo at a time when subregional collaboration between these two major South American powers was seen as an antidote to overwhelming U.S. power.[44] A series of stamps that must be seen with a certain irony are those (such as Scott Ecuador 639) issued to celebrate the 1958 South American trip of then Vice President Richard Nixon, who was met by hostile mobs in several countries.[45]

From one country honoring many, stamps sometimes honor national heroes, such as the Brazilian 1909 stamp (Scott 191) that features George Washington, San Martín, Simón Bolívar, Bernardo O'Higgins, and the Brazilian Jose Bonifacio Andrade de Silva. Recent Cuban stamps have included whole series honoring not only independence heroes of many Latin American countries (plate 15; Scott Cuba 3065–3089), but also cultural, scientific, military, and literary figures (plate 16; Scott Cuba 3151–3170).[46] Such stamps, issued in significant numbers, can be seen as an attempt to create Latin American solidarity in support of Cuba.

Major inter-American conferences are normally the subject of stamps issued by the host country, although others may also celebrate the meeting, sometimes on the occasion of an anniversary, such as the 1826 Amphyctionic Conference in Panama (Scott Venezuela 1148). Other examples include stamps of the 1936 Buenos Aires Peace Conference (Scott Argentina 152), the 1945 Chapultepec Conference on War and Peace (Scott Mexico 792–799), the 1947 Rio Treaty Conference (Scott Brazil c64), and the 1948 Ninth Inter-American Conference in Bogotá (Scott Colombia 560). Historically interesting are stamps issued by Ecuador for the proposed 1960 Inter-American Conference (Scott 661–669), which was never held because of political difficulties.

Conferences can also be controversial, and so can the associated stamps. The various Law of the Sea conferences, for example, frequently pitted the United States, which generally favored the smaller limit on sovereignty sea claims, against the Latin American nations (especially Peru and Ecuador), which favored two-hundred-mile limits (see Scott Peru 595, and Scott Ecuador C648–C650, which celebrates the Santiago Declaration supporting the two-hundred-mile limit).[47] Also controversial are the meetings of the oil-producing nations, OPEC (Scott Ecuador C533), the Third World Group of 77 (figure 5.6, Scott Peru C331), and the Sistema Económico Latinoamericano, SELA, which includes Cuba but not the United States.

Stamps featuring international organizations include global (United Nations), regional (Organization of American States), and subregional organizations, such as MERCOSUR, the economic grouping of Southern Cone nations (and their corresponding stamps): Argentina (figure 5.7, Scott 1975); Brazil (Scott 2646); Bolivia (Scott 1019); Paraguay (Scott 2564); and Uruguay (Scott 1681). Noticeably absent in MERCOSUR is Chile, which has chosen to put its economic emphasis in a direct bilateral relationship with the United States, possibly leading to inclusion in NAFTA (North American Free Trade Agreement).

Disasters often generate postage stamps, sometimes with charity surcharges to generate relief funds. Best known in this category is the 1944 Argentine stamp in support of the victims of the San Juan earthquake, whose political significance is that Colonel Juan Perón and actress Evita Duarte met at a disaster relief event in connection with this earthquake. More recently, Hurricane Mitch devastated large regions of Honduras, which shortly afterward issued a long series of stamps thanking the various countries which offered assistance (Scott C1044a–p, C1045a–p). The thirty-two stamps featured in this series included graphic presentations of the damage, as well as photographs of prominent visitors such as Hillary Clinton, former president George Bush, first lady Nilda de Zedillo of Mexico, and Prince Felipe of Spain.

Central America is in a geologically active zone, subject to numerous damaging earthquakes, which, in turn, have been met by international relief efforts. Stamps noting these efforts have included ones featuring the 1976 Guatemalan earthquake (figure 5.8, Scott C583), and the 1972 Nicaraguan one, which has political significance as the beginning of the end of the Somoza era, when the government was accused of profiting from international relief supplies by appropriating them and then selling them to the Nicaraguan victims of the quake (Scott 1248–1251).

In the "attacked nation" category, several countries issued stamps expressing solidarity with the United States after 9/11 and memorializing the victims of terrorism (e.g., figure 5.9).[48]

5 ARGENTINA

This chapter will examine the history, politics, and semiotics, where applicable, of Argentine postage stamps. Argentina is an especially appropriate country to begin this in-depth process since it has a rich history of postage stamps, as well as an equally rich production of stamps with political themes. Furthermore, the semiotics of Latin American postage stamps can be effectively illustrated with Argentine examples, and applying the tools of semiotic analysis to the postage stamps of this country can contribute to a greater understanding of Argentina's history, politics, and culture.

Argentine postal authorities have also made ample use of slogans on their stamp cancellations, a subject somewhat outside the scope of this work, but which will be considered in passing. These cancellations have included the patriotic ("San Martín consolidated the freedom of America with his sword"), the nationalistic ("Always ask for products made in Argentina"), the practical ("Don't dial the number until you have heard the dial tone"), the medical ("As Cervantes said, a tooth is worth more than a diamond—take care of yours"), and the promotion of public health and sanitation ("To spit on the floor is to sow microbes").[1]

Of all the Latin American countries, it is Argentina that has had the most prolific philatelic press, a reflection of the strong interest among collectors and the numerous philatelic organizations they have formed over the years. While the main concerns of these journals are the minutiae of individual stamp issues (especially the older classic ones), there are also many articles that provide research material for analysis of the historical and political themes on the stamps.[2] These philatelic journals have often carried editorials extolling the cultural value of postage stamps and calling for the teaching of philately as a required subject in primary schools, a suggestion that was not taken up by the federal authorities.[3] A somewhat different indicator of Argentine interest in stamps is the success of *Nine Queens*, a film made in

Argentina in 2002 featuring a con game surrounding rare stamps. The film showed some of the intricacies of dealing with rare and valuable postage stamps in an atmosphere of mistrust, fraud, forgeries, and financial irregularities set in contemporary Buenos Aires.[4]

From a semiotic perspective, Argentine stamps present both a problem and an illustrative example of the difficulties in using a graphic as icon. The problem is the official name of the country ("República Argentina"), and the fact that Argentine stamps carry this name (sometimes shortened to "Argentina") as a semiotic index taking the viewer to the country of origin. Argentina, like other Latin American countries, has not been able to come up with an icon or symbol that could also serve the indexing function of identifying the country. As noted in earlier chapters, Great Britain has done this with its reigning monarch, and France with the image of Marianne. These images have made it less necessary for Great Britain and France to put the name of their country on stamps. Since Argentina has not devised such a pictorial device, its postal administration has had to put the full name of the country on the stamps, thus taking up valuable space that could be used for iconic or symbolic purposes.

Argentine stamps offer several examples of the attempted use of a graphic as icon. One is the image of independence hero General José de San Martín, whose visage is familiar to every Argentine (and many Latin Americans), because he is a symbol of self-perceived Argentine values and nationhood. A second iconic graphic, albeit a politically slanted one, is the portrait of Evita Perón. After her death the only stamps that could be used in Argentina for a full year were the ones showing her portrait, and because of her iconic status it was not felt necessary to put her name on the stamps for a period of time.[5]

The cycle of Argentine military governments and elected civilian regimes permits useful observations regarding the appearance (or lack) of military themes on stamps and the use of themes such as arms limitations and peacekeeping when the country was under an elected civilian president.

Successive Argentine governments of various ideological tendencies have demonstrated a clear understanding of the political and cultural value of postage stamps. A recent decree authorizing a new series of stamps notes the recommendations of the National Advisory Commission, which receives and selects proposals for new stamps. The decree says that the commission is charged with developing themes for postage stamps that would play a significant role as expressions of the country's image, and as such will form part of the cultural heritage of the nation.[6] Finally, the panoply of Argentine stamps, and quasi-stamps issued for fund-raising purposes, provides interesting examples of their use, such as financing the costs of medical inspections for prostitutes, and the collecting of significant amounts of money (which subsequently disappeared) for a colossal statue of the *descamisado*, the iconic urban worker who came to symbolize Peronismo (figure 6.8).

THEMATIC ANALYSIS

A starting point in the study of Argentine postage stamps is the collection, classification, and analysis of data on the themes that have appeared on its postage stamps. As of late 2004, Argentina had produced a grand total of 3,229 different postage stamps in several different categories: regular mail, airmail, semipostal surtax issues, and stamps for official government correspondence.[7] This is in addition to a small number of early postage stamps (1856–1879) issued independently by several provinces, including Corrientes (8 stamps), Córdoba (2 stamps), and Buenos Aires (13 stamps). Many of these 3,229 stamps carry similar themes, and frequently the same graphic with a different face (monetary) value or color variation. As a result, the first step in the thematic analysis was to see how many design types were represented. A careful examination of the standard Scott catalogue, and the author's personal collection, yielded a total of 2,059 types between 1856 and late 2004.

From these, it was possible to classify the Argentine stamps under the major categories listed in table 2. The 2,059 designs were coded according to this scheme, with a total of 2,707 codings. The higher number for codings reflects the fact that in many cases a given stamp was coded in more than one category. For example, a stamp reiterating Argentina's Antarctic claim and showing wildlife of the region would be coded as international relations (Antarctica) as well as flora and fauna. Major sporting events, such as Olympic Games and Soccer World Cup championships, with clear implications for projecting a positive image of the country to the outside world would be coded as international relations as well as sports.

Calculations for these 2,707 codings were then made, producing the percentages indicated in the table. Some preliminary observations can be made based on this data. The four highest categories are (in order) culture, international relations, economics, and history. The highest subcategory in culture is art and architecture, reflecting the fact that many Argentine stamps are

Table 2: Thematic distribution of Argentine postage stamps, 1856–2004

Theme	Distribution (percent)
Culture	21.02
Art and architecture	5.62
Religion	4.77
Literature and journalism	3.58
Science and medicine	3.21
Music, radio, TV, stage, film	2.51
Culture (general)	1.33
International relations	16.07
Bilateral relations (includes honoring citizens of other nations)	4.10
International organizations and campaigns	3.35
Antarctica	3.29
International conferences (including sporting events)	3.18
Malvinas and South Atlantic	1.26
International relations, general	0.89
Economic	15.0
Communications and transportation	5.58
Tourism	2.62
Surtax	2.59
Agriculture	1.63
Commerce	1.29
Industry	1.29
History	10.27
Military	7.17
Flora and fauna	6.76
Nationalism, national identity	6.17
Postal	5.47
Sports	4.84
Geography	2.62
Politics and political figures	2.55
Other	2.06

reproductions of artworks.[8] Religion scores high because for the past several decades, stamps with religious themes were issued at Christmas. Graphic images of churches and patron saints (including those of military organizations) are also numerous. The subcategory of music, radio, TV, stage, and film includes a number of stamps featuring the tango great Carlos Gardel, who has become a quasi-icon.[9] In recent years comic strip characters such as Mafalda and Patoruzú have also been honored with postage stamps in the cultural category of literature and journalism.

International relations are well represented in several categories. "Bilateral relations" reflects the Argentine trend of honoring important figures from other countries such as Franklin D. Roosevelt, John F. Kennedy, Indira Gandhi, and Charles de Gaulle. The visit by a chief of state is usually the occasion for a commemorative stamp. Buenos Aires is an attractive site for hosting international conferences, and if the event is a significant one a stamp is usually issued. Argentina has had a good track record of supporting international humanitarian, scientific, and medical campaigns, especially if sponsored by the United Nations or one of its affiliated organizations, and a postage stamp is frequently one means of expressing this support. Finally, as noted in the previous two chapters, stamps have been issued with the obvious (though sometimes subtle) purpose of reminding the world of Argentina's position on the issues of Antarctic and Malvinas/Falklands sovereignty.

The economic category reflects a number of interests, especially making exportable Argentine products better known abroad. The higher percentage in the category of communications and transportation reflects the strong commitment to economic infrastructure (bridges, roads, airlines, etc.). The second highest is tourism, an obvious theme for postage stamps; these stamps frequently include Argentine national parks and well-known attractions that might appeal to the internal or international tourist.

The history category is common to the stamps of all nations, and Argentine issues are rich in this area. Anniversaries are especially suitable times for new stamps, which, of course, reflect the official version of the event concerned. The history category is often also coded as "military" if the theme is a battle or a military hero.[10] For a number of years in the 1960s and 1970s (coinciding roughly with periods of military rule), there was a stamp issued each year for Army Day and Navy Day, and occasionally Air Force Day. The army themes were usually uniforms of the independence fighting period, while the navy issues featured historic ships. This appearance of military service-themed stamps ended abruptly after the return of elected civilian rule in 1983, with the interesting exception of stamps honoring the soldiers, sailors, and airmen who died in the Malvinas/Falklands conflict, and stamps highlighting Argentine military participation in United Nations peacekeeping.

OUTPUT

Another perspective on Argentine postage stamps can be gained from the number of new stamps issued yearly, and by decade. In some of the nineteenth-century years no new designs were introduced. This highlights the phenomenon of long-lasting definitive series that reflect both financial stability (manifested by low rates of inflation) as well as a lack of interest in using new postage stamps to promote national goals. This situation changed with the 1910 centenary of independence commemorative series, and there is a slow rise in the number of new issues after that. In 1935 a new, and long-lasting, definitive series produced twenty-eight new designs, which were in use until 1951. The Perón years (1943–1955) saw a sharp rise in the number of new issues with political messages. In the decades since the first Perón regime there has been a constant increase in the number of new designs, to the point where at present questions can be raised as to the postal need for so many new stamps. Table 3 below gives the number of new issues per decade.

The data show notable increases in the yearly output of new stamps in the decades from the 1950s through the 1990s, and the present decade up to late 2004. The overall average in the last fifty years is 33.9 new stamps per year, and the current output in the 2000s is roughly double that.

THE "CLASSICAL PERIOD," 1858–1892

We turn now to a more detailed analysis of Argentine stamps as they evolved over time. The first period is the so-called classical one between the first stamps (1858) and the first commemorative (1892). Before delving into some of these features, we should note the earliest Argentine stamps, which were issued by the separate provinces of Corrientes (1856–1878), Córdoba (1859–1862), and Buenos Aires (1858–1859). The mere existence of these provincial stamps reflects the reality that Argentina was not an organized, single country in that period, but rather a loose federation of some very independent provinces. There is a charming story surrounding the preparation of the

Table 3: New Argentine stamp issues per decade

Decade	New stamp issues
1850s	1
1860s	4
1870s	7
1880s	8
1890s	9
1900s	2
1910s	23
1920s	16
1930s	58
1940s	66
1950s	105
1960s	211
1970s	238
1980s	390
1990s	411
2000–2004	678

Corrientes 1856 stamp: it was designed and engraved by a baker's delivery boy, Matías Pipet, who had served as an apprentice to a French engraver. Since no one else in the Corrientes provincial government had any experience preparing stamps, the boy was asked to undertake the task, and he simply copied the stamp he knew best, an early French stamp bearing the head of the Roman goddess of agriculture, Ceres (see figure 1.2).[11]

The first stamp of Argentina as a nation was a rather crudely lithographed seal of the Confederation (figure 6.1, Scott 1), followed in 1862 by the seal of the Argentine Republic (Scott 5). From 1864 to the first commemorative in 1892 a total of twenty-four different designs were issued. The majority of these stamp designs were small portraits of "próceres" (famous men), mainly from the independence period. The stamps had no identifying names for the *próceres*, so they would have meant little to anyone who was unfamiliar with Argentine history. Bushnell has analyzed the *próceres* appearing on these stamps, and concludes that they were primarily of the "liberal" current in

Argentine political history. These stamps reflect the principal trend after the fall of the dictator Juan Manuel de Rosas in 1852 at the battle of Caseros, and feature the dominant figure who was "the greatest of all the founders of Argentine liberalism, Bernardino Rivadavia."[12]

One "local" postage stamp from this period bears mentioning because it shows the lack of national consolidation, especially in the distant reaches of the territory that would eventually become Argentina: the Tierra del Fuego local stamps issued by an entrepreneurial Romanian mining engineer named Julius Popper. In 1891 he prepared his own stamp to cover the cost of postage from his scattered gold mining camps in Tierra del Fuego to the closest points of the postal systems of Argentina, or more frequently Chile (Punta Arenas/Sandy Point on the Strait of Magellan). Popper, labeled "the Patagonian Dictator" by one author, was a legendary figure who ran his mining camps with a heavy hand and had frequent run-ins with Argentine military and civilian functionaries who tried to control his activities. At the head of his own private army he fought numerous skirmishes with the local indigenous tribe (the Onas) and boasted of having killed many of them. Fictionalized biographies in the form of a novel and short story by Patricio Manns bring out his ruthless and cruel nature.[13] One of the anecdotes about Popper concerned his setting up straw scarecrows dressed as armed soldiers; he would deploy these around his camps to intimidate the Onas and the Argentine authorities. The Popper locals were not recognized by the central government in Argentina or Chile, which required that their own stamps be added once letters from the Popper mining camps entered their postal system. The stamp itself (figure 6.2, not catalogued by Scott) is well designed, with mining tools, the "Tierra del Fuego" label, and a partially hidden letter "P" for Julius Popper.[14]

THE FIRST COMMEMORATIVES (1892–1910)

The four-hundredth anniversary of Columbus's journey was the motive for much celebration in the Western Hemisphere, and in Argentine philately it was the occasion for the first commemorative, a small but well-designed graphic of Columbus's ships with the dates 12 October 1492 and 12 October 1892 (Scott 90–91). It was followed ten years later by a second commemorative celebrating the completion of port facilities in Rosario (Scott 143). In this period Argentina issued a stamp that could have become, in semiotic terms, index, icon, and symbol: the allegory of seated Liberty (Scott 122–138), in service from 1899–1903. The design was simple: Liberty rests her hand on the seal of Argentina and gazes out over the ocean to the rising sun. A second possible iconic stamp was the head of Liberty, with no allegorical symbolism, issued as a stamp for official mail (Scott 031–36; the prefix "O" indicates official mail). However, neither of these became generally accepted as a sufficiently strong symbol of the nation to become truly iconic.

More impressive was the high-quality 1910 centenary commemorative set (Scott 160–175)—a series of sixteen stamps that laid out the events and main characters of the 1810 break with Spain, then under Napoleon's control. The 1810–1910 dates make the purpose of the stamps clear, and they capture some of the more enduring images of independence: the monument in the Plaza de Mayo, and the rainy morning of 25 May 1810, when demonstrators outside of the Cabildo in that same plaza launched the independence movement. The stamps were well received by collectors and the general public, and the presidential resolution of 1 July 1909 authorizing the issue gives an indication of the increasing awareness of the propaganda value of stamps: "the postage stamp, besides serving as postage, will also permit the country's achievements to be known abroad."[15]

One unusual set of stamps in this period was the fiscal stamp series (i.e., revenue stamps not for postage) used to pay for the medical inspections of prostitutes in Rosario by the Servicio Sanitario or public health service, which were issued in that city between 1893 and the 1920s. Prostitution was legal and controlled during this period, and government regulations required a monthly medical inspection, for which the woman had to purchase a fiscal stamp to cover costs. The stamp would be placed on her medical identification card, which was required to be shown to customers, with a cancellation to indicate she was healthy, infected, or "under observation" (inconclusive). The fiscal stamps varied from 1.0 to 4.5 pesos, with the higher values presumably for late exams or failure to get treatment.[16]

THE 1910–1943 YEARS: LONG-RUN DEFINITIVES, COMMEMORATIVES, AND POLITICS

The years that followed the 1910 commemoratives saw a gradual increase in commemoratives, a number of long-running definitive stamps, and the first blatant entry of politics into the realm of Argentine postage stamps. Definitive stamps are ones that present general themes not linked to any particular anniversary. Accordingly, they are intended to be in service for extended periods and are usually issued in a broad range of denominations that cover postal needs from inexpensive internal mail to the higher value required for international, and especially airmail, postage. The first long-running definitive stamp was the 1911–1915 *labrador*, or agriculture icon (Scott 177), showing a farmer in his field looking past the furrows to a rising sun on the horizon. The Post Office director's decision to use this allegorical theme reflects the continuing search for a national icon: "Postage stamps should show, by means of an allegory, the outstanding characteristics of our national life."[17] However, the laborer, like the seated Liberty allegory before him, failed to be a sufficiently convincing icon, and in 1916 the new postal director felt that it was impossible to find a single symbol that could represent a complex nation with so many accomplishments in so many fields. He chose instead to use the figure of San Martín (Scott 226) as the one man who best represented Argentine ideals,[18] and this definitive theme in one form or another was used until 1933.

Commemoratives in this period began to be more numerous, and established certain themes that would reappear in future years. The 9 July 1816 Declaration of Independence in Tucumán was duly celebrated, although not to the extent of the 1810 independence commemoration. "Hispanidad" (the glorification of things Hispanic on the Iberian Peninsula as well as in the New World) was on the rise, and in 1929 the 437th anniversary of Columbus's voyage was celebrated with a three-stamp set honoring Spain. The decree authorizing the stamp was appropriately hyperbolic: "The discovery of America is the most transcendental event that humanity has carried out throughout all time . . . [and] Spain was the discoverer and conqueror who poured into this enigmatic and magnificent continent the bravery of its warriors, the fearlessness of its explorers, the faith of its priests, the perceptions of its geniuses, the work of its artisans."[19]

International relations themes also emerged. The 1928 centennial of peace between the Argentine Confederation and the Empire of Brazil was noted (Scott 369–370), as was the visit of Brazilian president Getulio Vargas in 1935. One stamp issued for that visit carried the iconic figure of Liberty with the crests of the two countries (Scott 416); a second stamp showed a handshake of peace and friendship set against both flags (Scott 417). Argentine-Chilean relations had been strained over border issues from time to time, but the occasion of the Eucharistic Congress in Buenos Aires was celebrated with a stamp picturing the massive statue of the Christ of the Andes located on the Argentine-Chilean border at the Uspallata Pass, one of the highest crossing points of the Andes (Scott 414).

The Eucharistic Congress was but one of many international meetings held in Buenos Aires in this period. These included the 1932 International Refrigeration Congress, for which a stamp was issued with a graphic showing a refrigeration compressor sitting on top of a globe (Scott 408). The Argentine philatelic press hailed the meat refrigeration theme of the stamps as an important symbol of Argentine cultural and economic development, arguing that the stamps would circulate throughout the world as an effective means of showing the progress being made in Argentina, a theme all too often neglected in the old world and North America. But the stamps were rather crudely printed, leading a U.S. philatelic writer to comment: "Argentina, in the true commercial spirit, presents us with a hideous set of poorly lithographed stamps to tell us about it."[20]

Aesthetically more pleasing were the stamps for the Universal Postal Union Congress of 1939, which featured scenic views of Argentine national parks, as well as an allegory of "Argentina, land of promise" (Scott 465). The 1936 Peace Conference in Buenos Aires was presided over by Argentine Nobel Prize winner Carlos Saavedra Lamas, and was attended by Franklin Roosevelt in the first visit a sitting U.S. president had ever made to South America. The commemorative stamp shows a shield of union and twenty-one flags representing the attending nations. However, to avoid protocol problems the designer deliberately omitted detailing the flags so that they could not be identified, and the end result was criticized by Argentine philatelists as not being up to the desired aesthetic standards.[21]

Two notable stamps in the "military" category date from this period. The first was an "aviation pioneers" label of 1912, which was a revenue-raising "voluntary" stamp that required regular postage, and that collected funds in support of an Argentine military aviation school. In 1936 the final voyage of the Argentine navy's sail-powered training ship, the *Sarmiento*, was commemorated (Scott 458); Deluca comments that the military was involved in the decision to issue it since the ship was the "Symbol of the Navy."[22]

Probably the most significant set of stamps in this 1910–1943 period was the 1935 definitive series, which was in use until 1951. The significance derives not only from this very long period of active use, but also from the variety of themes and the full realization of the economic, nationalistic, and political messages to be delivered by the postage stamps. In a November 1932 letter from the postal director to the minister of the interior discussing plans for the stamps, the following policy guidelines were expressed: the design of a postage stamp must have a determined purpose, be it patriotic, ideological, propagandistic, or commercial, but always with cultural and educational value for the people.[23] Economic themes should be stressed because this would be free advertising of unquestioned value, inasmuch as the postage stamp, circulating throughout all the countries of the world, would bring to mind the country of origin and its products and would thus awaken new markets. The same letter goes on to say that the lower face values such as that for the Manuel Belgrano stamp (Scott 418), which in general were to be used for internal domestic mail, should carry nationalistic and patriotic themes, while the higher values, primarily for international mail, would feature economic themes. These presented a balanced and comprehensive portrayal of the country's agricultural wealth, and included a prize bull (Scott 440), a laborer in his field similar to the 1911 *labrador* issue (Scott 441), a Merino ram (Scott 442), sugar cane and an "ingenio" sugar mill (Scott 443), fruit (Scott 447), wine grapes (Scott 449), and cotton (Scott 450). This series also included the previously mentioned infamous map stamps, which caused problems with Chile, Peru, and the United Kingdom (see figures 4.1–4.3).[24]

This period also saw the first blatant insertion of politics into a postage stamp issue. The event was the 6 September 1930 coup, which removed the aging and unpopular Radical president Hipólito Yrigoyen from office. The issuing decree of 30 September 1930 explains the reason for the stamp: "This is the most beautiful example of the communion of ideals between the army, the navy and the air forces joined with the people in their struggle to return full constitutional freedom to the country."[25] The semiotic messages contained in the two stamp designs make clear the notion of a joint civilian-military revolt: the first design (Scott 374–375) shows military and civilian revolutionaries standing side by side with the allegorical figure of Liberty in the background. The second design (figure 6.3 and Scott 376, 381–398) is larger in format and features a civilian flag-bearer in a dramatic pose in the foreground next to a military drummer leading a victory parade of intermingled civilians and military. The line of the horizon is broken by a pattern of raised arms, bayonets, naval ship masts, and soaring military aircraft. The stamps were prepared in haste and issued only three weeks after the coup, and as a result contain numerous errors and irregularities. A year later a corrected set was reissued with overprints ("6 septiembre 1930–1931"); the official issuing decree noted "the anniversary of this patriotic civic-military event, which put an end to the disastrous prior regime."[26]

THE FIRST PERÓN ERA, 1943–1955

The years of the first Perón era saw dramatic changes in Argentine postage stamps. Although Perón did not assume presidential office until 4 June 1946, any discussion of this period should begin with the military coup of 1943, which marks the start of his rise to power. The changes in the Perón era were in part quantitative, since a full 26 percent of all the postage stamps up to that time (1858–1955) were issued in the 1943–1955 period. However, more significant about this era were the changes in the stamps' design, size, quality, and especially their semiotic messages in support of the Peronista government. An intriguing explanation for these changes lies in the similarity between the Perón era stamps and many stamps of the Mussolini era in Italy. From 1938 to 1940 Perón was the Argentine military attaché in Rome, where he studied the techniques of the fascist movement, and developed an admiration for Mussolini.[27] Italian stamps of that period stressed the historical glories of Rome and the output of Italian industry and culture, as well as incorporating the symbols of fascism to the extent that semiotically these symbols began to assume the role of indexes pointing to the fascist government.[28] Some of the design features of Italian stamps of this period appear in Argentine stamps of the Perón years, such as classical and historical themes, and the heavy use of Peronista symbols of work, agriculture, and the icons that illustrate the Peronista movement's rise and consolidation of power. Italian cancellation markings in this period made heavy use of slogans, a feature that was also repeated in the Perón years in Argentina.[29] Walter B. L. Bose, the dean of Argentine philatelic writers, notes that an Italian design team came to Argentina shortly after World War II and was influential in the preparation of a number of important stamps in the Perón years.[30] Perón himself told the U.S. philatelic writer Ernest Kehr that he had "an amateur's interest in stamp collecting," and discussed Argentine stamps with Kehr during one of his visits to Argentina.[31]

Another philatelic legacy of the Perón years was Argentina's role in the creation of the United Nations Postal Administration (UNPA) and its subsequent U.N. stamps. These became the first stamps ever issued by an international organization, although in the 1920s the League of Nations did use Swiss stamps overprinted with "Société des Nations," as well as cancellations on mail from Colombia during the league's peacekeeping activities in the Leticia conflict between Peru and Colombia in the 1930s.[32] While it is not clear what role Perón himself had in this process, the record shows that his U.N. ambassador in 1947, Dr. José Arce, was an enthusiastic stamp collector, and as president of the General Assembly presented the original motion to create the UNPA, and lobbied to have it issue the first U.N. stamps.[33]

The 1943 coup/revolution

Compared to the 1930 revolution that brought down Yrigoyen (and the stamps that celebrated its joint civilian-military nature), the 1943 coup was considerably more militaristic, rejecting significant civilian participation and showing the strong influence of the Grupo de Oficiales Unidos (GOU—Group of United Officers), in which Perón had played a leading role. The first stamp celebrating the new regime in 1943 (Scott 508–511) was semiotically revealing: it featured a national crest, the date (4 June 1943), and the GOU slogan "Honesty, Justice, Duty." A first-anniversary stamp (Scott 518) used the same national crest, but omitted the slogan, leading critics to comment waggishly that the officers seemed to have lost their original revolutionary values. The stamp also used an allegorical figure of a female Argentina (with a resemblance to the French philatelic icon Marianne); the official decree authorizing the stamp cites the need "to commemorate the date because of the authentic and genuine democratic bases and the deep and spontaneous roots of the popular movement."[34]

The San Juan earthquake

One of the key moments in the early Perón years was the effort he organized as secretary of labor and social welfare to aid the victims of the devastating 15 January 1944 earthquake in the Andean province of San Juan. He met Eva Duarte at a benefit performance in support of earthquake relief, and their powerful political partnership dates from that encounter. Philatelically, a postal cancellation was prepared ("Ayude a las víctimas de San Juan"—"Help the San Juan victims"), and a set of surtaxed stamps (figure 6.4) was issued to raise funds. Over the years Argentina has made heavy use of surtaxed stamps, and the San Juan earthquake issue was one of the first. The basic

PLATE 1

1.1

1.2

1.3

1.4

1.5

1.6

1.7

1.8

1.9

1.1. The "bull's eye," earliest Latin American stamp, 1843 (Scott Brazil 1)
1.2. First Argentine stamp: Corrientes province stamp, 1856 (Scott Argentina, Corrientes 1)
1.3. A "classical" stamp: Columbus returns to Spain, 1894 (Scott El Salvador 103)
1.4. Celebrating Brazil's combat participation in World War II, 1945 (Scott Brazil 637)
1.5. Adolf Hitler portrayed by the U.S. Office of Strategic Services in World War II, 1944 (uncatalogued)
1.6. Maya ball game celebrating the 1968 Olympic Games in Mexico, 1968 (Scott Guatemala 399)
1.7. Chilean President General Augusto Pinochet gives a middle-finger salute to the British after his unhappy stay in that country, 2000. This satirical treatment is not an official British stamp. (Reproduced with permission of Michael Thompson, from Thompson and Michael Hernández de Luna, *Stamp Art and Postal History* [Chicago: Bad Press Books, 2000], 60.)
1.8. Cuauhtemoc, the last Aztec emperor, 1980 (Scott Mexico 1201)
1.9. Central figure of the Gate of the Sun, 1960 (Scott Bolivia 450)

2.1

2.2

2.3

2.4

2.5

2.6

2.7

2.8

2.9

2.1. Paraguayan President Alfredo Stroessner, 1972 (Scott Paraguay 1453)

2.2. Guatemalan presidential succession, 1951 (Scott Guatemala c185)

2.3. President Rafael Trujillo, 1937 (Scott Dom. Rep. c185)

2.4. Copper industry nationalization, 1971 (Scott Chile 423)

2.5. Anniversary of the 1973 fall of Salvador Allende, 1976 (Scott Chile 496)

2.6. Argentine guerrilla Ernesto "Che" Guevara, 1997 (Scott Argentina 1978)

2.7. Anniversary of the death of Karl Marx, 1982 (Scott Nicaragua 1182)

2.8. "No more *mordidas* [bribes]" issued by the Vicente Fox administration, 2002 (Scott Mexico 2291)

2.9. Battle of Santa Clara during the Cuban Revolution, 1959 (Scott Cuba c200)

3.1

3.2

3.3

3.4

3.5

3.6

3.7

3.8

3.9

3.10

3.1. Peruvian Revolution, soldier and Inca, 1970 (Scott Peru 534)
3.2. Oil industry nationalization, 1968 (Scott Peru 513)
3.3. Mineral exports, 1986 (Scott Chile 728)
3.4. "A country free from hoof-and-mouth and BSE," 1998 (Scott Argentina 2008)
3.5. Brazilian victory in World Cup, 2002 (Scott Brazil 2848)
3.6. Pelé's 1000th goal, 1969 (Scott Brazil 1144)
3.7. Machu Picchu, 1980 (Scott Peru 726)
3.8. Diego Rivera's design for the 1968 Olympic Games, 1966 (Scott Mexico 983)
3.9. U.S. censor seal during World War II
3.10. Lance Wyman's continuous strip for the 1968 Olympic Games, 1967 (Scott Mexico C329)

4.1

4.2

4.3

4.4

4.5

4.6

4.7

4.8

4.9

4.10

4.11

4.1. "With borders" stamp, 1935 (Scott Argentina 445)

4.2. "Without borders" stamp, 1937 (Scott Argentina 446)

4.3. Perón administration sequel, 1951 (Scott Argentina 594)

4.4. Map with Haitian border moved west, 1900 (Scott Dom. Rep. 111)

4.5. President Oscar Arias, author of the Esquipulas Peace Treaty, 1987 (Scott Costa Rica 395)

4.6. Amputee soccer championship, 1989 (Scott El Salvador C546)

4.7. "Ecuador has been, is, and will be an Amazonian country," 1961 (Scott Ecuador C377)

4.8. Momotombo volcano, 1900 (Scott Nicaragua 129)

4.9. Anniversary of the 1961 Bay of Pigs victory, 1991 (Scott Cuba 3308)

4.10. "U.S. genocide in Vietnam," 1966 (Scott Cuba 1163)

4.11. Guatemalan claim on Belize, 1967 (Scott Guatemala 396)

5.1

5.2

5.3

5.4

5.5

5.6

5.7

5.8

5.9

5.1. Bolivia's captive seacoast, 1979 (Scott Bolivia 634)

5.2. Condor looking to the sea, 1925 (Scott Bolivia 155)

5.3. Easter Island moai, 1986 (Scott Chile 720)

5.4. Bolivian Chaco, 1928 (Scott Bolivia 191)

5.5. "The Chaco has been, is, and will be Paraguayan," 1932 (Scott Paraguay 323)

5.6. Group of 77 meeting in Peru, 1971 (Scott Peru C331)

5.7. South American Common Market (MERCOSUR), 1997 (Scott Argentina 1975)

5.8. Thanks for relief aid in the 1976 earthquake, 1976 (Scott Guatemala C583)

5.9. In memory of the victims of 9/11, 2002 (Scott Costa Rica 560)

6.1

6.2

6.3

6.4

6.5

6.6

6.7

6.8

6.9

6.10

6.11

6.1. First national Argentine stamp, 1858 (Scott Argentina 1)
6.2. Local mining camp, 1891 (uncatalogued)
6.3. The 1930 Revolution, 1930 (Scott Argentina 376)
6.4. San Juan earthquake, 1944 (Scott Argentina B6–9)
6.5. Juan Perón's first inaugural, 1946 (Scott Argentina 552)
6.6. Centennial of Juan Perón's birth, 1995 (Scott Argentina 1902)
6.7. Peronista loyalty day, 1946 (Scott Argentina 556)
6.8. Fund-raising non-postal stamp for Peronista monument, 1946 (uncatalogued)
6.9. Evita Perón, 1952 (Scott Argentina 616)
6.10. Evita stamp harshly cancelled after Perón's fall, 1955 (Scott Argentina 615)
6.11. Celebration of Perón's fall, 1955 (Scott Argentina 647)

7.1

7.2

7.3

7.4

7.5

7.6

7.7

7.8

7.9

7.1. Evita, "eternal in her people," 1974 (Scott Argentina 1003)
7.2. Martín Fierro, gaucho epic poem, 1972 (Scott Argentina 983)
7.3. U.N. development conference, 1976 (Scott Argentina 1194)
7.4. Patoruzú, comic strip character, 1998 (Scott Argentina 2017)
7.5. U.N. peacekeeping, 1998 (Scott Argentina 2000)
7.6. Profile of Evita Perón on the fiftieth anniversary of her death, 2002 (Scott Argentina 2191)
7.7. Jorge Luis Borges, author, 1977 (Scott Argentina 1972)
7.8. Diego Maradona, soccer player, 2002 (uncatalogued)
7.9. Condom and anti-AIDS campaign, 1992 (Scott Argentina 1986)

8.1

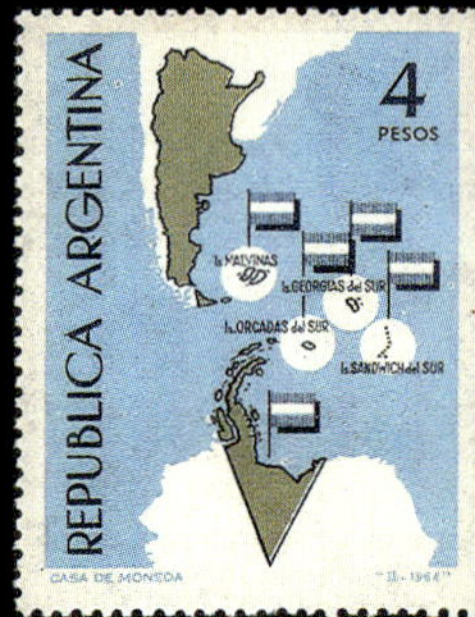

8.2

8.3

8.4

8.5

8.6

8.7

8.8

8.9

8.1. Map of the Falkland Islands Dependencies, 1946 (Scott Falkland Is. Dependencies 1L1)

8.2. Tricontinental Argentina, 1964 (Scott Argentina 758)

8.3. “Las Malvinas son Argentinas,” 1982 (Scott Argentina 1338)

8.4. Grytviken, South Georgia, 1933 (Scott Falkland Is. 70)

8.5. Map of the Falkland Islands, 1933 (Scott Falkland Is. 69)

8.6. Map of the Malvinas, 1964 (Scott Argentina C92)

8.7. Duke of Edinburgh on a gaucho saddle, 1977 (Scott Falkland Is. 254)

8.8. First Argentine flag on the Malvinas in 1820, 1976 (Scott Argentina 1131)

8.9. “First recovery” of the islands, 1982–1983 (Scott Argentina 1411)

9.1

9.2

9.3

9.4

9.5

9.6

9.7

9.8

9.9

9.1. Raising the British flag in 1833, 1983 (Scott Falkland Is. 360)
9.2. Argentine wildlife, 1994 (Scott Argentina 1839)
9.3. King penguins with emperor chick, 2003 (Scott Argentina 2183)
9.4. British mine disposal, 1987 (Scott Falkland Is. 459)
9.5. Twentieth anniversary of the British landing, 2002 (Scott Falkland Is. 810a)
9.6. South American Missionary Society, 1994 (Scott Falkland Is. 622)
9.7. Sir Ernest Shackleton and the rescue ship *Yelcho*, 2000 (Scott Falkland Is. 760)
9.8. Argentine cruiser *Belgrano*, sunk in 1982, 1992 (Scott Argentina 1767)
9.9. Old sealing ships on South Georgia, 1999 (Scott South Georgia 226)

10.1

10.2

10.3

10.4

10.5

10.6

10.7

10.8

10.9

10.1. British Antarctic science, 1969 (Scott BAT 20)

10.2. Argentine Antarctic claim, 1947 (Scott Argentina 561)

10.3. Raising the flag at the Orcadas Antarctic station in 1904, 1954 (Scott Argentina 621)

10.4. Argentine rescue of Swedish Antarctic expedition in 1903, 1953 (Scott Argentina 620)

10.5. Argentine base on Deception Island, 1998 (Scott Argentina 2012)

10.6. Chilean Antarctic claim, 1958 (Scott Chile 305)

10.7. Antarctica in sixteenth-century “La Araucana” poem, 1958 (Scott Chile 310)

10.8. Captain Pardo’s rescue of Shackleton’s expedition, 1967 (Scott Chile 361)

10.9. Tordesillas Treaty of 1494 and Antarctica, 1958 (Scott Chile 311)

11.1

11.2

11.3

11.4

11.5

11.6

11.7

11.8

11.9

1.1. Chilean Antarctic "colony," 1984 (Scott Chile 672)

1.2. Lt. Marsh Antarctic air force base, 1981 (Scott Chile 592)

1.3. Brazil's first Antarctic expedition, 1982 (Scott Brazil 1845)

1.4. Brazilian Air Force in Antarctica, 1987 (Scott Brazil 2096)

1.5. Humboldt penguin in Antarctica, 1986 (Scott Peru 853)

1.6. Peruvian Antarctic expedition, 1991 (Scott Peru 1005)

1.7. British expedition at the pole in 1912, 1987 (Scott BAT 140)

1.8. Scottish National Expedition: bagpiper and penguin, 2002 (Scott BAT 317)

1.9. Admiral Richard Byrd's Antarctic Expedition, 1934 (Scott U.S. 733)

12.1

12.2

12.3

12.4

12.5

12.6

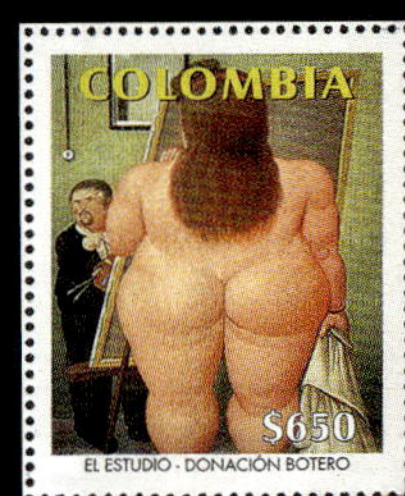

12.7

12.8

12.9

12.10

12.11

12.1. Condom, anti-AIDS campaign, 1997 (Scott Brazil 2624)

12.2. Environmental conservation, 1976 (Scott Brazil 1474)

12.3. Pablo Neruda, poet, 1991 (Scott Chile 980)

12.4. President Salvador Allende, 1990 (Scott Chile 912)

12.5. Jorge E. Gaitán, politician, 1998 (Scott Colombia 1140)

12.6. Colombian soldiers in the Korean War, 1955 (Scott Colombia 635)

12.7. Fernando Botero, painter and sculptor, 2001 (Scott Colombia 1069)

12.8. Victory of the Cuban Revolution, 1959 (Scott Cuba 613)

12.9. Fidel Castro's landing of the *Granma*, 1956 (Scott Cuba 626)

12.10. Celia Sánchez, seventieth birthday, 1990 (Scott Cuba 3223)

12.11. Che Guevara in Africa in 1965, 2000 (Scott Cuba 4069)

13.1

13.2

13.3

13.4

13.5

13.6

13.7

13.8

13.9

13.10

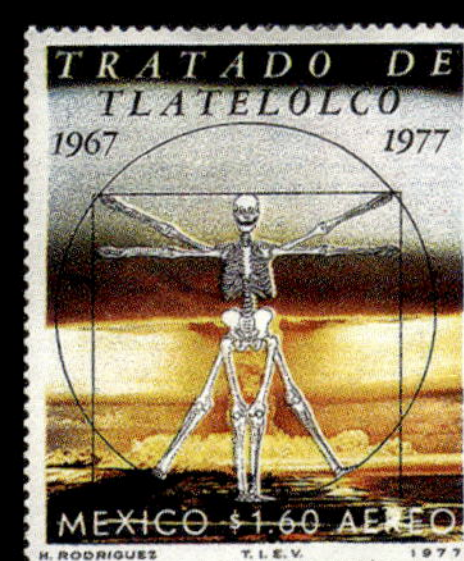

13.11

13.1. Salvador Allende and the burning presidential palace, 1983 (Scott Cuba 2605)

13.2. Fidel Castro's speech on the fortieth anniversary of the revolution, 1999 (Scott Cuba 3983)

13.3. Soviet icebreaker and penguins, 1972 (Scott Cuba 1752)

13.4. Grenada: research on UFOs, 1978 (Scott Grenada 885)

13.5. Emperor Maximilian, 1866 (Scott Mexico 27)

13.6. Mexican Revolution stamp, 1914 (Scott Mexico 427)

13.7. José G. Posada, engraver, 1963 (Scott Mexico C278)

13.8. Sor Juana Inés de la Cruz, nun and author, 1996 (Scott Mexico 1911)

13.9. Diego Rivera, muralist, 1986 (Scott Mexico 1464)

13.10. Frida Kahlo, painter, 2001 (Scott Mexico 2228)

13.11. Tlatelolco Treaty of 1967, 1977 (Scott Mexico C533)

14.1

14.2

14.3

14.4

14.5

14.6

14.7

14.8

14.9

14.10

15.1

15.2

15.3

15.4

15.5

15.6

15.7

15.8

15.9

5.1. José de San Martín, Argentina, 1988 (Scott Cuba 3065)
5.2. Simón Bolívar, Venezuela, 1988 (Scott Cuba 3084)
5.3. Miguel Hidalgo, Mexico, 1988 (Scott Cuba 3078)
5.4. José Artigas, Uruguay, 1988 (Scott Cuba 3083)
5.5. Bernardo O'Higgins, Chile, 1988 (Scott Cuba 3069)
5.6. Antonio José de Sucre, Ecuador, 1988 (Scott Cuba 3074)
5.7. Antonio Nariño, Colombia, 1988 (Scott Cuba 3070)
5.8. Tiradentes, Brazil, 1988 (Scott Cuba 3068)
5.9. José Martí, Cuba, 1988 (Scott Cuba 3071)

16.1

16.2

16.3

16.4

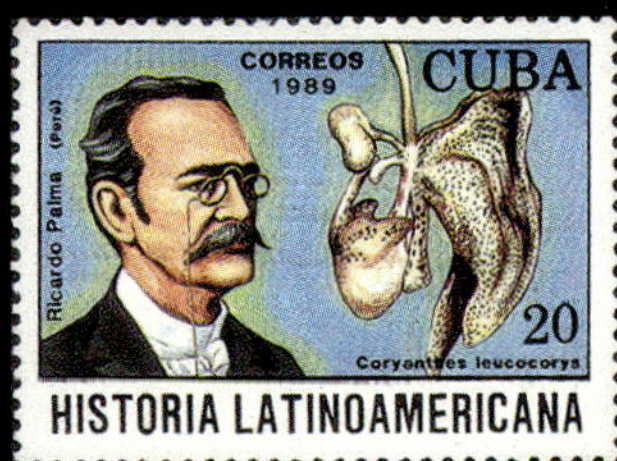

16.5

16.6

16.7

16.8

16.9

16.1. Domingo F. Sarmiento, Argentina, 1989 (Scott Cuba 3151)

16.2. Jorge Isaacs, Colombia, 1989 (Scott Cuba 3154)

16.3. Rubén Darío, Nicaragua, 1989 (Scott Cuba 3164)

16.4. José E. Rodó, Uruguay, 1989 (Scott Cuba 3169)

16.5. Ricardo Palma, Peru, 1989 (Scott Cuba 3166)

16.6. Alfonso Reyes, Mexico, 1989 (Scott Cuba 3162)

16.7. Miguel Angel Asturias, Guatemala, 1989 (Scott Cuba 3160)

16.8. Alejo Carpentier, Cuba, 1989 (Scott Cuba 3155)

16.9. Pablo Neruda, Chile, 1989 (Scott Cuba 3156

stamp value was five centavos (the going postal rate for internal mail), but the surcharges were available in four denominations: five and ten centavos, and one and twenty pesos. At the time the exchange rate was four pesos to the dollar, so the higher value represented a considerable amount of money. Despite the charitable and political significance, the stamps did not do well: a total of 3,600,000 were printed, but only about 278,000 were sold, and the rest were destroyed. The twenty-peso value had especially modest sales: of the 100,000 printed, fewer than 14,000 were sold.[35]

The 1946 inaugural

Perón's presidential inaugural on 4 June 1946 was commemorated with an allegory showing Liberty standing in front of an Argentine flag and administering the oath of office to Perón, who is represented by only his right hand resting on the constitution (figure 6.5). This ingenious design device was used to get around the Argentine philatelic tradition (shared with the United States) of not placing the face of any living person on a postage stamp. A first-anniversary stamp features an allegory of justice, but no Perón hand.

The 17 October "Loyalty Day"

A major landmark in the history of Peronismo is the 17 October 1945 Loyalty Day, when massive demonstrations by Peronista workers in Buenos Aires forced the military to release Perón from jail, and launched him on a virtually unstoppable trajectory to the 1946–1952 presidential term. The first anniversary stamps (figure 6.7, Scott 556; Scott 553–557), issued on 17 October 1946, show an allegory of Argentina receiving acclaim and popular support from the masses of Peronista supporters, including workers, professionals, women, children, and the elderly. Two years later the anniversary was noted by a commemorative (Scott 581) showing Liberty surrounded by the symbols of Peronista progress, with a strong resemblance to Mussolini-era Italian stamps.

The focus on San Martín

The Perón administration made heavy use of the figure of independence hero General José de San Martín, converting him into something of a semiotic symbol to stand for the Argentine nation at home and abroad.[36] Perón himself was often associated with San Martín, and compared to him by his followers.[37] Besides the definitive sets featuring San Martín (especially the five-centavo red stamp, which was by far the most commonly used postage stamp in this period), these years saw a lavish and well-designed set of stamps honoring San Martín on his death centennial (1950, Scott 587–593), which was proclaimed "Year of the Liberator San Martín." The transfer of the remains of his parents to Argentina was also celebrated (Scott 569–570), and several other issues featuring San Martín followed (Scott 628–631, 642). Numerous cancellations in this period also honored San Martín, with slogans such as "America gives eternal homage to General San Martín," "Glory to the Liberator General San Martín on the Centennial of his death," "San Martín's triumph in the Battle of Maipú determines the independence of Chile," and "San Martín lives eternally in the Argentine people."[38]

The Peronista constitution and the Perón stamp

Unique philatelic circumstances surround the Peronista constitution of 1949 and the Perón stamp that never was (until after his death). A major development in the Perón years was the rewriting of the old national constitution and its replacement by the Peronista constitution of 1949. The engraved stamp commemorating the new constitution (Scott 585) is attractive and well designed, the product of the visiting Italian design team mentioned by Bose. The head of the allegorical figure of Liberty dominates the central medallion, which is surrounded by the symbols of Peronismo: agricultural products, drafting tools, a hammer, the cogs of industry, a blacksmith's anvil, the scales of justice, and a medical caduceus; the symbols representing industry and agriculture are to the left, and those of the arts and sciences are to the right. There is a story behind the design. The original proposal of the Italian designer Renato Garrasi portrayed the head of Perón in the central medallion, but the president apparently rejected that idea based on the policy that no living Argentine appears on a postage stamp. The sequel is that when the Carlos Menem administration sought to honor Perón on the 1995 centennial of his birth the 1949 constitution stamp was resurrected and the Perón head was indeed placed in the center of the design (figure 6.6, Scott 1902). Although Perón never appeared on an Argentine stamp during his lifetime, he, along with his friend General Alfredo Stroessner of Paraguay, did appear together in an April 1955 series of Paraguayan stamps (Scott 486–490 and C221, which were printed in the Argentine Mint) celebrating Perón's visit to the neighboring country.[39] Only a few months later Perón was to flee into exile on board a Paraguayan gunboat conveniently positioned near Buenos Aires on the River Plate.

The descamisado voluntary label

One of the scandals of the Perón era, the dimensions of which emerged only after his fall in 1955, was the scheme to raise funds for an enormous monument in the central Plaza de Mayo dedicated to the descamisado, the prototypical and mythological urban worker supporter of Perón who was supposedly too poor to even own a shirt. To raise funds for the project, the Post Office printed over 7.5 million stamps (figure 6.8), which were technically "nonpostal labels" since they would not actually carry the mail (regular postage was required in addition to the descamisado label). The labels were placed on sale in early 1947, and there is no publicly available data on how many were sold and how much money was collected. The face values of the labels ranged from five centavos (equivalent to the normal letter postage rate) up to one hundred pesos (equivalent to twenty-five U.S. dollars). To increase the likelihood that they would be purchased, the government decreed that no charity seals or other nonpostal labels (used to support other campaigns such as the fight against tuberculosis) would be sold for the next several years. There were also no surtax stamps sold between 1944 and 1950. I was living in Buenos Aires during this period and recall the energetic campaign to place these "voluntary" stamps on all mail in these years, when it was generally assumed that postal patrons wishing to get their mail past pro-Peronista mail clerks had best include a generous amount of the descamisado labels next to their regular postage stamps on letters. The monument itself was never built, and presumably the funds raised went into the Peronista political coffers, or individual secret bank accounts.[40]

International themes

These were well represented in the Perón years, and many of them simply reflect international congresses or anniversaries, as might be expected. Others carried political messages, such as those related to the Malvinas issue or Antarctic sovereignty, which will be analyzed in the two following chapters. The 1946 stamp honoring U.S. president Franklin Roosevelt (Scott 551) was somewhat surprising, considering the often strained state of Argentine-U.S. relations during those years. These strains peaked during the 1946 election campaign, when Perón accused the United States of interfering with the process through the actions of Ambassador (and later Assistant Secretary of State) Spruile Braden. A possible clue to the interest in honoring Roosevelt lies in the legend on the stamp, which calls him "the standard-bearer for new social justice," a label that Perón often applied to himself. A year later a set of three stamps celebrating Argentine children's crusade for world peace (Scott 571–573) seemed innocuous enough, but according to a contemporary Argentine philatelic journal they were issued to support a Perón speech calling for world peace that same year.[41]

Economic themes

These continued in one sense via the previously mentioned 1935 set of definitive stamps, which were in use through 1951, featuring the basic strengths of Argentina's agricultural economy in the higher values of the twenty-four-stamp set, intended for use abroad. National Agriculture Day was celebrated with a 1948 stamp (Scott 580), as were wheat and cattle in the new definitive series of 1954–1959.

However, the Perón administration was more interested in promoting Argentine economic development, which would compete with the first world's, and in reinforcing the image of a modernizing, industrializing, and technologically advanced nation. And so we have stamps honoring Argentine industry (1946, Scott 559; and 1954, Scott 636), aviation (1947, Scott 566; and 1955, Scott 645), including a celebration of the tenth anniversary of the state-owned airline (1951, Scott C59), the nationalization of the railway system (1949, Scott 584), communications, including television (1954, Scott 624), and the National Productivity and Social Welfare Congress of 1955 (Scott 644). Most notable in the economic category are the stamps issued to propagandize the Plan Quinquenal (Five-Year Plan), in 1951 (Scott 595–597, C60). These were created by the Italian team, and feature elegant designs that mixed mythological figures and wildlife to illustrate the major features of the plan: Pegasus is shown racing a train (transportation), Mercury is set against communication equipment, a dolphin is following a vessel of the national steamship line, and a condor is accompanying a modern airplane.

The influence of Evita

It was Perón's wife Evita, María Eva Duarte de Perón, who had the most significant direct and indirect impact on Argentine stamps of the Peronista 1943–1955 period. Evita was instrumental in achieving voting rights for women, and this event was celebrated by a well-designed stamp showing the allegorical figure of a female Argentina accompanying and protecting a woman on her way to vote, a ballot in her hand (Scott 598). The building housing the Fundación Eva Perón appeared on a 1954 stamp (Scott 637), and an extraordinarily high surtax stamp to support the foundation was produced in 1951. The stamp itself (Scott CB6) is an attractive presentation of Michelangelo's *Pietà*, showing the Virgin Mary cradling the body of Christ. But the air postage rate of 2.45 Argentine pesos was surtaxed with 7.55 pesos destined for the Eva Perón Foundation, costing the postal patron an even 10 pesos to mail a letter normally costing 2.45. The decree authorizing the stamp explains the reason: "This stamp has as its purpose to exalt the laudable work of universal transcendence carried out by this institution, and providing it with funds coming from the users of the stamps as well as philatelists."[42]

But it was Evita's tragic death of cancer at the young age of thirty-three in 1952 that had the greatest philatelic impact. Evita stamps were but one among the many tributes that reflected and stimulated the paroxysm of national grief at her death. To honor the president's wife the Postal Administration proposed (and Perón accepted) the suggestion that a whole series of stamps bearing her likeness would be immediately issued, and that no other stamps would be sold or be valid for the period of one year, and an executive decree gave the suggestion the force of law.[43] Besides the emotional and political aspect, there was a financial consideration, since all other stamps were useless for one year, and persons holding stocks of these older stamps were forced to buy the Evita stamps and thus provide the government with additional revenue. Although the idea was new to Argentina, other countries had also promulgated edicts that prohibited all but certain types of stamps for specified periods of time. A European example was Franco's stamp portrait, which was the only one authorized in Spain for a period of several months in 1941.[44]

The Argentine stamps bear the attractive likeness of a young and smiling Evita (figure 6.9 and Scott 599–618), and they immediately raised the troubling question of how they were to be canceled. It would clearly not do to have the beautiful and venerated face of Evita insulted by an ugly black cancellation mark. However, there was a precedent for the solution reached by Argentine postal authorities: in the nineteenth century, King Ferdinand II of Sicily ordered that his likeness on stamps not be touched by black ink cancellation marks, and so the Post Office prepared a special hand-cancellation device that had a cut-out to prevent this from happening (in philatelic lore these canceled stamps are known as the "Bomba Heads," using the unpopular monarch's irreverent nickname). A similar approach was taken with Spanish stamps of Queen Isabella II.[45] In Argentina the order went out in postal channels that clerks had to be extremely careful not to cancel the face of Evita, under severe penalties, which could include being fired. Cancellations of the Evita stamps in this period show a generally careful attempt to have the black ink touch only the frame, and not the face of Evita. When Perón fell in September 1955 the Evita stamps were still in circulation (although not exclusively), and some cancellations with dates after September 1955 show a deliberate attempt to cancel the stamp squarely on Evita's face (figure 6.10, Scott 615).[46]

FROM THE MID-1950S TO THE END OF MILITARY RULE (1983)

The period since the fall of Perón in 1955 is characterized by a significant and constant rise in the number of new postage stamps. As indicated in table 3, the average annual production of new Argentine stamps in the 1950s was around eleven new stamps per year, increasing to twenty-one per year in the 1960s, around twenty-four in the 1970s, thirty-nine in the 1980s, forty-one in the 1990s, and approximately sixty-eight in the 2000s (up to late 2004). This growth pattern is not unique to Argentina, whose increase was modest compared to countries such as Paraguay and some of the former Commonwealth Caribbean nations. But the sheer volume of stamps leads one to wonder how many of them saw actual serious postal usage, and how many were produced for the philatelic sales market, or to satisfy the requests of key individuals or organizations. Due to this large number of new issues, my analysis here will be limited to selected items that merit consideration for their political, historical, semiotic, or design features.

Politically significant stamps

When the military "Liberating Revolution" deposed Perón in September 1955, a celebratory stamp was produced in little over a month (figure 6.11). It was an allegory of a seminude Liberty breaking her chains, which, according to some irreverent observers, was supposed to be Evita or a female *descamisada*. A second stamp was issued on the first anniversary (Scott 657), and this time the allegorical female figure was fully clothed. The military government also celebrated the 104th anniversary of the battle of Caseros, when the tyrannical strongman Juan Manuel de Rosas was defeated by General Justo José de Urquiza. Commemorative stamps are usually issued on centennials, and not the 104th anniversary, but there is a political reason for this anomaly.

Perón was often associated with Rosas, and emphasis was placed on similar aspects of their regimes, such as ruling with a strong hand and the centralization of national authority. Presumably Perón's regime could not contemplate issuing a stamp on the centennial of Rosas's defeat in 1852.[47] When the military government that overthrew Perón in 1955 issued the stamp commemorating the battle of Caseros and featuring General Urquiza (Scott 649), the regime was reminding the nation that it too had defeated a tyrant. A similar motive was probably behind the Esteban Echeverría stamp of 1957 (Scott 666), since romantic author Echeverría (1805–1851) had written bitter essays against Rosas, the most notable being "El matadero," in which a slaughterhouse is a metaphor for the Rosas dictatorship. The 1956 journal of the Argentine Communication Ministry noted that the history of the previous few years (i.e., the Perón period) had forgotten Echeverría, and this honor was due him with an added urgency.[48] The 1955–1958 military government also moved to do away with the 1949 Peronista constitution, and commemorated this effort with an allegorical stamp showing the head of Liberty (Scott 667). The issuing decree noted that this accomplishment (reform of the Peronista constitution) "was an event of indubitable historical repercussion, and will make manifest the unbreakable will of the Nation to recover democracy, and that therefore the issuing of a stamp will perpetuate this process and will also symbolize the return of Argentines to the path shown by the forgers of our nationality."[49]

Presidential successions (except for ones caused by military coups) were all noted by stamps in this period. When the post-Perón military government headed by General Aramburu turned power over to the elected Radical Party candidate Arturo Frondizi in 1958, there was hope that this would mean the end of military involvement in politics (a vain hope). The three-stamp set issued to commemorate Frondizi's inauguration (Scott 673–675) featured an allegorical figure of Argentina, the Argentine flag (mounted on a shaft decorated with a sprig of wheat, symbolizing Argentine economic wealth), and the words "Liberty and Democracy." The issuing decree noted that "the officials elected by the vote of the people in exemplary and absolutely democratic elections will take charge of the destinies of the nation, and for this reason it is opportune to provide for the issuing of commemorative postage stamps that will remember and perpetuate the event."[50] Frondizi's tenure was cut short by a coup, and after a short interim government, the new president, Arturo Illia, took office, with a commemorative stamp (Scott 751) featuring the Casa Rosada (government house). During Illia's presidency the previously much maligned Radical Party leader and president Hipólito Yrigoyen (Scott 1916–1922, 1928–1930), whose removal from power in 1930 was the occasion of numerous stamps, was honored by a stamp (Scott 779). Presumably neither the Peronistas nor the military regime wanted to see him so honored during their tenure in office, and thus it took the inauguration of Illia, a Radical Party leader, to do so. As happened with Frondizi, Illia's term in office was cut short by a coup that led to a series of military presidents (Generals Onganía, Levingston, and Lanusse), none of whom commemorated their accession to power with a postage stamp, although, as we shall see below, the military governments had other ways of leaving their mark on philately.

By the early 1970s it had become clear that neither elected Radical Party leaders nor generals could effectively run Argentina, and the military's last president in this period (General Alejandro A. Lanusse) reluctantly allowed the Peronista Party functionary Hector Cámpora to run for the presidency on the slogan "Cámpora a la presidencia, Perón al poder" ("Cámpora to the presidency, Perón to power"). Cámpora's accession to the presidency was noted by a stamp (Scott 1000) featuring the chair of Bernardino Rivadavia, semiotic symbol of the presidency,[51] along with the national crest and colors. A stamp honoring Evita was quickly issued (figure 7.1, Scott 1003), showing her delivering one of her fiery speeches, with the words "Eva Perón—Eternal in her people" printed below. The Cámpora presidency was short-lived, and was quickly followed by the second administration of Juan Perón, which, oddly enough, was not marked with a postage stamp on his assumption of office. Instead, the anniversary of the 17 October 1945 Peronista Loyalty Day was celebrated (Scott 1075), with a stamp showing the blue and white colors of the Argentine flag taking the shape of an eternal flame.

Military themes in the 1955–1983 period

As noted above, the military did not issue stamps upon taking power in a coup, except for the September 1955 removal of Perón. Shortly after the celebratory 1955 stamp showing Argentina breaking the chains of Peronismo, the military government issued a stamp (Scott 648) with symbols of the army, navy, and air force and the words "Brotherhood of the Armed Forces of the Nation," apparently to suggest the unified front of the military in the face of divided civilian political factions represented by the Radicals and the still-powerful Peronistas.

An analysis of the presence of military themes among new stamps for the various periods of military government shows a marked tendency for this theme to appear more frequently in years of military presidents. In the 1955–1958 years of direct military rule there were thirty-seven military themed stamps, which represented 27.0 percent of all issues. In the following years of 1958–1966, which represented the civilian regimes of Frondizi (1958–1962), and Illia (1963–1966), military themes were only 9.8 percent of the total. The 1966–1973 return to direct military rule (Generals Onganía, Levingston, Lanusse) again saw a sharp increase, during which military stamps were 20.7 percent of the total. The brief administrations of Juan and then Isabelita Perón (1973–1976) saw this drop to 13.4 percent, only to rise to 17.7 percent during the years of the military "Proceso" government of Generals Videla, Viola, and Galtieri.

The most common stamps with military themes celebrated Army Day, Navy Day, and, less frequently, Air Force Day. A typical Army Day stamp would feature a soldier wearing the uniform of an independence regiment (Scott 1133). Navy Day stamps usually featured a historic ship (Scott 858), while the Air Force Day design frequently used one of its early aircraft (Scott 1157). Military-themed stamps also often featured patron saints of units or branches of the service. Saint Barbara is the traditional patron of artillerymen (supposedly because her martyrdom was accompanied by lightning bolts that killed her torturers), and in 1967, during the presidency of General Onganía, a stamp (Scott 849) declaring her as such was issued. During that same presidency another stamp (Scott 854) declared Archangel Gabriel the patron saint of the Army Communications Corps. Gabriel was selected because it was he who brought God's message to the Virgin Mary at the Annunciation, and Leonardo da Vinci's painting of the event was featured on the stamp. The use of religious symbols in support of the military on stamps presumably had another purpose: to remind the populace that the generally conservative (and anti-Peronista) Catholic Church in Argentina was behind the military in its often violent efforts to rid Argentina of Peronista (and, later, Marxist) influences.

International military conferences were also noted in this series of military-themed stamps: the Seventh Conference of American Armies (held in Buenos Aires) was celebrated with a colorful map stamp (Scott 810) featuring the flags of all the attending nations. The issuing decree, signed by President-General Onganía, noted "the significance of the issuing of a commemorative postal stamp, destined to show America and the world the joint decision of its armies to fight together for the peace and liberty of the continent."[52] A similar air force conference in 1982, during the regime of President-General Leopoldo Galtieri, was also commemorated by a stamp (Scott 1340). During the period 1976–1983 Argentina was wracked by increasing violence between armed groups on the left and right of the political spectrum, as well as from the military itself, which was increasingly involved in what became the anti-leftist "dirty war" during these years of military rule. Postage stamps were occasionally issued to note the assassination of key military figures by opposition guerrillas. As an example, when a military housing unit was named in honor of a junior officer killed by guerrillas, a stamp was issued to commemorate it (Scott 1240), as was one honoring President-General Pedro Aramburu (Scott 1272) after his assassination by Peronista Montoneros, supposedly because of his role in hiding the corpse of Evita after the fall of Perón in 1955.

Historical and nationalistic themes in this period included the 150th anniversary of the 1810 and 1816 independence declarations, as well as the same anniversary of the defense of Buenos Aires against the "English Invasions" of 1808–1809 (Scott 664), an event that in Argentine military history is only one of several times they have defeated the British. The issuing decree noted that the event had "indubitable historical repercussions,"[53] and the historic memory of this victory against the British could have led the Argentine military to believe they could defeat the English once again in 1982, when Argentina launched the Malvinas/Falklands War.

International themes in this period included the honoring of notables from other nations, such as John F. Kennedy (Scott 760), and the king and queen of Spain during their visit to Argentina (Scott 1225). Major conferences held in Buenos Aires were celebrated by stamps, such as the Cuenca del Plata (River Plate Basin) meeting of 1974 (Scott 1022), and the 1957 Inter-American Economic Conference (Scott C66), in which the map of the hemisphere included Argentina's Antarctic claim. Some of the design and semiotic features of the internationally themed stamps in this period are notable. The celebration of the twenty-fifth anniversary of the Organization of American States (Scott 1020) featured the names of the member states (including Cuba, which is a member of the OAS as "a people," but not as "a Marxist-Leninist government") in a colorful design surrounding the letters "OEA." A U.N. technical cooperation conference (figure 7.3, Scott 1194) showed a young tree grafted onto an older root stock, delivering the semiotic message that developing countries could gain strength from the more established nations of the world.

Economic themes continued to stress agriculture and traditional exports, using in one case a well-known mural by the artist Quinquela Martín, showing the loading of grain on ships in the port of Buenos Aires (Scott 724). Economic development stamps featured the Atocha Nuclear installation (Scott C116) and various infrastructure projects (Scott 1023–1025).

In the culture category of this classification scheme we see the celebration of Argentine Nobel Prize winners (Scott 1135–1137), its major newspapers, such as *La Nación* and *La Prensa* (Scott 906–907), writers (Scott 774–778), and the powerful national icon of the gaucho as personified in the poem "Martín Fierro," who was dramatically portrayed (figure 7.2, Scott 983; Scott 984). Postage stamps were also used to support public health campaigns, such as vaccination programs (Scott 1066) and antismoking efforts (Scott 1282), which imaginatively featured a heart with a hole in it being pierced by a cigarette. Religious themes usually involved one or two stamps at Christmastime, but also politically significant events, such as the 1982 trip to Argentina by the pope during the Malvinas/Falklands conflict (Scott 1367).

Finally, there were numerous stamps, many of them well designed, issued in this period to celebrate major sporting events. Among them were the 1982 World Volleyball Championships (Scott 1394), and the 1983 Pan American Games, with a stylized track curving through the main frame of the stamp (Scott 1445). But the most significant sport stamp series was associated with the 1978 Soccer World Cup held in Buenos Aires, when a dictatorial military government, anxious to present a positive image to the world, and also to distract its own people from the regime's failures and the violent excesses of the dirty war, used the games for political purposes. This included the production of a large number of postage stamps and souvenir sheets (Scott 1147–1148, 1179–1184, 1188–1192), culminating in a rapidly issued overprint (Scott 1193) proclaiming "Argentina/Campeón." The Argentine stamps and philatelic souvenir sheets of this period feature stylized soccer players, stadiums, and tourist views of each of the venues where games were played. Politics intruded in the stamp production process: a preliminary design of the 1978 World Cup stamps had been prepared toward the end of the second Perón era in 1976, but when the military government examined the designs, the generals felt they contained Peronista political symbols and the stamps were replaced with a more nationalistic icon showing cupped hands in blue and white holding a soccer ball (Scott 1147).[54]

THE CURRENT PERIOD, FROM 1983

Argentine postage stamps in this last period continue the trends observed in the 1955–1983 years: an increasing number of commemoratives and other issues, which make a detailed analysis of individual stamps cumbersome and difficult. Accordingly, this section will select representative and significant issues for consideration.

Political themes

The current period encompasses the elected civilian administrations of the Radical Raúl Alfonsín and the Peronistas Carlos Menem and Néstor Kirchner. Stamps were issued for all three of these presidential inaugurations (but not for the luckless Fernando de la Rúa, who oversaw Argentina's economic collapse): Alfonsín's 1983 stamp (Scott 1455) featured a nineteenth-century coin with the inscription "Union and Liberty"; Menem's 1989 inaugural (Scott 1659) used the reproduction of a congressional bronze bust of the republic, and Kirchner's showed the Casa Rosada and the presidential sash (Scott 2253). The serious inflation taking place at the end of Alfonsín's term meant that the stamp commemorating the transition to Menem had to be overprinted with a higher value before being usable for postage. During the Menem administration several Peronista icons appeared on stamps. There was, for example, the 1995 centennial of the birth of President Perón (figure 6.6), which used the design of the 1949 constitution stamp. This was followed by a 1997 Evita stamp issued to celebrate the fiftieth anniversary of women's suffrage in Argentina (Scott 1974). Evita was honored again late in this period on the fiftieth anniversary of her death, with a series of controversial stamps criticized by some as presenting an unduly harsh image of Evita (figure 7.6, Scott 2191).[55]

The free market policies of the Menem administration had their impact on Argentine postage stamps when the national postal system was privatized in 1997. A dual series of postage stamps were used: those in the privatized mail network of the Andreani/OCA company, and the Correo Oficial ones, which continued to be issued by the government. The latter maintained the attractive appearance and semiotic messages of the previous administrations, are recognized by collectors, and are listed in standard catalogues. The privatized stamps are generally unattractive, functional, semiotically thin, and sometimes crassly commercial, with messages that include advertising and publicity for contests. They are not listed in most catalogues and collectors shun them because of their high prices and uninteresting appearance. The company handling the bulk of privatized mail went into bankruptcy in 2001, and the whole privatization scheme was terminated by the Kirchner administration in late 2003.[56]

Military themes

The number of military-themed stamps dropped sharply in this post-Proceso period, a not surprising trend in light of the withdrawal of the military from active political life after the disastrous experiences of the Malvinas conflict and the dirty war. A set of three stamps commemorating the fallen in the 1982 conflict was issued, one each for army, navy, and air force personnel (Scott 1767–1769). One for the Prefectura Naval (Coast Guard, Scott 1797) was later authorized. Perhaps the most significant military-themed stamp was one issued in 1998 honoring United Nations peacekeepers (figure 7.5, Scott 2000), since the Argentine military (and especially the army) had been actively involved in several U.N. peacekeeping missions as a way of restoring some of its lost prestige and "reinserting" the nation into the international political system as a respectable member.[57] The U.N. peacekeeping stamp was followed a year later by a stylized graphic of two figures embracing over the legend "The new millennium without weapons" (Scott 2071). The contrast with the dirty-war years was further illustrated by observance of the fiftieth anniversary of the Universal Declaration of Human Rights; the stamp (Scott 2036) showed a bewildered child surrounded by the detritus of violence and the legend "Enojarse mata" ("Anger kills").

International relations themes continued to be present in this period, not without some controversy. Brazilian-Argentine relations showed a notable and historic improvement in these years, in contrast to a geopolitical and economic rivalry that stretched back to the days of the 1494 Treaty of Tordesillas. A 1988 stamp (Scott 1621) symbolized closer relations between these two countries by means of a clever design showing building blocks with the national colors of Argentina (blue and white) and Brazil (yellow and green), accompanied by the slogan "together for growth."

Ecology, conservation, and the natural world were also emphasized. In contrast to earlier periods, when stamps would simply show native Argentine wildlife, there was an increasing emphasis in linking wildlife and the natural world to the need to protect and conserve them through national parks (Scott 2073–2077),[58] and high-tech means such as the SAC-C satellite (Scott 2155). An eye-catching set of two stamps promoting forest conservation showed first a lush and healthy forest, while the second stamp portrayed the destructive results of a forest fire by presenting a large, black-bordered hole in the middle of the stamp (Scott 2274a and b).[59] To further emphasize the point, there is a time line showing the disappearance of millions of hectares of Argentine forests between 1914 and 2004. Equally dramatic was the sad portrayal of a Magellanic penguin (Scott 2043) covered with oil spilled or dumped from passing tankers in the South Atlantic.

Economic themes stressed tourism (Scott 1543–1548), Argentina's national airline (Scott C151–154), soon to be privatized by Menem, and Argentina's main agricultural products in connection with a series of conferences organized by the United Nations Food and Agriculture Organization. Stamps in the cultural area showed some refreshing originality in this period. Characters from comic strips, such as Mafalda (Scott 1730) and Patoruzú (figure 7.4, Scott 2017) were honored, as were the famous authors (figure 7.7, Scott 1972; Scott 1973) Jorge Luis Borges (with a picture of a maze) and Julio Cortázar (with a hopscotch game), both symbols of their most famous literary works. Argentine films were celebrated (Scott 1500, 1779–1783), as was the iconic tango singer Carlos Gardel (Scott 1502–1504), whose career tragically ended in an airplane accident in Colombia. Gardel was honored by stamps in a number of countries, including Uruguay (which claims he was born on its soil) and Spain, which used his image to celebrate "the day of Argentine Hispanidad," linking the two countries together.[60] Tango dancers appeared on numerous stamps, sometimes paired with the national dancers of second countries as a celebration of a shared event or conference (Scott 2255), especially those dealing with philately. Postage stamps were used extensively in public health campaigns, including those to prevent blindness (Scott 1551) and breast cancer (Scott 2161), to avoid drugs (Scott 1681, 1776), and prevent AIDS (figure 7.9, Scott 1986). The last presented a rather startling comic drawing of a wiggling condom, with the legend "I am a defense [against AIDS]. Protect yourself."

The world of sports was well represented in Argentine stamps in these years, including various World Soccer championships (Scott 2001), and the celebration of two of Argentina's best-known athletes: the race-car driver Juan Manuel Fangio (Scott B154), and the soccer player Diego Maradona (figure 7.8, issued by privatized Argentine mail and not catalogued by Scott), called “the most famous Argentine in world philately.” This comment was made by a Spanish news service, which researched the number of times prominent Argentines have appeared on stamps around the world, and listed Maradona first (forty-three stamps of thirty-three countries), followed by General José de San Martín (thirty stamps), and Che Guevara (twenty-four stamps).[61] Placing living sports figures on stamps ran counter to Argentina’s traditional policy of not honoring personalities this way until after their death, a policy followed by only a few hemispheric nations, including the United States. One curious use of sport postage stamps was to publicize Argentine hopes of being selected as the site of the 2004 Summer Olympics. On two occasions stamps were issued (in 1996, Scott 1927–1928; in 1997, Scott 1965) listing Buenos Aires as a candidate for the honor; the second stamp noted that Argentina was a finalist in the competition. Unfortunately, Buenos Aires was not selected.

6 THE FALKLANDS/MALVINAS

We turn now to a more detailed consideration of the relationship between postage stamps and two geographical areas that have seen their share of conflict, as well as some international cooperation: the Falklands/Malvinas and other South Atlantic islands (this chapter) and Antarctica (chapter 7).[1] Both involve Argentina. The Falklands/Malvinas stamps fall into two obvious categories: those issued by British authorities in the period from their 1833 initial permanent settling of the islands, and those issued by Argentina with Malvinas themes. We should note that the British administration since 1833 was interrupted by the seventy-four-day occupation by Argentina from 2 April to 14 June 1982.

The British stamps follow the pattern of crown colony stamps established over many years of imperial rule, and at present the Falklands are among the very last crown colonies left from the old British empire. The stamps begin with the classic issues of 1878, showing the reigning monarch Victoria (Scott 15), with no themes reflecting events, geography, or life on the islands. From a semiotic perspective the stamps are simple. The indexing function is fulfilled by the portrait of the monarch and the notation "Falkland Islands," since all British colonies are identified by their name, even though Great Britain is not. The icon is also the portrait of the monarch, which in turn becomes the symbol of nation or colony, especially if the sovereign has an extended reign, as was the case with Queen Victoria (1837–1901), the longest reigning British monarch. The message of the stamp is equally simple: this is British territory, albeit with a status different from that of the mother country.

This stamp pattern changes dramatically with the 1933 issue celebrating the centennial of permanent British occupation, a set of stamps that had significant political implications for the Argentine-British relationship with the islands and with each other. Since that date British Falklands stamps have provided comprehensive windows into the geography, history, flora and fauna, economics, and social life of the islands—all, of course, from the British perspective.[2] As a crown colony the Falkland Islands Postal Administration also issues stamps as part of the so-called omnibus series in which each crown colony (and many members of the Commonwealth) celebrates some major event in British life, usually a royal wedding or jubilee anniversary, with a common design for all crown colonies (Scott 326). Up to the 1982 war there was a slowly increasing but not unreasonable output of well-designed and well-produced Falklands stamps, which came to represent an important source of revenue for the colony. The production and sale of Falklands postage stamps rose sharply after the 1982 conflict for two reasons: renewed interest in the islands, and the increase in the population of about 2,000 civilians to approximately 2,700 at present, plus a significant military garrison estimated at about 1,000.[3] In 1984 the sale of postage stamps to collectors surpassed the government's income from wool as the principal source of revenue, with nearly $1.5 million in profits.[4] Since then the sale of fishing licenses to foreign ships has become the main source of the crown colony's income, but postage stamps remain significant.

The Argentine stamps focusing on the Malvinas are more sporadic, and frequently have obvious and sometimes blatant political themes. These are often linked to Argentina's claim not only to the Malvinas, but also to related islands (South Georgia, South Sandwich) and its claim in Antarctica, which overlaps with the British, as well as the Chilean, claim (see map 1). The Argentine government is well aware of the propaganda value of postage stamps in the political and diplomatic battle with Great Britain over the islands, and articles on philately as a means of asserting Argentine claims frequently appear in the popular press as well as in specialized philatelic journals.[5]

The British Falkland Islands stamps also include a somewhat complicated set of derived issues linked to other stamp-emitting entities, collectively designated "Falkland Islands Dependencies." Over the years these have included the islands of South Georgia, South Sandwich, South Orkneys, South Shetlands, and British Antarctica—Graham Land (see figure 8.1 for a dependencies map stamp, which shows the relationship between the various islands and Antarctica). The South Georgia and Sandwich Islands are politically and geographically associated more closely with the Falklands proper, while the South Orkneys, Shetlands, and Graham Land are associated with the British Antarctic Territory. At present only three philatelic entities issue

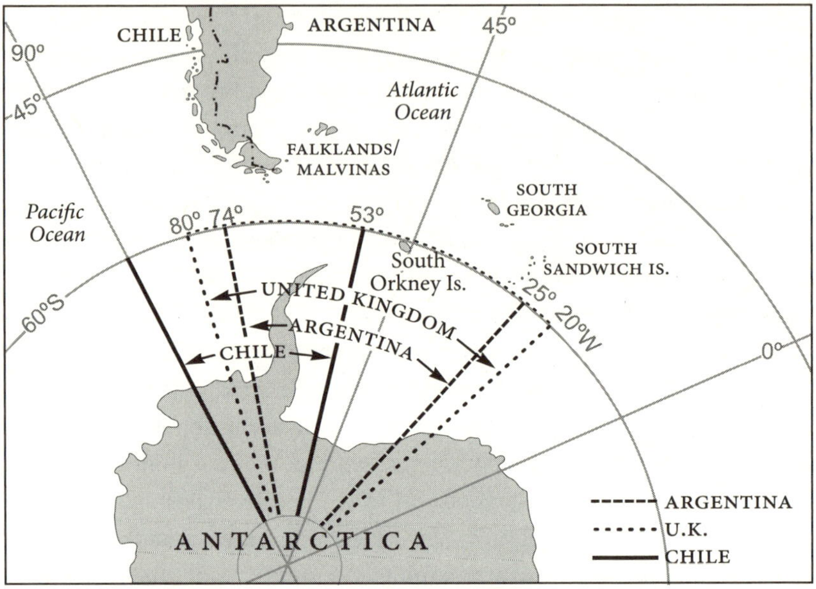

Map 1. South Atlantic and the South American quadrant of Antarctica

stamps: Falkland Islands, South Georgia/South Sandwich, and British Antarctic Territory. Because of the very small population of the latter two dependencies,[6] which are governed from Port Stanley on the Falkland Islands, it is clear that one of the main reasons for issuing these stamps is a political one: to reassert British claims over these territories and remind everyone that the British claim is alive and constant.

OUTPUT

Not counting the stamps of the Falkland Islands Dependencies, the British issued about 990 Falkland Islands stamps from 1878 to early 2005, with a total of more than 800 designs (see table 4). As with Argentina, most of the early stamps, such as the Queen Victoria 1878–1904 series, had a single basic design with numerous color and value variations.

The very small number of new stamps in the decades from the first stamps in 1878 to the 1930s was due to the basic design featuring the reigning monarch surrounded by the same (or very similar) decorative frame. Thus, the Queen Victoria stamps were the only ones from 1878 until the stamps marking the accession of her son Edward VII in 1904, followed by his son

Table 4: New Falkland Islands stamp designs issued by Great Britain per decade

Decade	Number of designs
1870s	1
1880s	0
1890s	1
1900s	2
1910s	2
1920s	2
1930s	26
1940s	4
1950s	14
1960s	46
1970s	77
1980s	183
1990s	228
2000 to early 2005	305

George V in 1912. The basic design for King George V was the same as for Edward VII, with the new monarch simply replacing the old in the central vignette of the stamp (Scott 22, 30).

The sharp tenfold increase in the decade of the 1930s was due to the 1933 centennials and the 1938–1946 definitives, to be discussed below. After the 1930s there is a relatively slow increase each year until another sharp increase in the 1980s, reflecting the impact of the war with Argentina. The rate of increase has continued, with an average of over thirty new stamp designs per year at present. Considering that we are dealing with a population of under three thousand (with an additional one thousand military) and a geographical area the size of Connecticut, this is a remarkably high number of new stamps per year per inhabitant. It suggests that the real purpose of the stamps is financial, political, and semiotic (the message that the islands are British), and that the real intended targets are the tourist, the philatelist, and the outside world, not merely the islanders. This phenomenon is even more pronounced for Antarctica, which is vastly larger in territory and has no permanent human inhabitants; there are only a few scientists and support personnel at a small number of research stations. Again, the targets are the tourist, the philatelist, and the outside world.

THE 1933 CENTENARY ISSUE AND ITS REPERCUSSIONS

The beginning of the strains between Argentina and Great Britain over Falklands/Malvinas postage stamps can easily be traced to the British 1933 series celebrating the centennial of permanent British occupation of the islands. Ironically, even though the Argentines have made the most blatant use of postage stamps as propaganda, it was the British who started the chain of events with this 1933 issue. The 1933 stamps were a remarkable departure from the previous classical period, which featured only the monarch's portrait, with the minor exception of small portrayals of a whale and a penguin in the 1929–1932 issue (Scott 54–64). These earlier stamps were dominated by the large visage of King George V. There were twelve stamps in the 1933 series (Scott 65–76), with twelve very different designs, including a sheep, an iceberg, a whaling ship, a whale, a penguin, views of the Port Louis settlement, South Georgia, Government House, the Port Stanley World War I Battle Memorial, a map of the islands, and the colony's coat of arms. Each stamp carried the dates 1833–1933. The occasion and the centennial dates were bad enough in Argentine eyes, but the map stamp (figure 8.5), the portrayal of the early British settlement at Port Louis (Scott 68), and the inclusion of South Georgia made it very clear that this was a pointed reminder of British possession of islands that the Argentines felt were taken from them unjustly in 1833. The stamps were beautifully engraved and produced, and some of them, for example the orange-tinted sunset view of South Georgia (figure 8.4), rank among the most aesthetically pleasing stamps ever issued. The semiotics of the stamps were now becoming more complicated, since the icons were carrying deeper political messages. Additionally, several of the stamps carried obvious symbols of British possession, such as the map, the Government House at Port Stanley, the colony's coat of arms, and the full portrait of a stern-looking King George V. The value of the 1933 centennial set has risen considerably; the 2006 Scott catalogue lists it at $4,508, with half of that representing the highest value stamp of the set, the one-pound stamp featuring King George V. The set is by far the most expensive one in the Falklands series, and this rise in price reflects the relative scarcity of the stamps, as well as increased interest in the islands since the 1982 conflict.

The aesthetics of the 1933 stamps were wasted on the Argentine government. The regime at the time was authoritarian and unpopular, and as in 1982, presumably would have welcomed an external diversion to distract the nation from internal economic and political problems. Buenos Aires newspapers expressed indignation at the British stamps: "The printing of these stamps compels our authorities to do or say something that will make it clear that the British Government has no right whatever to do so."[7] The Argentine government did indeed protest, and the British Foreign Office noted that the stamps caused considerable and unfortunate comment among the Argentines, who saw the issue as a provocative act that could not be ignored.[8] The International Postal Union was informed by the Argentine postal director that Argentina would not accept the stamps as valid for postal purposes, and that any mail carrying them into Argentina would be subject to paying regular postage plus a fine.[9]

The stamps also caused some internal British government friction, as noted by Paul Goodwin.[10] The British Foreign Office was eager to avoid stirring up nationalistic Argentine passions over the islands, especially as the 1933 centenary neared, and suggested that the whole controversy might have been avoided if the Colonial Office and the Falkland Islands authorities had consulted with the Foreign Office on the details of the centenary set before it was issued. The Foreign Office requested that it be informed before the issuance of any other stamps that might possibly be annoying to Argentina. Several of the 1933 stamps had been designed by residents of the Falkland Islands, working in collaboration with the governor and crown authorities on the islands, suggesting that, as in 1982, there was a certain cross-purpose between officials in London and the crown representatives residing in Port Stanley, who tended to be allied with the permanent residents of the islands, who were in turn often characterized as being "more British than the British."

Argentine philatelic reaction was conveyed by that country's two map stamps of 1935 (Scott 445) and 1937 (Scott 446), which remain as classics in anyone's collection of postage stamps with political repercussions. As noted in chapter 4, stamp 445 (the "with borders" stamp) showed the frontiers of all the South American nations. Although it did not name or label the islands as Argentine, it did shade the Malvinas/Falkland Islands the same color as the Argentine mainland, which caused some unhappiness in London, and a consequent British protest to Buenos Aires. The Argentine government was not willing to disown the stamp, or change the shading of the Malvinas Islands, because to do so might imply that it was retreating on the Malvinas claims situation.[11] As the director of the Argentine Postal Office put it in a 22 April 1936 memo to the ministry of the interior: "The withdrawal of the stamp could lead to the belief that the Argentine Republic was backing off from its rights to the Malvinas Islands."[12] *Time* magazine described, in its inimitable style, the response of the Argentine foreign minister to the British protest:

> In Buenos Aires the next day, villainously mustached Argentine Foreign Minister Carlos Saavedra Lamas in effect hissed that if that proud beauty Britannia continues to think the Falkland Islands are hers, that is perfectly all right with him. "In Britain they always maintain that the Islands are theirs, just the same as we always maintain they are ours," explained the Foreign Minister. "It is a century-old controversy, but they have admitted, and we consider that Mr. Eden has just admitted again, our 'assertion of claim.'"[13]

BRITISH FALKLAND ISLANDS STAMPS OF THE 1933–1982 PERIOD

The Foreign Office's headache over Falkland stamps was apparently not going away, since in 1937 there were rumors that a special coronation issue (for King George VI) would include a map of the islands, which would surely bring a repeat of the Argentine reaction to the 1933 issue. As Goodwin notes, the Foreign Office, while not objecting to a coronation issue for the Falklands colony (along with all the other crown colonies), asked that the stamp not be provocative, and not include a map, which it did not.[14] A map was also apparently planned for the new definitive series of 1938–1946, but was not included in the final set of designs (Scott 84–96), which featured mainly wildlife and a few innocuous views of the Falkland Islands and dependencies (Scott 84–85, 96).

British Falkland Islands stamp designs in the period between the 1933 centenary set and the 1982 war continued to be unremarkable and unprovocative, stressing the unique wildlife and some of the more interesting geographic features of the area. There were no Falklands map stamps until 1977 (Scott 257), and the 1981 historic map series (Scott 318–323) just before the conflict. Prevailing themes were wildlife, flowers, historic ships, transportation and communications vehicles, and the wool industry. Historic themes included the World Wars I and II naval victories over the Germans and the sesquicentennials of Darwin's 1833 and 1834 visits to the islands (he was not particularly impressed by either the topography or the biology). The Darwin set includes a portrait of the scientist (Scott 344); the warrah, an extinct Falklands fox (Scott 346); and the HMS *Beagle* (Scott 347). The Darwin visit came at a politically delicate time in the history of the islands, just as the British were beginning their permanent occupation; there was suspicion in Argentina that the presence of the scientific party on board the HMS *Beagle* was a cover for the political purposes of the trip.[15]

Some Falklands issues in this period stand out as curiosities. The stamp commemorating the visit of Prince Philip, the duke of Edinburgh, in 1957 (figure 8.7, Scott 254) showed the prince riding a horse on a gaucho sheepskin saddle. The saddle is a carryover from the early nineteenth-century period when the Argentine settlers worked the wild cattle introduced on the islands by the Spanish during their brief eighteenth-century presence. In 1847 a Uruguayan merchant interested in exploiting the feral cattle had brought over some one hundred gauchos from South America, complete with their typical saddles. The gaucho saddle, called a *recado*, is a simple leather and wood frame with a sheepskin thrown over the top for comfort. When sheep became abundant on the islands it seemed logical to continue using the saddle, and the prince may not even have been aware of its Argentine origins. The gaucho saddle also shows up in a 1970 stamp commemorating the local defense forces (Scott 188) and a 1981 one showing sheep herding.

Although Argentine authorities did not protest the 1981 Falkland Islands old historic map stamp series (Scott 318–323), any map stamp is potentially provocative. These 1981 ones were perhaps linked to strains that were building as the 150th anniversary of British occupation in 1983 neared, and which erupted in the South Georgia diplomatic crisis in 1982 that led to the April–June 1982 war. The maps show charts of the eighteenth century produced by British and French cartographers, who are identified by name on each stamp. The series shows the way in which the islands were seen over the years of the century in the eyes of the French and British, and emphasized the early settlements of the French (who gave the name Malouines to the

Islands) and the British. None of the maps carry any indications of Spanish settlement, which is the basis for the Argentine claim as inheritors of the Spanish colonial possessions.[16]

Semiotic analysis of the stamps in these years shows that the indexing function continued to be carried out by the legend "Falkland Islands," with this index confirmed by either the profile of the monarch (King George VI and Elizabeth II), or the royal cipher (E II R). The icons provide a long series of windows into the wildlife, flora, geography, and history of the Islands, but with few exceptions these icons would not be familiar enough to most outside recipients of the stamps to be able to rise to the level of being strong symbols of the islands.

ARGENTINE STAMPS IN THE 1933–1982 PERIOD

The Argentine stamps of 1936 and 1937 that caused political repercussions were noted above. After that period came the Perón regime (1946–1955), which was strongly nationalistic, and one of the themes of this nationalism was Argentine sovereignty and possession of the Malvinas (and associated islands), and Argentina's Antarctic claim. In 1954 Argentina reissued the infamous South American map stamp (figure 4.3) showing the Malvinas Islands and the other South Atlantic islands in the same color as mainland Argentina, as was the Argentine Antarctic claim.

Some of the most openly political and even provocative Argentine stamps in this period were the three-stamp series of 1964. The first two (figure 8.6, Scott C92; Scott 757) showed maps of the Malvinas Islands and the other South Atlantic islands (South Georgia, South Sandwich, and South Orkneys), with an Argentine flag on each stamp to make the indexing and symbolic function perfectly clear. Even more direct was Scott 758 (figure 8.2) showing five Argentine flags planted on the islands and the Antarctic claim. This latter stamp presents Perón's geopolitical concept of a "tricontinental Argentina" consisting of South American Argentina, Antarctic Argentina, and Insular Argentina (Malvinas, Georgias del Sur, Sandwich del Sur, Orcadas, and the Shetlands along the Antarctic Peninsula), which link the other two Argentinas across "Mar Argentino."[17] In 1965 a new "national territory" was declared, similar to a province, but directly under federal government control due to its small population and special status: it was to include Tierra del Fuego, the South Atlantic islands, and the Antarctic claim. Two stamps, one featuring an Argentine navy icebreaker being observed by a penguin in

Antarctica, and the second showing the General Belgrano Antarctic base, were issued to celebrate the occasion (Scott 769–770).

Toward the end of this period before the 1982 conflict, Argentina issued a colorful stamp (figure 8.8, Scott 1131) to commemorate the raising of the national flag for the first time on the islands in 1820. The left pane shows the frigate *Heroina*, under the command of Colonel David Jewett, an American in the service of Buenos Aires. Argentina was not yet an organized country, and would not be so until various wars between semi-independent provinces wound down in the 1850s. Until then the closest thing to a national government was the United Provinces of the River Plate, under the leadership of Buenos Aires. The right pane shows a map of the islands, with the Spanish/Argentine names for the two major islands (Soledad and Gran Malvinas), and the legend "Taking of possession and the first raising of the national flag on the Malvinas, 6 November 1820." An Argentine philatelic journal noted that this event constituted juridical confirmation of Argentine sovereignty on the islands, which had been without effective government since Argentina gained its independence from Spain in 1810.[18] The Jewett expedition was motivated in part by concern in Buenos Aires that in 1820 the Spanish were mounting an expedition to recover their lost colonies. Jewett was a colorful character who had to put down a mutiny, control an epidemic of scurvy, and overcome the loss of his second in command before reaching the islands. He executed the Englishman who headed the mutiny and then sailed to the islands, with a crew much reduced by scurvy. Upon arriving at the Malvinas/Falklands he found some fifty ships engaged in sealing, hunting, and fishing without the permission of the Buenos Aires government. He communicated to the captains of these vessels that he had "been commissioned by the supreme government of the United Provinces to take possession of the islands in the name of the country to whom they belong by natural law."[19]

THE 1982 ANGLO-ARGENTINE WAR

Events during the seventy-four-day conflict (2 April to 14 June 1982) are reflected in the postage stamps and postal history of that period, and indicate that the Argentines consciously relied on stamps, mail, and cancellation slogans as propaganda instruments. Argentina has always regarded the islands as part of its national territory, to the extent that it proclaims anyone born there to be an Argentine citizen (whether they accept it and appreciate that citizenship or not—and it is invariably not).[20] Thus, unlike the British, the government does not consider it necessary to issue special stamps for the Malvinas, although, as we have seen, postage stamps indicating Argentine possession of the islands had been a frequent theme prior to the 1982 invasion, or "recovery," as the Argentines called it. Apparently no thought was given to having Malvinas-themed stamps available for the invasion itself. The first new Malvinas-related stamp was not issued until early June, indicating that it was a high-priority item rushed to production once the invasion/recovery occurred.

Cancellation slogans are a different matter. They can be prepared, distributed, and put into service in just a few days, and indeed this is the first evidence of postal propaganda activities in support of the April invasion. The Central Post Office in Buenos Aires actually stamped some mail on 2 April 1982 with the slogan "The Malvinas are Argentine." Samples of other propagandistic cancellations used as early as the first days of April 1982 are contained in Argentine philatelic journals.[21] The cancellations include one indicating that mail passing through Argentine naval postal installations was being censored for security reasons.[22]

Overprints are also fairly easy to make on a rush basis, and the Argentine postal authorities selected a somewhat undistinguished seventeen-hundred-peso stamp showing the Argentine national colors in an *escarapela* (rosette) for this same overprint, "Las Malvinas son Argentinas." Figure 8.3 shows this stamp (Scott 1338) canceled with Argentine Islas Malvinas markings. The print of this 17 April 1982 stamp run was substantial: two million. A special envelope with maps of the Malvinas, South Georgia, and Sandwich Islands was also prepared and released on 22 April.

As a symbolic gesture a postal code designation for Argentine Malvinas (code 9409), similar to U.S. zip codes, had existed for many years. It had never been used on actual mail until it was activated by a 2 April 1982 decree in Argentine-occupied Port Stanley. On 4 April, two Argentine postal officials traveled to the islands with stamps and a cancellation device carrying the 9409 Islas Malvinas designation and an Argentine flag.[23] Various Argentine stamp clubs also organized special exhibits and activities in support of the "recovery" of the Malvinas. The volume of mail handled by Argentine postal office 9409 in Puerto Argentino (the name given to Port Stanley by the Argentines) was substantial. During April there was a daily average of 5,000 ordinary letters, 2,000 pieces of registered mail, and 400 packages; one day saw the arrival of 150 sacks of mail. This peak diminished in May and June due to the British naval blockade, which forced the Argentines to limit the amount of mail carried by their principal means of transportation, Air Force C-130 cargo planes.

Postal office 9409 was faced with the problem of what to do with mail carrying the old British Falkland Islands stamps, which were still in the hands of the islanders, or which had entered the postal system just before the 2 April invasion. Argentine postal authorities initially delivered some of this mail, but laboriously drew "X" marks on the British Falkland stamps to indicate they were not acceptable stamps (canceling them with the regular markings would have implied acceptance of the stamps as legitimate). Each envelope was also rubber-stamped "Las Malvinas son Argentinas" before delivery to the Falklander concerned. Within a few days the Argentine administrators decided to reject all mail carrying British or British Falkland stamps, requiring Argentine stamps if the item was to be mailed from Puerto Argentino. Any reference to "Falkland Islands" or "Port Stanley" on the address would be obliterated by hand.[24]

Interestingly enough, the Argentine postal authorities permitted their British Falkland Islands colleagues to continue functioning, albeit in a very limited way.[25] They were allowed to retain and secure stocks of prior Falklands stamps, which of course could not be used in the April–June period of Argentine occupation. These Falkland clerks also assisted the Argentines and their fellow islanders in the process of converting their pound sterling currency into Argentine pesos for the purchase of the required Argentine stamps. Three clerks were involved, and they were praised by the Argentines for their sense of postal solidarity as they labored to keep the overloaded mail system functioning.

Postal history of the three-month period of Argentine occupation is rich, and reveals the deliberate use of the mails by the Argentines for propaganda and morale purposes. Military commanders are well aware of the value of mail from home as a factor in maintaining the spirit and fighting edge of their troops, and the Argentine soldiers on the islands were given free mail privileges (the envelopes were stamped "Correo de Soldado"), eliminating the requirement for postage stamps; British forces in the campaign had the same privilege. At the same time, Argentine authorities on the mainland engaged in a massive campaign to send supportive letters and postcards to the soldiers on the islands, to the point that this volume swamped the system and had the unfortunate effect of delaying, and in some cases blocking, the delivery of personal mail from the soldiers' relatives. Soldiers frequently complained of the lack of personal mail from relatives, so in a sense this massive campaign may have backfired. John Davis, a Falkland Islander who has extensively studied this mail, argues that the government organized an intensive and well-orchestrated campaign that involved mainly schoolchildren, but also the general public, provincial and municipal authorities, other countries, and perhaps even the Catholic Church.[26] The children's mail is especially revealing. Some of the letters and cards were apparently original thoughts and words, but Davis shows that many of them carry similar wording, suggesting that these were written at the direction of the Ministry of Education through the educational administrative chain down to individual classroom teachers and children. In some cases schoolchildren were asked to draw their impressions of what the soldiers were doing as they defended Argentine sovereignty. Davis notes that one particular set of cards he holds was packaged in an envelope with the official stamp of the school and forwarded to Puerto Argentino under an "Official Paid" cover. The general public was also encouraged to write a personal letter to "An Argentine Soldier serving on the Malvinas," and after the Argentine surrender in June 1982 Davis found many samples of these in Port Stanley, some of them undelivered and unopened. Davis believes they reflect the "typical nationalistic fervor of the South American continent, fanned no doubt by frequent exhortation through the media," adding that "the speed with which letters were written and posted suggests that the planning for the 'Operation Rosario' [the invasion] included the mobilization of public opinion and a propaganda campaign, described by one British commentator as 'hysterical nationalism,' which was pursued relentlessly."[27]

A typical message reads:

> Dear friend, Argentine soldier,
>
> From the depths of my heart, today I send you these few lines and hope that as you receive them you find yourself in very good health. I hope that in defending our sovereignty you do it for love of God and love for the Motherland.
>
> Every day we pray that God help you and that it might end soon, we are proud of you.
>
> /signed/ Mario Ruben Quiñonez, 3rd grade[28]

On 12 June 1982, just days before their forces were defeated on the islands, the Argentine postal authorities issued a pair of Malvinas-related stamps to commemorate the 153rd anniversary of the creation of the Malvinas Civil and Military Command (Scott 1365) and its first incumbent, Luis Vernet (Scott

1366).[29] The event had also been celebrated previously in 1979 at the 150th anniversary point with a souvenir sheet (Scott 1280). A design similar to 1365 was issued a year after the defeat and carried the inset notation written on an Argentine flag: "First Recovery of the Malvinas, Georgias and South Sandwich" (figure 8.9), implying that a second and presumably more successful "recovery" was to follow at some future time. Both stamps show Cape Horn Island as belonging to Argentina, which mystified and irritated the Chileans, who have had possession of the island for many years. They had been prepared to fight to retain possession in 1978 when it appeared as though Chile and Argentina might face off militarily over the Beagle Channel Islands.[30] Argentine-Chilean relations have been tense at times, and accounts of Chilean assistance to the United Kingdom in the 1982 conflict fueled the strains.[31]

After the surrender of Argentine forces on 14 June 1982, postal office 9409 was closed down and its civilian officials sent home to Argentina via a hospital ship. Mail coming from mainland Argentina had dropped off sharply with the British naval blockade around the islands, and some fifty thousand kilos of packages and letters never left the Comodoro Rivadavia distribution center on the Argentine mainland. Included in this massive amount of mail were large quantities of postcards from supporting countries, especially Venezuela and Peru. The Peruvian postcards were preprinted ("Cartas al Soldado Argentino"), with room for a brief personal message.[32]

POST-1982 STAMPS

After the defeat in June 1982 Argentine postal authorities on the mainland issued a decree stating that any mail passing through the mail system that carried the words "Falklands" or "Stanley" would be returned to sender after the offending words had been replaced with "Malvinas" or "Puerto Argentino." Envelopes would be rubber-stamped with the following: "RETURN TO SENDER. Postal communications have been interrupted with the Malvinas Islands, South Georgias and South Sandwich due to the illegitimate occupation by Great Britain of these islands, which form part of the Argentine Republic and belong to its sovereignty."[33]

Postconflict postage stamps reflected the new reality of hardening positions on both sides.[34] Before the 1982 invasion the British authorities had been struggling with how to mark the 150th anniversary of the beginning of their permanent occupation, remembering the problems caused by the 1933 centenary issue, and realizing that the 150th anniversary was an important symbolic event for both countries (in fact, a popular slogan in Argentina was that the Malvinas had to be recovered one way or another before 1983). One design for the lowest value of the sesquicentennial set (figure 9.1, Scott 360) was thought to be especially controversial since it showed the raising of the British flag at Port Louis in 1833. Other indexing and iconic elements in the series included the dates (1833–1983) and the profiles of Queen Elizabeth II and the reigning monarch at the time of the event being celebrated. The British Crown Agent Philatelic Office noted that "the whole concept of the issue was causing considerable perturbation in official quarters and the [design] Committee agreed to alter some potentially inflammatory wording and review the lowest value design [one penny]. An alternative was produced and adopted—only to be finally rejected in favor of the original, when fear of offending Argentina was no longer such an overriding concern."[35] The stamps of the 1983 sesquicentennial of British occupation also included ones portraying Government House at Stanley (Scott 364), the World War I battle of the Falklands (Scott 365), contributions to the World War II effort (Scott 367), the visit of the duke of Edinburgh, and the Royal Marines in 1833 and 1983 (Scott 369).

Other post-1982 British Falkland stamps relating to the conflict included a September 1982 "rebuilding" one-pound surcharge (Scott B1) on a one-pound stamp (a similar stamp was issued for South Georgia). On the "First Anniversary of Liberation" a four-stamp set (Scott 375–378) was issued honoring the British Army, Royal Air Force, Royal Navy, and Merchant Navy. The opening of the military base and airport at Mount Pleasant was celebrated in 1985 (Scott 425–428); this was an event that had political and military significance since it could accommodate large supply and troop aircraft that could reinforce the islands quickly in case of another military threat posed by Argentina. The Royal Engineers (and their work clearing mines of the 1982 war) were honored in 1987 (figure 9.4, Scott 459; Scott 457–460) as were the British military forces on the tenth (Scott B2–B5) and twentieth (figure 9.5, Scott 810a) anniversaries of the victory.

Many of the post-1982 British stamps of the Falkland Islands are not politically semiotic, but rather are high-quality portrayals of the unique wildlife of the islands, frequently drawn by talented native Falklanders such as Ian Strange (Scott 744) and Tony Chater (Scott 822a). My conversations with these two stamp designers during trips to the Falkland Islands in the 1986–1999 period indicate that part of their motivation was to show the outside world the special and unique nature of Falkland Islands wildlife and to convey their strongly held belief that the Argentines would destroy this paradise if the islands passed to their control. A third Falklander cited the rumor (never substantiated) that during the occupation the Argentines used king penguins for target practice.[36]

Numerous historical themes have been portrayed on Falkland Islands stamps in recent years. The California Gold Rush was one such theme, important because before the opening of the Panama Canal in 1914 ships from the Eastern United States had to use the Cape Horn route to reach California, and usually this involved a stop at Port Stanley. If the ship had suffered severe damage during horrendous Cape Horn storms it would be repaired at Stanley, or, worse yet, be condemned and prohibited from leaving the islands. This helps account for the large number of nineteenth- and early twentieth-century wrecks around the islands (Scott 745). A second historical theme concerns the activities of the Anglican South American Missionary Society, which used the Falklands as their base of operations in their attempt to Christianize the native peoples of Tierra del Fuego (figure 9.6, Scott 622). Several of these missions ended tragically, with death due to starvation or violence at the hands of indigenous Tierra del Fuegans. Sir Ernest Shackleton was also celebrated in stamps. He had stopped at Port Stanley for supplies and repairs on two of his Antarctic expeditions, as well as during the attempt to rescue his men stranded on Elephant Island (figure 9.7).

Argentine post-1982 stamps were also subdued. Any map of the nation featured on a stamp included, of course, the Malvinas and Southern Islands as well as the Antarctic claim. The provocative mention of the "first recovery" of the islands on the 1983 stamp was not repeated, although a map of the islands prepared during the period of one of the Spanish governors was issued in 1987 (Scott 1606). The tenth anniversary of the war saw a three-stamp set (figure 9.8, Scott 1767; Scott 1768–1769) showing a soldier, the lost cruiser *Belgrano*, and a Pucará fighter aircraft; the twentieth anniversary was observed with a stamp honoring "los caídos por la Patria" ("those who have fallen for the fatherland"). This latter stamp, issued by the OCA private mail company, shows a family of four Argentines standing on the eastern shore of Argentina gazing toward the Malvinas Islands across the South Atlantic; a ghostly figure of an Argentine soldier is in the background along with an Argentine flag.

One postwar set of stamps featured wildlife of the Malvinas (figure 9.2, Scott 1839; Scott 2180–2183). Besides keeping the Malvinas issue in the

Argentine public eye, these sets were part of the Argentine "seduction campaign" intended to win over the Kelpers (the very pro-British inhabitants of the islands). The Argentine foreign minister sent the stamps, along with small gifts, to individual Kelpers with a short personal note; the items were not well received by the Kelpers, and one Stanley leader said he would place the gifts on top of the next Argentine mine to be detonated.[37] One unfortunate aspect of the stamp showing a king penguin (figure 9.3, Scott 2183) depicts a chick whose characteristics mark it not as a king penguin, but rather an emperor penguin, which is not found on the Malvinas. Privately printed stamps of the Falklands also exist. One of the more notable such stamps was prepared by Leonard Hill and called attention to conservation efforts in 1970 on Jason Island (Falkland Islands); it featured a gentoo penguin.[38]

STAMPS OF SOUTH GEORGIA AND THE SOUTH SANDWICH ISLANDS

Argentina has never issued any special stamps for South Georgia and the South Sandwich Islands, although they are included as part of the sovereignty claim under the titles of "Islands of the South Atlantic," and are shown as such on relevant maps and map stamps (Scott 757).

Early (1944) British stamps for these jurisdictions were Falkland Islands overprints reading "South Georgia Dependency of Falkland Islands" (Scott 3L6). A 1946 map stamp series (Scott 1L1–8) labeled "Falkland Islands Dependencies" and showing the link between the Falkland Islands and South Georgia, South Sandwich, and the British Antarctic Territory, was seen in Argentina as "a threat to our sovereignty," and led to a demand (ignored by the British) that these stamps be withdrawn.[39] In 1962 British Antarctic Territory became a separate philatelic entity, and in 1982 South Georgia/South Sandwich Islands became a separate colony, so that since that date there are three distinct philatelic issuing authorities: Falkland Islands, British Antarctic Territory (BAT), and South Georgia and the South Sandwich Islands.

South Georgia and South Sandwich stamp issues are rich in local historical themes, such as Captain James Cook, who (according to the British but not the Argentines) discovered the islands in 1776: 1975 (Scott 41–43) and 1979 (Scott 52–55). Also portrayed is Sir Ernest Shackleton, who started his fateful 1914 expedition from South Georgia and is buried there; one stamp (Scott 254) shows the launching of the small lifeboat that carried him and five of his men on an incredible voyage across many miles of the South Atlantic to South Georgia.

Scenes from around the abandoned whaling factory and settlement at Grytviken feature the whaling industry (Scott 166–169, 194–197) and the whaling museum, open to occasional passing tourist ships. One stamp (figure 9.9, Scott 226) shows two seal catcher vessels tied up at a collapsing dock. They once belonged to the Compañía Argentina de Pesca, a firm incorporated in Buenos Aires with British and Norwegian capital that is cited by the Argentines as important evidence of their sovereignty over South Georgia. The seal catchers (the *Albatros* and the *Dias*) have since been refloated and preserved as part of the whaling museum. Of interest in the wildlife category is a stamp showing reindeer imported from Norway (Scott 219a) by whalers from that country. Norwegians were the principal source of workers at the various South Georgia whaling factories, and they craved meat other than whale or seal, or penguin eggs. The reindeer were turned loose and, with no natural enemies, have thrived.

South Georgia stamps with direct or indirect references to the 1982 war include the 1992 "10th Anniversary of Liberation" set (Scott B1–4), with the surcharge going to benefit soldiers', sailors', and airmen's families' associations, and depictions of various ships, including the *Queen Elizabeth II*, which called at Grytviken, South Georgia, in connection with the conflict.[40] The continuing relevance of the Malvinas/Falklands and South Atlantic Islands dispute in Argentine-British relations was highlighted again in mid-2005 when the Argentines protested the inclusion of the islands in an annex to the European Constitution as part of "British Antarctic Territory."[41] The Argentine protest was made in several forums, including the United Nations Decolonization Committee and the OAS Annual General Assembly. The British ignored the protests.

7

SOUTH AMERICAN ANTARCTICA

It is legitimate to question why Antarctica should be included in a consideration of Latin American postage stamps. As I have argued elsewhere, for many of the nations of the Southern Cone of South America, especially Argentina and Chile, their continent does not end at Tierra del Fuego or Cape Horn, but rather in Antarctica, which lies only six hundred miles away across the Drake Passage.[1] Further, the two South American countries closest to Antarctica, Argentina and Chile, have sovereignty claims on pie-shaped sectors of Antarctica that end at the South Pole.

These two sectors substantially overlap with the British Antarctic claim, which is inextricably tied to the British possession of the Falklands and other South Atlantic Islands (South Georgia, South Sandwich, South Orkneys, South Shetlands). The linkage can also be explained this way: whichever country (Argentina or the United Kingdom) possesses the Falklands and other South Atlantic Islands greatly strengthens the credibility of its Antarctic claim, in geopolitical, cartographic, diplomatic, psychological, and logistical dimensions. It is hard to imagine the British maintaining their Antarctic activities without their base of operations on the islands, and this may in fact be one reason why they so strongly resisted, and eventually defeated, the Argentine "recovery" or invasion of the Malvinas/Falkland Islands in 1982. Concomitantly, this may have been one reason (among several) explaining Argentina's strong desire to recover them.[2]

Within this complicated geopolitical framework the postage stamp plays a role in strengthening sovereignty claims and making the country's own citizens, as well as those of other nations, aware of Antarctic interests and activities. They represent a kind of symbolic administration of territory, which is one of the generally accepted ways to establish or strengthen a sovereignty claim under international law.[3] As Richard Bagshawe has argued in his work on the postal history of the area, it should not be surprising that

Antarctica has produced an abundant variety and range of philatelic materials, many of which are produced for reasons that are "frequently political, often financial, sometimes philatelic, but rarely postal."[4] The limited legitimate postal use of such materials stems from the very small human population in Antarctica, which is generally limited to scientific bases, with visits in the summer season by a growing group of tourists.

Four non-Latin countries have separate postal jurisdictions for their territories claimed in Antarctica, and for the philatelist these are considered separate "nations" or philatelic entities: the United Kingdom (British Antarctic Territory—BAT), France (French Austral and Antarctic Territories—TAAF), Australia (Australian Antarctic Territory—AAT), and New Zealand (the Ross Dependency). The latter two entities issue relatively small numbers of stamps, and they and the TAAF will not be considered in this chapter since they lie outside of the so-called South American quadrant of Antarctica. The British Antarctic Territory will be discussed below since it is in the quadrant, and has close links to other British possessions in the area, most notably the Falkland Islands.

All the remaining countries with an Antarctic claim or interest use their regular postage stamps to move Antarctic mail, but they also issue regular commemorative stamps with Antarctic themes. These countries include the United States, the former Soviet Union (and now Russia), Ukraine, Japan, both Koreas, both Germanies (now unified), Norway, Sweden, South Africa, Poland, Spain, Belgium, India, Pakistan, Bulgaria, the People's Republic of China, several South American nations (Brazil, Uruguay, Peru, and Ecuador), and, most important for our consideration, Argentina and Chile. The most prolific producers of such Antarctic postage stamps are these last two countries, which have made a deliberate effort to use postage stamps to support their Antarctic claim, to develop the "Antarctic conscience" of their citizens, and to inform the rest of the world of their Antarctic presence.

Although we will not be considering it here, there is also a limited but rich postal history associated with Antarctic expeditions, existing bases, and tourism. Of considerable historic significance are the postal communications related to the early Antarctic expeditions, especially those of Robert F. Scott, Roald Amundsen, Ernest Shackleton, and Richard Byrd. These explorers were not above using philatelic entrepreneurship to raise funds, and the British explorer Scott openly stated that this would be one of the ways he would finance his 1910 expedition.[5] A further indicator of the significance of Antarctic philately is that it is one of the recognized topical areas that collectors focus on, and that an organization (the American Society of Polar Philatelists) exists to promote the study of the subject, complete with its own journal, *The Ice Cap News*.

Antarctica is unique in that it is the only significant land surface on earth whose sovereignty has still not been resolved. True, for the seven countries that have claims the issue is "resolved" in that they claim parts of it, but these claims are generally not recognized by the remaining nations of the world. There is no "government" in Antarctica except the loose agreement to cooperate in environmental protection and scientific study that is embodied in the 1959 Antarctic Treaty, its associated protocols and agreements, its bodies, and their periodic meetings. One key article in the Antarctic Treaty establishes the principle that the seven territorial claims existing before the treaty was signed in 1959 are not denied, but neither are they acknowledged, and that new claims cannot be made by treaty members, nor can existing claims be expanded. The treaty thus represents an internationalizing of the continent, but with enough wiggle room so that the seven claimant nations can continue to argue the validity of their claims, especially for internal national audiences. One of the ways this is done is through maps on postage stamps which show the national claim. The nonclaimant nations of the Antarctic Treaty System, which make up the majority of the forty-two signatories, and which include some of the diplomatically and militarily most powerful countries, do not recognize the seven claims, and would prefer that any map of Antarctica show it as an undivided whole, with no sectors.

For this reason, the map of Antarctica on any official Treaty System document is always the undivided one, delivering the semiotic message that it is a single whole continent, belonging to no one and to everyone. In this sense Antarctica is a "global commons" and the common heritage of all humankind, similar to the air we breathe, the open ocean, and outer space. This sensitivity to the cartographic representation of Antarctica, especially as it pertains to postage stamps, appears in exhortations by most nations of the Antarctic Treaty System (i.e., those without claims) that stamps bearing Antarctic maps show an undivided continent.

When the members of the Antarctic Treaty System met in a periodic consultative meeting in 1968, one of their agenda items was the way in which the tenth anniversary of the coming into force of the treaty would be celebrated in 1971. Stamps were recommended, with the proviso that "the most prominent feature of the stamp should be the Antarctic Treaty emblem representing a map of Antarctica, which appears on the official documents of consultative meetings" and "that any additional matter should be consonant with the provisions and the spirit of the Antarctic Treaty."[6] The system has no effective mechanism to enforce recommendations of this kind, and as shown below, the stamps of Chile and Argentina did comply with this request for only the treaty commemorative stamps. Their other stamps with Antarctic themes continued to show their claimed sectors.

The base map of Antarctica published by the United Nations shows the pie-shaped sectoral claims of seven nations: Argentina, Chile, United Kingdom, Norway, Australia, France, and New Zealand.[7] The map also shows another large triangular sector from 90 to 150 degrees west longitude as not claimed by any recognized sovereign nation. The unrecognized "Dominion of Melchizedek" mentioned in chapter 4 in connection with Clipperton Island has claimed this sector of Antarctica. As I noted in chapter 4, the main activity of this domain appears to be fraudulent banking and insurance schemes; there is even an "embassy" of the domain, which has a Washington phone number and an entry in the phone book.[8]

OUTPUT

When examining the output of Antarctic-themed stamps, we must distinguish between those countries that issue separate stamps for their Antarctic stations and those that do not. The countries that do issue separate stamps create separate philatelic "entities" or "nations" that merit a separate section in standard catalogues. The nations that do this and their output (to early 2005) are the Australian Antarctic Territory (AAT): 127; British Antarctic Territory (BAT—the only one present in the South American quadrant of Antarctica): 345; French Austral and Antarctic Territories (TAAF): 492; and New Zealand (Ross Dependency): 74.

Nations of relevance to this project with a presence in the South American quadrant of Antarctica that use their regular stamp issues have produced the following quantities of Antarctic-themed stamps: Argentina: 93; Brazil: 8; Chile: 68; Ecuador: 2; Peru: 6; Uruguay: 2; and the United States: 9.

ARGENTINA

With the exception of the British BAT and French TAAF postal administrations, which are dedicated solely to Antarctica, Argentina is the country with the most prolific Antarctic stamp activity.[9] As with the Malvinas/Falklands, it was apparently an Argentine reaction to a British stamp that began the process. As noted in the last chapter, the British 1933 Falklands stamp set and its map stamp led the Argentines to issue the "frontiers" South American 1935 map stamp, as well as official postcards showing a map on which an Argentine flag was placed on the South Pole itself.[10] In the Antarctic case, it was the British Falkland Islands Dependencies map stamp (1946, figure 8.1), which clearly showed the cartographic relationship between the Falkland Islands, the other South Atlantic islands, and the British Antarctic claim, which was then known as Graham Land.[11] The timing was fateful: the nationalistic administration of Juan Perón (1946–1955) seized upon the related themes of Argentine sovereignty in the Malvinas, the southern islands, and Antarctica as a rallying cry for Argentine patriotism, especially directed against Great Britain.

This first Argentine Antarctic stamp (figure 10.2, Scott 561; Scott 562) carried, in addition to the map of the territorial claim, what might seem to be a curious legend: "First Antarctic mail. 1904—22 February—1947." The story behind the slogan is highly significant in Argentine eyes, and is one they take some delight in pointing out to the British.[12] The reference is to the date on which William Bruce, leader of the 1902–1904 Scottish National Antarctic Expedition, turned his scientific base on the South Orkney Islands over to the Argentines, who promptly inaugurated mail service to and from that outpost. The explanation for Bruce's generosity lies in tensions between Scotland and England. London had opposed Bruce's expedition, and did nothing to assist him. He passed through Buenos Aires on his way to Antarctica, and the Argentine authorities were helpful, a gesture that was repaid handsomely in 1904 when Bruce turned his base over to them. This makes the Argentine Orcadas (South Orkneys) base not only the oldest postal installation in Antarctica, but also the oldest continuously manned Antarctic site. For the Argentines this strengthens their sovereignty claim at the expense of the British, and numerous Argentine stamps over the years refer to this fact. The two identical stamps (figure 10.2, Scott 561–562) include a small inset icon of the Argentine navy ship, the corvette *Uruguay*, which transported the personnel staffing the new Argentine outpost in 1904. This was the same ship that was involved in the other major event in Argentina's Antarctic history of the period: the rescue of the stranded Swedish expedition on the Antarctic Peninsula. The issuing decree for these stamps, signed by President Perón, noted that this "first Antarctic postal service" would consolidate the unquestionable Argentine rights to its Antarctic sector, as well as the Malvinas Islands.[13]

In 1954 the Argentines issued a rather dramatic large-format stamp (figure 10.3, Scott 621) on the fiftieth anniversary of the acquisition of the Orcadas base, showing a heroic figure planting a large Argentine flag in the ice. The seventy-fifth anniversary was the occasion for a twelve-stamp set and souvenir sheet, which featured Antarctic wildlife and the contemporary Orcadas base (Scott 1279); 1983 and 1986 saw similar souvenir sheets (Scott 1456a–l and 1559a–l), which included references to the Orcadas base as part of Argentina's Antarctic activities. The centennial in 2004 was the occasion for two more stamps (Scott 2271). The political significance of the 1904 Argentine Orcadas base was spelled out in an Argentine Post Office magazine: "In founding the Antarctic Post Office they established a civil administrative function which affirms its sovereignty in the aforementioned lands of its sector."[14] The article notes that many nations have set up stations in Antarctica, and while their work has been important, "none of them can present the characteristics of a permanent station with permanent personnel as that in the Orcadas, which gives Argentina just and valid title over that region which is considered the national Antarctic sector." A comment in the official journal of the Argentine Antarctic Directorate noted that the Orcadas meteorological station and the post office "were in reality two acts of sovereignty, and that for whatever nation possessed these islands, this represented effective occupation on our part, which is in fact sovereignty."[15]

The Orcadas postal and radio stations were cited by the Argentine government as justification for putting these areas under Argentine postal control in a memo to the Universal Postal Union. The memo adds that the Argentine postal jurisdiction also includes the Malvinas Islands, but that the jurisdiction cannot be exercised in practice due to the illegal British occupation of the islands.[16] The Argentines maintain a small museum at the Orcadas base that stresses its long Antarctic history, with prominent displays of postal history materials (stamps, envelopes, correspondence, canceling machines, pouches, etc.). Commemorative plaques sent by various schools, government agencies, and civic groups are also displayed in abundance. A short distance away are the ruins of Bruce's original station, with a plaque explaining its history. Tourist groups are made to feel welcome, are given briefings explaining the history of Argentine Antarctica, and are provided opportunities to buy souvenirs, including stamps and commemorative envelopes.[17] Not mentioned by the Argentines (but noted by the British) is that the Orcadas postal facility was inactive from 1905 until 1942.[18]

In Argentina it is illegal to show a map of the country without including the Malvinas, the South Atlantic islands, and the Antarctic sector. Thus, a number of map stamps not related to Antarctica have carried the Antarctic claim as a reminder, even though the basic theme of the stamp might not have anything to do with Antarctica. These stamps have included a 1948 pan-American cartographer's conference (Scott C56), the 1957 Inter-American Economic Conference (Scott C66), the national census of 1960 (Scott 719), the 1979 centenary of the Military Geographic Institute (Scott 1255), and participation in a campaign against indiscriminate whaling (Scott 1323).

The infamous 1951 redrawn map of South America under the Juan Perón administration reflected this legal requirement, and included the Argentine Antarctic sector shaded in the same color as mainland Argentina, the Malvinas, and the other islands. The equally significant 1964 series of three map stamps (figures 8.2 and 8.6), celebrated the sixtieth anniversary of the Orcadas station with Argentine flags distributed among the "three Argentinas" (mainland, Antarctic, and insular) and continued this trend.[19]

Another significant event was noted in 1953 with an attractive large-format stamp (figure 10.4, Scott 620): the fiftieth anniversary of the rescue of the Swedish Antarctic expedition by the *Uruguay*. As with the Scottish expedition, the event was related to Argentina's geographic proximity to Antarctica, and the fact that the Swedes, under Otto Nordenskjold, stopped in Buenos Aires on their way south for provisions in 1901. Argentine authorities persuaded the Swedes to take a naval ensign (José M. Sobral) with them, and his presence on the marooned expedition was undoubtedly a factor in the Argentine willingness to mount a rescue expedition when the Swedes did not return the following year after their ship, the *Antarctic*, was caught in ice in the Weddell Sea and crushed. In 1999 an attractive souvenir sheet (Scott 2093) commemorating the *Uruguay*, and noting its 1903 activity, was issued. After their ship sank, the crew of the *Antarctic* was able to reach Paulet Island at the tip of the Antarctic Peninsula, build a crude stone hut, and live off penguins and seals for a season until they were rescued by the Argentines. A plaque installed by Argentine authorities stands next to the remains of the hut, which has now been taken over by Adelie penguins.[20] In 2003 the Argentine rescue of the marooned Swedes was commemorated by an exhibition of philatelic materials and memorabilia from the expedition. It was held at the Argentine Antarctic Museum, with ceremonies on board the *Uruguay*, anchored nearby in Buenos Aires harbor as a national historical monument. The event was attended by President Nestor Kirchner and Swedish authorities.[21]

Argentina participated in the 1957–1958 International Geophysical Year (IGY), and noted the event with a stamp (Scott 677) showing a map of the whole continent of Antarctica, with the Argentine claim shaded differently. The decree issuing the stamp, signed by President Aramburu, notes that the Argentine sector would be visible on the stamp's map of Antarctica, and that Argentina had been present in planning and preparatory activities for the IGY, as well as carrying out scientific activities in Antarctica during that year.[22] The Antarctic Treaty (signed 1959, in force as of 1961) grew out of this IGY collaborative scientific effort, and in a departure from its usual practice Argentina did respect the recommendation of the Antarctic Treaty Consultative Meeting that stamps celebrating the tenth anniversary of the Antarctic Treaty carry a map showing the continent not divided into sector claims (Scott 973). However, in all other map stamps the Argentine sector was clearly shown. One somewhat provocative example, which occurred less than three years before the Malvinas/Falklands invasion, was the "Toward the Frontiers" stamp of late 1979 (Scott 1254) showing two children looking at a map of Argentina (including the Antarctic sector and the Malvinas) with the slogan "Argentinos: Marchemos Hacia las Fronteras" ("Argentines, we must march to the frontiers"). The semiotic message was clear: Argentines should not cling to the population centers around the capital, but should focus more on the "frontiers" of Antarctica and the South Atlantic islands.

Many of the Argentine Antarctic stamps commemorate expeditions, such as the army's 1966 overland one to the pole, where they planted the flag (Scott 813);[23] historic first flights (Scott 853), including the first to join South America and Australia across Antarctica; the launching of experimental rockets (Scott C105); and military ships and aircraft involved in supporting Argentine Antarctic activities (Scott B165a–b, 1948). Each major Argentine base has also been the object of at least one stamp: General San Martín (Scott 731), General Belgrano (Scott 770), and Almirante Brown (Scott 852). In semiotic terms each of these stamps usually contains an icon with a graphic of the event, vehicle, or station involved, as well as a map of the Antarctic claim that serves both as index (back to Argentina) and symbol of the nation and its Antarctic aspirations. Significantly, each base was named after a military hero of the independence period, and each base is controlled and staffed by a military department.

In 1966 (Scott 797) and again in 1994 (Scott 1844) stamps were issued showing the territory of Tierra del Fuego, Antarctica, and the South Atlantic islands, which became a separate province in 1994. The iconography of the province's seal in 1994 includes penguins and other reminders of the extension of Argentina to the far south; the 1996 commemorative stamp shows the three regions involved, from Tierra del Fuego, just across a narrow strait from the mainland, through the arc of the South Atlantic islands to the Antarctic claim, ending at the South Pole. Semiotically the message was the geopolitical one noted previously: that Argentina is a tricontinental nation, with the mainland linked to Antarctica through the chain of South Atlantic islands.

An event in Argentine Antarctic history that was celebrated by a special cancellation and envelope, although not a stamp, was the birth of the first human being in Antarctica in the history of the world.[24] Since Antarctica was never visited by humans until the 1820s and never had a native population, it was only a question of time until someone concluded that such a birth, and the registry of that birth in an official document, would also be an act of sovereignty for a country with an Antarctic claim. On 7 January 1978 the wife of the Argentine army captain commanding the Antarctic base at Esperanza (Hope Bay) gave birth to a boy, Emilio Palma, who fulfilled that requirement. The Palmas had been sent to Antarctica as part of an Argentine project to colonize their claim by sending families, and not just scientists, military men, and support personnel. Argentine authorities set up a civil registry that recorded the birth, along with marriages and other births to come later.

In their zeal to commemorate Antarctic events and activities, the Argentine authorities sometimes exaggerate or present somewhat distorted versions of reality. The main Almirante Brown Antarctic base, for example (Scott 1109), continues to be featured as a major active base even though it was burned down in April 1984 by a mentally unstable Argentine doctor who believed that by damaging the base slightly, the staff (including himself) would not be left there to winter over. The doctor did indeed get to go home early, but was institutionalized.[25] The base has been partially rebuilt with container units, which are occupied sporadically in the summer. A second example of misrepresentation concerns Deception Island off the west coast of the Antarctic Peninsula. In 1998 a stamp was issued (figure 10.5, Scott 2012) to celebrate the fiftieth anniversary of the Deception Island Argentine Antarctic base, with the implication that it was still functioning. However, it had been abandoned during the volcanic eruption of 1969 and never reoccupied, although the island is frequently visited by tourists and various Antarctic vessels from Argentina and several other countries.[26] The official Argentine description of their bases lists Deception as a "summer-only" base; the reality is that the base no longer exists and that the Argentine presence is limited to short stays lodged in temporary quarters. The volcano continues to show signs of activity, including thermal springs used by tourists who want to claim that they have "swum in Antarctica."

CHILE

Chile follows Argentina in terms of the number of Antarctic stamps issued in the 1947–2005 period.[27] Even though the numbers may be fewer, Chilean Antarctic stamps have some unique characteristics. A Chile Antarctic claim map is featured prominently in an early stamp in 1947 (Scott 247–248), as well as one commemorating its participation in the International Geophysical Year, 1957–1958 (figure 10.6, Scott 305).

This latter stamp immediately caused problems with Argentina. In part this was because of the overlapping claims of the two countries, but also because of the way the words "Océano Pacífico" are placed on the stamp. From a design perspective the placement of the words makes sense since they are centered on the stamp. But extending the Pacific Ocean this far east violates one of the most cherished Argentine-Chilean geopolitical dictates in this sensitive area: the so-called bi-oceanic principle under which Chile has primacy in the Pacific and Argentina in the Atlantic.[28] The stamp suggests that the Pacific Ocean (and thus Chile's primacy) extends well into the South Atlantic region considered by the Argentines to be their "mare nostrum." It is possible that the stamp design was an innocent error, but it was not so perceived by many Argentines, and the Chileans were careful not to repeat this typographical false step.

Chilean-Argentine strains on the mainland and in the Beagle Channel area over border issues have carried over into Antarctica. In the 1940s and 1950s there were tensions not only between Argentina and Great Britain but also between Argentina and Chile over presence and sovereignty claims in Antarctica and surrounding waters. The claims overlap problem seems to defy solution, and the most promising approach appears to be the one evolved in 1948 under which Argentina and Chile recognize that each has Antarctic interests, but agree to disagree on the limits of each other's claim.[29]

Although Chilean-British relations have generally been good, and even though Chile has historically tended to side with Great Britain on matters involving Argentina (such as the Malvinas/Falklands issue), the Chilean government protested the British 1949 overprinted stamps (Scott 2L1–8 and 4L1–8) for Graham Land (mainland British Antarctica) and the South Shetland Islands respectively. The Chilean protest argued that these areas were Chilean Antarctic territories. The Chileans soon responded philatelically with their own Antarctic stamps, as noted above. Diplomatic communications between Chile and Great Britain (as well as Argentina) illustrate the seriousness with which the governments concerned viewed the issuing of these postage stamps.[30]

In 1958 two stamps were issued that provided a unique perspective on Chile's Antarctic interests. The first (figure 10.7, Scott 310) quoted lines from the epic poem of the conquest of Chile, "La Araucana" by Alonso de Ercilla y Zúñiga (1533–1594), in which the poet-soldier refers to the country as "Chile, fértil provincia y señalada / En la región antártica famosa. ("Chile, fertile and well-known province / In the famous Antarctic region"). Ercilla could not have known about the existence of Antarctica, nor Chile's relationship to it, in the sixteenth century, and was simply using the word "antártica" in the sense of the region's being "antiarctos," that is, the antipodal polar opposite of the Arctic region. Nevertheless, the Chileans, by placing the lines from the poem next to a map of their Antarctic claim, are in effect using poetry written centuries ago to emphasize their Antarctic interest.

The second 1958 stamp (figure 10.9, Scott 311) uses the 1494 Treaty of Tordesillas to argue that Spain had "ancient sovereignty" in Antarctica, so by inference and the doctrine of *uti possidetis, ita possideatis* (as you possess, so may you possess) Chile should inherit Spain's Antarctic sovereignty. In case the point is missed, the line of the treaty of 1494, which divided the Portuguese and Spanish empires, is drawn "from pole to pole," as the treaty stated, showing how Chile projects to Antarctica along the line.[31]

In a 4 July 1958 note from the Chilean minister of foreign affairs to the minister of the interior, he notes the importance of stamps as a universal medium for making Chile's Antarctic territorial rights known. He goes on to refer to the role stamps could play in supporting the Chilean theory regarding the border between Atlantic and Pacific Oceans along the "arc of the Southern (Austral) Antilles." This thesis would define the eastern limit of the South Pacific area of Chilean primacy all the way out to the South Sandwich Islands and would in effect undercut the Argentine notion of itself as a con-

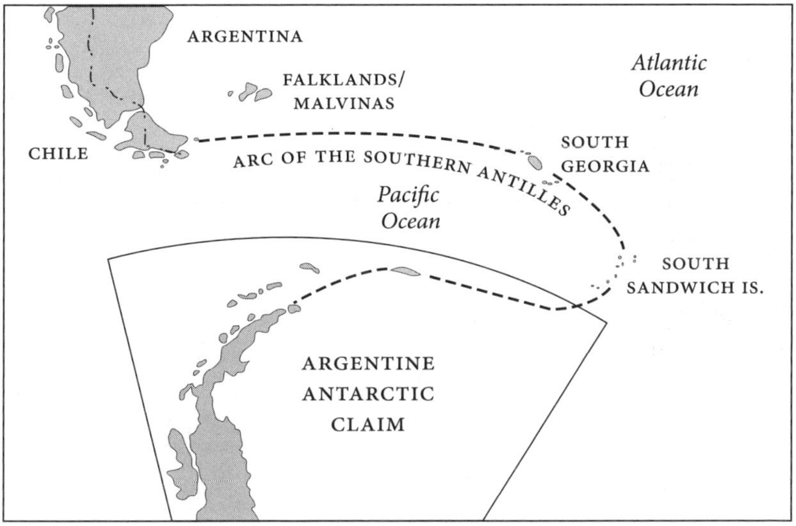

Map 2. The arc of the Southern Antilles

tinuous tricontinental nation.[32] Map 2 and figure 8.1 show this "arc of the Southern Antilles."

Paralleling the Argentine experience in rescuing the Swedish Antarctic expedition in 1903, the Chileans played an important role in rescuing the men Ernest Shackleton left on Elephant Island, when he undertook his harrowing open-boat odyssey to South Georgia to get assistance. Shackleton made several attempts to mount a rescue effort from South Georgia and Uruguay, but it was not until he obtained the Chilean government's support, and the use of the small cutter *Yelcho* under the command of Piloto (Captain) Luis Pardo, that he was able to get his men safely back to civilization. The Chileans are justly proud of their involvement in this effort, and have issued several stamps celebrating Captain Pardo (e.g., figure 10.8). The Chilean Naval Museum in Valparaiso and the Postal Museum in Santiago both emphasize the Chilean role in the Shackleton saga, including postal aspects and the commemorative stamps. As with the Argentines, the geographic reality of proximity to Antarctica gives Chile logistical and geopolitical advantages as exemplified by this rescue effort.

Chilean stamps commemorating the Antarctic Treaty on its various anniversaries also respected the recommendation that the map shown be that of an Antarctica not divided into national sector claims (Scott 974). Also paralleling Argentina's Antarctic stamps, Chile has issued ones featuring its bases (Scott 434, 592, 742–743) and its research activities (Scott 765b, 836, 1109–1110). The visit to Antarctica by President-General Augusto Pinochet, who expressed considerable interest in Chile's Antarctic activities and claim, was noted with a stamp featuring the base he visited with his wife in 1977 (Scott 497). The Chileans argue that they have in fact "colonized" Antarctica, establishing the first Antarctic "cities" that include families, post offices, banks, churches, civil registries, and many other features typical of a small town, not normally expected in an Antarctic base. To make this point, a set of stamps (figure 11.1, Scott 672; Scott 671–673) was issued in 1984 featuring "Villa las Estrellas" ("Villa of the Stars"), the evocatively named housing area at the Teniente Marsh base on King George Island.[33] Two stamps show a Chilean women's expedition to Antarctica, and a Boy Scout troop visit. The third shows a couple with their child looking out over the housing area of Villa las Estrellas. The joke making the rounds was that since the Argentines had beaten the Chileans in the race to have the first human being born in Antarctica, the Chileans were sending recently married couples to Villa las Estrellas with orders not to return until the first human being both conceived and born in Antarctica was produced. With little else to do over the long Antarctic winter, there would be ample time and opportunities for this to occur. The story may be apocryphal, but Chilean military and civil service couples have stayed in the base for a year at a time, and have had children born there.

One sometimes overlooked feature of many Antarctic programs, and especially the South American ones, is the key role played by the military. There are good reasons for this high profile, mainly that the military has the logistic, communication, and transportation infrastructure to mount and support Antarctic stations. Indeed, the U.S. Antarctic effort for many years was a military one, which has gradually been turned over to nonmilitary government organizations and civilian contractors. Many of the Chilean (as well as Argentine) bases carry the names of military heroes and are identified as being army, navy, or air force bases. Visitors to some of these Antarctic bases have noted the military uniforms and presence, although in deference to the Antarctic Treaty, no weapons are visible. An example of the military aspect of an Antarctic base is shown in a Chilean stamp (figure 11.2, Scott 592) celebrating the "Antarctic Lieutenant Marsh Air Base," and featuring as the graphic icon a Chilean air force C-130 transport aircraft. As is the case in Argentina, Chile's Antarctic programs are run by a national Antarctic Directorate, which is part of the Ministry of Defense.[34]

In recent years Chilean Antarctic stamps have emphasized wildlife, especially penguins, realizing that these appeal to topical collectors of that species. An original use of polar wildlife appeared on a 1989 Chilean stamp (Scott 865) issued in honor of a major stamp show in Washington; the stamp featured a map of the hemisphere, with a polar bear semiotically representing North America, and penguins doing the same for South America.

OTHER SOUTH AMERICAN NATIONS

In addition to Argentina and Chile, four other South American nations have an Antarctic presence, albeit minimal compared to these two. Two of them (Brazil, Uruguay) have each had a permanent (year-round) base in Antarctica since the early 1980s. Peru and Ecuador each have a summer-only base, to which they return each year. The stamp issues produced by these countries are correspondingly fewer than those of Argentina and Chile.

Brazil had participated in the 1957–1958 International Geophysical Year, but did not send scientists to the area. A Brazilian Antarctic Institute was created some years later, and did assign personnel to work on U.S. ships and scientific bases. It was not until 1982 that the Brazilians launched an expedition on their research ship the *Barão de Teffé*, an event that was commemorated with a stamp (figure 11.3, Scott 1845) showing the ship being observed by penguins on an ice floe.[35] A year later their Comandante Ferraz base on King George Island was completed, and appears on a commemorative stamp (Scott 2044). The Brazilian Antarctic effort, like those of all the South American countries, is heavily dependent on the military, and a 1987 stamp titled "Participation of the FAB [Brazilian Air Force] in the Brazilian Antarctic Program" (figure 11.4, Scott 2096) shows an FAB C-130 Hercules transport aircraft taking off alongside a large Brazilian flag and attentive penguins. The youthful and dynamic president of Brazil, Fernando Collor de Mello, visited the Ferraz base in 1991, and a stamp (Scott 2304) was issued in commemoration of the event. Since Brazil has not made an Antarctic claim, and cannot now that it has signed the treaty, any map of Antarctica on a Brazilian stamp is the undivided one favored by the Antarctic Treaty System. Brazil's Antarctic stamps have included numerous high-value souvenir sheets, suggesting that the intent was not normal postal usage as much as sales to collectors, tourists visiting the Ferraz base, and any other "Antarcticans." These sheets, which include a stamp usually accompanied by a map and descriptive materials, have covered a range of themes: in 1988, scientific research in Antarctica and a map of the area around the Ferraz base (Scott 2127); in 1990, the Antarctic Research Program and wildlife (Scott 2235); in 1997, the Antarctic Program (PROANTAR), a research vessel, a map of South America, and a detailed map of the South Shetland Islands showing the Ferraz base with a Brazilian flag (Scott 2630); and in 1999, the exploits of the sailor Amyr Klink, who completed the first solo circumnavigation of Antarctica (Scott 2746).

Despite having had a permanent scientific base (Artigas) since the mid-1980s, Uruguayan Antarctic stamps are relatively few in number, and follow the general theme of showing the base (Scott 1239) along with wildlife in the area, especially penguins. The most ambitious set was a four-stamp series issued on the tenth anniversary of the Artigas base in 1995, showing an albatross, support aircraft and ships, and the base itself (Scott 1589). The Uruguayan flag and the national colors are prominently featured. The fifteenth anniversary stamp (Scott 1803) stressed the base's scientific activities, and the Web page announcing the stamp carried a long explanation of the various research projects.[36]

Peru's Antarctic philatelic output features a semiotically imaginative stamp (figure 11.5, Scott 853) that shows a Humboldt penguin sitting on an ice floe under the slogan "Peru Present in Antarctica." The imaginative aspect involves the fact that when the stamp was issued in 1985, Peru had not yet mounted an expedition, and that the Humboldt penguin is a warm-water species native to northern Chile and southern Peru. The semiotic message was that the Peruvian penguin was soon to be transported philatelically to colder waters as a symbol of national interest in Antarctica. An expedition had been planned for the 1983–1984 season, but it did not materialize until several years later, whereupon a commemorative stamp was issued (1988, Scott 935) showing the research ship *BIC Humboldt* and a map with Peru and Antarctica prominently displayed. The second Peruvian Antarctic expedition was celebrated with a three-stamp set (figure 11.6, Scott 1005; Scott 1006–1007) showing bird wildlife, whales, and a researcher approaching penguins (inexplicably, one penguin appears to be flying). Each stamp carries a Peruvian flag and shows the temporary (summer-only) base station.

Ecuador, like Peru, only has a summer base, which it shows (Scott 1344–

1345) along with a flag and an undivided map of Antarctica. A later stamp shows wildlife and the base, which is named after the eighteenth-century Spanish geographer Pedro Vicente Maldonado,[37] who was active in exploring large areas of Ecuador. Ecuadorian-Peruvian strains have also involved their Antarctic programs, with each nation arguing that the other was attempting to illegally make an Antarctic claim, and each recognizing that the principal reason for setting up an Antarctic program was in part a political one designed to ensure that they would achieve voting status in the Antarctic Treaty System, which they did in 1991.[38]

BRITISH ANTARCTIC TERRITORY

Although not as aggressively nationalistic in Antarctica as Argentina and Chile, the British are also keenly aware of the propaganda, financial, and geopolitical value of postage stamps to reinforce their claim in the area.[39] The 1946 British Falkland Islands Dependencies map stamp (figure 8.1) clearly showed the cartographic relationship between the Falkland Islands, the other South Atlantic islands, and the British Antarctic claim (Graham Land). In 1962 the Falkland Islands Dependencies were divided up into British Antarctic Territory (BAT) and the South Georgia and South Sandwich Islands.

After this somewhat provocative beginning, one might expect a series of BAT map stamps making very clear what the British territorial claim is, and how it relates to the Falklands and South Georgia. However, the BAT stamps from 1963 to the present have refrained from including maps, except the undivided map favored by the Antarctic Treaty System. BAT stamp themes have also tended to be innocuous, stressing anniversaries of the Antarctic Treaty, scientific activities, wildlife, geology, fossils, and atmospheric phenomena (figure 10.1, Scott 20). Historical themes have included the expeditions of Robert F. Scott in 1902–1904 and the especially fateful one in 1910–1912 (figure 11.7, Scott BAT 140), and of Sir Ernest Shackleton (Scott 285–287), as well as the trans-Antarctic expedition in which the British Commonwealth's conqueror of Mount Everest (Sir Edmund Hillary) completed Shackleton's dream of traversing the continent (Scott 288). Even though the British might still have reason to be annoyed at the 1904 Scottish expedition of William Bruce and his gift of the Orkneys station to the Argentines, the BAT did feature a series on him, showing the iconic portrait of a king penguin patiently listening to the bagpiper Gilbert Kerr (figure 11.8, Scott 317). Unlike the photograph on which the stamp illustration is based, the short rope tying the penguin to the piper to prevent its escape is not shown.

Particularly striking, well prepared, and helpful to the student of Antarctic history was the BAT's 1975–1980 "Explorers" series (Scott 45–59), which showed all the major Antarctic explorers with their ships (and aircraft, in the case of more recent ones). Illustrative stamps that relate to our area of interest, the South American quadrant of Antarctica, include those of Captain James Cook and the *Resolution* (Scott 45)—Cook was the first person to circumnavigate Antarctica, and discovered the island of South Georgia; Otto Nordenskjold and his ship *Antarctic*, whose sinking led to Argentina's rescue effort on the *Uruguay* (Scott 53a); the Scot William Bruce and the *Scotia* (Scott 54a); and Sir Ernest Shackleton and the *Endurance* (Scott 56).

Another two stamps (Scott 62–63) focus on the then secret World War II Operation Tabarin (named after a Paris nightclub, supposedly because it was always kept dark), which responded to British concern over possible German naval activities in Antarctica and the sub-Antarctic islands during World War II. Claiming these were scientific activities, Prime Minister Winston Churchill directed the British military and Antarctic establishments to set up a series of bases, mainly along the Antarctic Peninsula, whose purpose in fact was to monitor possible Nazi activities, which some feared might be supported by Argentine Nazi sympathizers.[40] After World War II, Operation Tabarin was transformed into the Falkland Islands Dependencies Survey, and finally became a crown colony, the British Antarctic Territory, but the political and strategic tension persisted to some extent, reflecting the continued strain between Britain and Argentina over the territory. Beck quotes from 1947 British government instructions: "The primary objective of the Survey is to strengthen His Majesty's title to the sector of the Antarctic known as the Falkland Islands Dependencies by maintaining British occupation parties there. There are strategic reasons for this occupation. . . . The secondary objective of the Survey is to continue scientific work in the Antarctic."[41]

In early 2005 the draft European Union Constitution listed the British Antarctic Territory in an annex that also included the Falkland Islands, identified as British. This provoked the Argentine foreign minister Rafael Bielsa to protest and reject the inclusion of these areas, stressing that Argentina would wait four, forty, or four hundred years to work the problem out. "We have to have the same patience as the colonial powers had."[42]

Like stamps of the Falkland Islands and South Georgia, those of the British Antarctic Territory (which are processed in the same facilities at Port Stanley, Falklands) are of high quality and generally include themes relevant to the history, geography, and science of the area. First-day covers (stamped envelopes) with inserts are an attractive and valuable source of information. Because of the very small population of BAT (a maximum of about one hundred in the summer and perhaps a third of that for winter maintenance), very few BAT stamps are actually used for postage, except for items mailed by tourists. The base most frequently visited by tourists is Port Lockroy, which has been restored to its Tabarin-era appearance by a historic trust. Here the BAT postmaster may process as many as five thousand first-day covers yearly; the permanent staff of the base is four.[43] BAT postmasters follow the tradition of early British polar expeditions, which used postage stamps, postcards and envelopes, and mail cancellations to partially fund their activities. Shackleton was especially meticulous in handling these, and in many cases added personal notes. Steve Pendleton notes that Shackleton even went out of his way to answer letters addressed to "Mr. Seal."[44]

OTHER MINIATURE MESSAGES FROM SOUTH AMERICAN ANTARCTICA

Several other countries have research stations in Antarctica that document and propagandize their activities using postage stamps. These comprise the United States, Russia, Poland, and the People's Republic of China, whose base, along with the Russian, is close to the Chilean base at Teniente Marsh.

The United States has a major presence in Antarctica, with three large year-round stations, including one at the South Pole. Palmer Station (named after a New England sealing captain) is on the Antarctic Peninsula, in the area where the Argentine, Chilean, and British claims overlap. Despite this major effort involving study and presence in Antarctica, the United States has issued very few stamps with Antarctic themes.

The first of these was a stamp (figure 11.9, Scott 733) whose design was suggested by President Franklin D. Roosevelt, an ardent philatelist. The map stamp shows the American continent and Antarctica, with a dotted line representing the route of Admiral Byrd's 1933–1934 expedition to "Little America." In order to show the terminus of the trip (across from New Zealand) the designer had to distort Antarctic geography. More recent U.S.

stamps have celebrated the Antarctic Treaty and its tenth anniversary (Scott C130), as well as four Antarctic explorers (Scott 2386–2389): Charles Wilkes, Nathaniel Palmer, Lincoln Ellsworth, and Richard E. Byrd. The designs are basically the same, showing the bust of the explorer and his ship or plane set against a map of Antarctica; a white line shows the explorer's route. Since the United States makes no Antarctic claim and recognizes none, the map shows no sectors. Finally, the environmental organization Greenpeace produced fund-raising "stamps" in connection with an Antarctic base that it maintained for several years on the Antarctic mainland.

8 OTHER MINIATURE MESSAGES OF NOTE

Several other Latin American countries have issued stamps that contain political or semiotic messages of interest. Because of the large number of stamps issued, I will review only a very few of the total available stamps, using the criterion of significant illustrative value in terms of the politics, history, and semiotics involved.

BOLIVIA

In 1981 the administration of General Luis García Meza, which had come to power in a coup and was marked by harsh antisubversive measures, issued a set of four stamps (Scott 657–660) commemorating his "revolution." The semiotic messages of the stamps were striking, reflecting García Meza's ideological stance. They made ample use of the Bolivian flag, and slogans such as "Neither colony nor satellite, but a sovereign patria" and "The Armed Forces and the people will liberate Bolivia from extremism." One stamp in particular shows a soldier and an indigenous man (wearing a peasant hat) holding a large Bolivian flag, whose shaft is destroying the hammer and sickle of Communism. The courageous president of the Bolivian Philatelic Federation pointed out that the rules of the Universal Postal Union prohibited the issuing of stamps that offended a member country of the UPU, in this case the Soviet Union. Two of the stamps were indeed withdrawn from circulation, but a total of about seven thousand of the print run of one hundred thousand were sold before the withdrawal and destruction of the remainder. A few months later the government of García Meza fell.[1]

A curious anomaly with political implications, which reflects the economic realities of inflation, surrounds the Bolivian stamp commemorating a joint Bolivian-Brazilian railroad project and two presidents (Victor Paz Estenssoro of Bolivia and Getulio Vargas of Brazil). A January 1954 meeting between the two presidents was scheduled at their common border to inaugurate the international railroad between Corumba and Santa Cruz, and the Bolivian postal administration issued a stamp with the faces of the two presidents set against a locomotive in the background. But the 1954 presidential meeting never took place, and the stamp was withdrawn that year. However, it was later released in 1960 (Scott C227) with a surcharge to accommodate inflation of postal rates. The railroad was a long-planned project originally proposed in 1884 as part of a link between the Brazilian Atlantic port of Santos and the Chilean Pacific port of Arica. The 2,500-mile rail line would open up large areas of Brazil and Bolivia to development under an arrangement in which Brazil would build the line in exchange for oil and mineral rights along the Bolivian stretch of the line. Construction started in 1939 and was not completed until 1955 because of enormous difficulties with the terrain, disease, and hostile indigenous tribes. Once finished, operating the railroad revealed a basic economic flaw: there was not enough traffic or demand for transportation to justify the expensive construction and operation of the line. Some 1,180 employees were hired to take care of one round trip per week, and the project soon faced bankruptcy. The 1954 stamp was not issued because Brazilian enthusiasm for the project had diminished by the time of the now canceled meeting at the border.[2] However, the stamps had been printed, they represented a substantial expenditure, and eventually the Bolivian government decided to use them, even though four years had passed since the supposed inaugural ceremonies, and Bolivian inflation required a surcharge of twelve hundred bolivianos on the original ten-boliviano stamp.

Considering the fundamental importance of mining to the economy and sociopolitical structure of Bolivia, it is not surprising that stamps noting this activity have been common. The best of these issues, an attractive engraved set, was produced in 1943 (Scott 290–296) and shows various mining activities (drilling, moving ore, etc.), as well as some of the major mining centers, such as Potosí. Later stamps portray the nationalization of the mining industry (Scott 377, C253), which was a major goal of the Bolivian MNR (Nationalist Revolutionary Movement) that came to power in 1952.

The MNR has been celebrated with many stamps since 1952. The most prevalent semiotic messages dealt with nationalization of mines and agrarian reform (Scott C252), as well as the major leaders of the MNR going back to Gualberto Villaroel and Victor Paz Estenssoro (Scott 381), and continuing through René Barrientos (Scott 481), and Hugo Banzer (Scott 539), although it can be argued that some of these later leaders strayed considerably from the original revolutionary goals of the MNR.

BRAZIL

Brazil has a long and rich tradition of issuing postage stamps with significant political, historical, and economic themes. Brazil was the first Latin American nation (and the second in the world) to produce postage stamps, only three years after England's pioneering effort. However, these early stamps were susceptible to counterfeiting, and after two decades of stamps with no iconography the Brazilian authorities decided (after consultation with U.S. banknote-printing companies) that having a portrait of the monarch on their stamps would make them harder to falsify. Accordingly, in 1866 Emperor Dom Pedro II made his appearance, although there was an anomaly: on one of the stamps the emperor is shown as a man much older than his forty years. This pattern of showing an older emperor was repeated some ten years later, when at age fifty his appearance with a full white beard made him look older than his age. Philatelists have provided no explanation for this phenomenon.[3] When the empire was replaced by a republic in 1889 the remaining stamps bearing the face of Dom Pedro were replaced with the so-called republican issues bearing themes such as the Southern Cross constellation and an allegorical head of Liberty.

In chapter 3 it was noted that the national colors of Brazil (yellow and green) provided continuity between the old empire and the new republic. C. W. Hennan tells a most likely apocryphal story that provides an alternate explanation for the two colors.[4] According to him, there were two Irishmen involved in the printing of Brazilian stamps at the Continental Bank Note Company of New York. One was an Orangeman, and the other was "a loyal wearer of the green." Their religious and political differences led to constant squabbling and attempts to place their favorite colors (yellow or green) on stamps they were designing. Finally, to shut them up an official of the company put both colors on the stamps they were designing, much to the satisfaction of the Brazilians; it was the country's first bicolor stamp.

Brazilian postal officialdom has a well-developed sense of the significance of the messages carried by its postage stamps. A statement by the minister of communications argues: "The postage stamp, in and of itself, is a calling card and a part of the history of the country that issues it. The stamp is an indispensable presence on all the messages and objects sent by mail, traveling throughout all Brazil and the world. The beauty of its colors, the care taken in its preparation, and an appropriate selection of themes will serve to positively represent the country and all that is part of it."[5] The Brazilian postal administration backs up this notion by preparing well-designed presentation albums of new stamps, explaining their political and historical significance, and distributing them widely within Brazil as well as to foreign governments and national libraries abroad.[6] The sensitivity to the impact of postage stamps is not limited to official sources. The Bloch Editores publishing empire prepares inserts to its popular magazines, which invite the reader to better know Brazil through its postage stamps, regarding stamps as cultural objects with educational value.[7] The Bloch inserts were mainly historical, but also included economic and international themes, as well as celebrations of Brazilian painters, musicians, and artists.

Although not as blatant as the examples of Trujillo in the Dominican Republic, Stroessner of Paraguay, or the Somozas of Nicaragua, several presidents of Brazil have not been shy about putting themselves on postage stamps. The earliest example is Getulio Vargas, whose first democratically elected administration turned into the more authoritarian Estado Novo. To make his presence on a postage stamp more acceptable (and perhaps to stroke his ego), Vargas would authorize stamps in which he would be accompanied by (and thus be associated with) a major historical figure, such as Dom Pedro II or Franklin Roosevelt (Scott 485, 487).[8] Vargas also used stamps to commemorate major events of his tenure, such as the creation of Petrobras, the Brazilian oil monopoly; the stamp has a semiotic message when it shows Vargas holding up his hand dripping with a black substance, presumably oil (Scott 883). The tendency of presidents to put themselves on postage stamps (called philatelic "self-homage" by a critic)[9] was particularly notable during the 1964–1985 years of the military "revolution" (Scott 996). After the restoration of democracy this tendency was continued, starting with the luckless Tancredo Neves (Scott 2025), who died before assuming office, José Sarney (Scott 2238), and Collor de Mello (Scott 2304). Past presidents have also been honored, and a particularly dramatic stamp shows a large head of Juscelino Kubitscheck looming over the presidential palace in the city he created, Brasília (Scott 2079).

One notable Brazilian stamp with a significant semiotic message is the tribute to the Frenchman Auguste Comte (Scott 854), who is regarded as the father of the positivist school of philosophical thought that was to have so much influence in Brazil in the nineteenth century. Positivism is credited as being a major moving force behind the shift from empire to republic, and the Brazilian national motto (enshrined in its flag) is the positivist theme of "order and progress."

In a similar vein are the stamps honoring air pioneer and national hero Alberto Santos Dumont (Scott C18–20), who designed, built, and flew a number of dirigibles and fixed-wing aircraft in Brazil as well as France. Using his dirigible, he won a 1901 competition in Paris involving an eleven-kilometer course around the Eiffel Tower, making him, in the words of the Brazilian Postal Administration, "the most important aeronaut of his times."[10] Santos Dumont had great hopes that aviation would serve to unite people from different cultures, but grew despondent when he saw aircraft being used as weapons in World War I as well as in a Brazilian armed revolt in São Paulo state. Shortly afterward he committed suicide.

A third stamp series with a significant semiotic message is that of the São Paulo revolutionary issues of 1932 (Scott 364–374), which were issued by a separatist military revolt in that state.[11] The revolt was settled peaceably, and, contrary to what might have been expected, the Federal Government recognized the stamps and accepted them for general use.

Stamps were also issued to celebrate Brazil's participation in World War II, in two rather different sets, one produced immediately after the war in 1945 (Scott 635–639), and a second twenty-five years later, in 1970 (Scott 1172). The earlier stamps have a semiotic message emphasizing Brazil's role in collaboration with (indeed subordination to) U.S. forces in the conflict. Three of the stamps carry the unit patch of the U.S. Fifth Army, to which the Brazilian Expeditionary Force was attached, and one stamp is dominated by a large U.S. flag (figure 1.4). Four of the five stamps also carry the unit patch with the BEF's "smoking cobra" symbol. However, the 1970 stamp, reflecting perhaps a greater sense of Brazilian independence from U.S. influence, shows only Brazilian military symbols.[12]

Inflation has been a problem at times in Brazil, and, as noted in chapter 3, this affects postage stamps because they must increase in face value to accompany the inflation rate in order to avoid losing revenue. In 1988 the Brazilian Post Office devised a creative way to handle the problem: they issued stamps with no face value, with each stamp identified by a single letter of the alphabet. So if stamp "A" was to cover a basic postal rate of one hundred cruzeiros it would be worth one hundred cruzeiros. But if inflation pushed the postal rate up to two hundred cruzeiros, then the government would announce that stamp "A" would now be sold for two hundred cruzeiros and would still cover the basic postal rate.[13] These so-called nonmonetized stamps have been used in the United States for a somewhat different purpose, namely at the start of a period of new postal rates when the postal system lacks enough stamps of the correct monetary value.

Starting in the 1970s Brazil's stamps began to display bolder and more distinctive graphic designs. The military dictatorship from 1964 to 1985 made sure that themes on its agenda were prominent, including those honoring the military "revolution" of 1964 (Scott 1215), the armed forces (with many celebrations of Army, Navy, and Air Force Days and Weeks; Scott 1182, 1193), and compulsory military service (Scott 1073, 1113). The military government's push for economic development was also prominent in stamps such as those noting the national oil industry Petrobras (Scott 1098), steel mills (Scott 1017), the Itaipú Dam (Scott 1847), and the Trans-Amazonian Highway (Scott 1189–1190). Perhaps the most blatant of these themes was captured in stamps such as the one honoring the army as promoter of development (Scott 1134), and the contribution the armed forces made to civilian services (Scott 1541–1543). Also notable was the stamp honoring Brazil's participation in United Nations peacekeeping missions (Scott C88).

The emphasis on bolder designs, starting in the 1970s and continuing to the present, can be seen in stamps celebrating Carnival (Scott 1150–1154), soccer (Scott 1230), folklore (Scott 1234), and popular dances (Scott 1758). Typical of the design innovations was the 1997 stamp (figure 12.1, Scott 2624), which was part of the worldwide campaign calling for increased attention to the fight against AIDS. As was the case in the parallel Argentine stamp, the Brazilians used a condom, but inside the condom is the red ribbon symbolic of the campaign against AIDS, thus signaling semiotically that the condom is a barrier to the transmission of the AIDS virus.

One suggestive theme in Brazilian stamps of the last two decades has been ecology and conservation (figure 12.2, Scott 1474), which came about at a time when there was increasing criticism that Brazil was guilty of basic environmental sins, especially the deforestation of the Amazon. In 1992 a special commemorative album was designed around a set of stamps (Scott 2367–2369) issued for the United Nations Conference on the Environment (Earth Summit 92), held in Rio that year.[14] The topics included celebration of the Botanical Society of Brazil, the Yanomani indigenous people, the forests and plants of Brazil, and Brazil's ecological research program in Antarctica.

Some of the reaction to Brazilian ecological themes was on the cynical side. Denis Altman, for example, noted: "Sometimes these stamps may represent a genuine concern of the issuing government. But it is also true that it is very easy to issue a stamp—certainly a lot easier than saving a rain forest. . . . There is sad irony in the juxtaposition of two Brazilian issues in 1988, one for 'protected animals' and one for the National Confederation of Industry."[15]

As might be expected in a nation that has dominated international soccer so long, this sport has appeared in numerous forms in Brazilian stamps, and Brazil's triumph in World Cup events has been lavishly noted. The summer 2002 championship shows the priority that soccer gets on stamps. Barely two days after Brazil's victory over Germany, a stamp appeared celebrating this fifth World Cup for Brazil. Because of the normal lengthy design and printing process, this meant that the stamp had been prepared well before the final soccer game, and that the government was betting on a Brazilian victory. The design includes the Rimet Cup itself, five stars (for Brazil's five victories), and the flags of the host countries for the victories, all set against a background of the Brazilian national colors (figure 3.5).

CHILE

Chile's early stamps (from the first in 1853 until the independence centennial issue of 1910) are an oddity: almost all the iconography is related to Christopher Columbus (e.g., Scott 10), despite the fact that Columbus was never anywhere near Chile, and has no special association with that country. As with most of the Spanish-speaking Latin American countries that date their independence back to 1810, an important change occurred with the centenary, when an iconographically rich set of commemorative stamps was issued. In the next several decades Chile showed a typical increase in the placing of historically and politically significant icons on its stamps. Cultural values are also present, and a major study of artworks that appear on stamps was prepared by a distinguished philatelist who is also an art critic, noting that the serious study of postage stamps is an "auxiliary science of history."[16]

Of special interest in our consideration of the semiotics and politics of postage stamps are some issues produced during the years of Salvador Allende (1970–1973), the military dictatorship that followed (1973–1990), and the restoration of democratically elected presidents after the long years of de facto authoritarian rule. In 1972 Chile hosted a meeting of the third

United Nations Conference on Trade and Development (UNCTAD), and the stamp issued to celebrate the occasion was a pair of joined stamps in which the upper one contained an icon of a group of Chilean workers in various fields (agriculture, mining, industry, science, etc.), along with the legend "Masters of our own destiny" (Scott 418–421). The lower stamp was devoted entirely to a quotation from President Salvador Allende: "Chile will only progress on the base of an organized, disciplined and conscientious people who will work more and produce more." Shortly afterward that same year a stamp was issued to commemorate the Allende administration's nationalization of the Chilean copper industry, an event that contributed significantly to the increasing strains with the Nixon administration in Washington (figure 2.4 and Scott 423). Allende's relationship with the military was also strained. Up until that time the Chilean military had a long tradition of abstaining from direct political activities, and there had not been a serious coup attempt in almost four decades. Within the military, however, there was an increasingly sharp division between those who remained loyal to this tradition, and those who were being influenced by important sectors of the middle and upper class, who called for a coup to remove Allende. Among the former was the commander of the army, General René Schneider, who was assassinated and subsequently honored by a stamp during the Allende years (Scott 428).

The 11 September 1973 coup that brought down the Allende government also brought a change in the postal issues of Chile. As noted previously, the anniversary of the coup (declared an official holiday during the dictatorship) was often celebrated by a postage stamp noting how many "years of freedom" Chile had enjoyed since 1973. Particularly lavish were the postage stamps for the third and tenth anniversaries (figure 2.5 and Scott 656–659), which featured an allegorical angel breaking the chains of Communism, a young couple with the Chilean flag, and a family group with the torch of freedom.

Armed forces days, and the celebratory days of the individual armed forces (plus the militarized police—the *carabineros*), were often noted with stamps during these years, along with important military anniversaries celebrating the centennial of the War of the Pacific in 1979 (Scott 537–539).[17] There were numerous stamps noting Chilean Antarctic activities in this period, and many of the stamps issued showed that the bases were established and maintained by each of the main branches of the armed forces (Scott 592, 594, 691).

Economic themes were also prevalent during the 1973–1990 military dictatorship as the regime moved Chile's economy from the state-directed Marxist approach of the Allende years to the more open model advocated by Milton Friedman and the "Chicago Boys." These stamps with economic themes featured traditional exports such as minerals (Scott 728a–d), as well as those products (mainly seasonal fruits such as grapes or apples, Scott 439) in which Chile enjoyed a comparative advantage in the U.S. market due to the reversal of seasons in the northern and southern hemispheres (Scott 830–833). The excellent Chilean wines also were featured in stamps such as one that carried the legend "Chile exports wines" (Scott 439–440).

After the military turned power back to elected civilian presidents in 1990, the philatelic emphasis shifted again. There were no more stamps celebrating the 1973 coup, and the number of stamps honoring the military diminished. In 1991 the Nobel literature laureate Pablo Neruda, a committed Marxist who died shortly after the 1973 coup, was honored with a stamp (figure 12.3, Scott 980; Scott 981), something that would not have been possible under the military regime. A second stamp honoring him was issued in 1996 (Scott 1200). Neruda's fellow Nobel literature laureate Gabriela Mistral has also appeared on Chilean stamps (Scott 300). After his death Salvador Allende was featured on the postage stamps of a number of nations, including Cuba, the Soviet Union, several Eastern European nations, and (after 1979) revolutionary Nicaragua. His first appearance on a Chilean stamp was in 1990, as one of a series of stamps featuring the last ten elected presidents (figure 12.4, Scott 912). Pointedly, General Pinochet was not included.

COLOMBIA

Early Colombian postage stamps, like those of Argentina, reflect the difficulties the nation had in consolidating a central government in the face of strong regional political currents that favored a less binding federal system. But while Argentina had three provincial governments, which issued stamps for only a few years, Colombia had six such administrations, and their postal issues continued into the early years of the twentieth century. Colombia's difficult mountainous topography contributed to this sense of fragmentation, and it is not surprising that Colombia was one of the first Latin American countries to develop an efficient airmail system, and has had many airmail postal issues (see Scott C869). Some of these were privately issued by the airlines handling the mail, such as the Sociedad Colombo-

Alemana de Transportes Aéreos (SCADTA), which had a heavy infusion of capital from Germans residing in Colombia. Colombian postal authorities, working closely with stamp clubs, have also strongly supported philately, evincing a sensitivity to the educational and cultural values involved. Several ministers of communication have been collectors, and have encouraged Colombian philatelic organizations to become involved in organizing programs promoting stamp collecting at the high school level.[18]

Political themes on Colombian stamps are numerous. David Bushnell has analyzed how, responding to either official ideology or popular culture, postage stamps in general, and those of Colombia in particular, demonstrate a definite choice of themes, frequently with political implications.[19] Practically all the Colombian presidents have appeared on postage stamps, sometimes as individuals, and occasionally as part of series (Scott 1110a–t). Political *caudillos* and militant leaders of both major parties have also been featured. Unfortunately, Colombia also has a history of assassinated political leaders who probably would have reached the presidency, but who were cut down before that goal could be reached. The most noteworthy of these was Jorge Eliécer Gaitán, whose murder set off the "Bogotazo" riots in 1948; he is featured on several postage stamps (Scott 698–699, C319–320). In his most recent appearance on a 1998 stamp (figure 12.5, Scott 1140) one of his statements is featured: "I am not an individual, I am a people." More recently, the presidential hopeful Luis Carlos Galán was honored on a stamp (Scott 1031) after his assassination during a political rally.

The Colombian military makes the expected appearances on postage stamps through celebration of heroes, historical battles, and military institutions, but also includes a commemoration unique in Latin America: their participation in the Korean conflict, where they were the only Latin American nation to do so. The first of these stamps appeared in 1955 shortly after the war ended (figure 12.6, Scott 635; Scott C255, C269), and were featured on a souvenir sheet that also commemorated the General Gustavo Rojas Pinilla coup of 1953 as part of an "homage to the armed forces of Colombia" (Scott 637a). The ceremonies surrounding the issuing of the Korean War stamp involved the presence of all three commanders of the Colombian infantry battalion in Korea.[20]

Cultural icons on Colombian stamps have been numerous, featuring poets, authors, and painters. The issue celebrating the 1982 Nobel literature prize for Gabriel García Márquez (Scott 917, C731–732) is striking in its design, showing a ghostly gray pencil drawing of the author set against a white background. Equally dramatic was a 2001 series honoring the painter Fernando Botero (figure 12.7, Scott 1069), and later when he donated a series of paintings (some his and some by other famous painters) to museums in Bogotá and Medellín;[21] the stamps were issued in a souvenir set of twelve of the paintings, and featured several of his better-known paintings, including his signature rotund human figures, some nude.

CUBA

Any analysis of Cuban stamps is complicated by the very large number of stamps that have been produced since the triumphant 1959 Castro Revolution. In the first century of Cuban stamps (1855–1958) the total number issued was a little over eight hundred, or about eight a year. In the period from January 1959 to late 2000 over thirty-six hundred stamps were produced, for an annual average of about eighty-seven a year, or almost eleven times the average before the revolution. This pattern follows that of the Soviet Union, and the sheer volume suggests that most of these stamps were not actually used for postage, but rather for financial and political reasons. In terms of popular culture criteria, they would seem to fall short of qualifying, since the intended audience was probably international, and not domestic. Nevertheless, they do form part of the official Cuban stamp record, and merit our consideration as indicators of the image the Cuban government wished to project abroad. A further complication involving post-1959 stamps (to be considered below) is the restriction the U.S. government has placed on their importation.

Pre-1959 Cuban stamps are not particularly distinguished by any unique features. They show the typical range of nationalistic, patriotic, and cultural themes, limited in scope because Cuba's independence was achieved considerably later than that of the other Latin American nations. Thus, from 1855 to 1898, when Cuba was under Spanish control, Cuban stamps carried the faces of Spanish monarchs (for example, Queen Isabella II, on Cuba's first stamp in 1855), or abstract allegories of Spain, its national crest, and other symbols determined by Madrid. For a brief period in 1898–1899 U.S. stamps with the overprint of "Cuba" were used, followed by stamps prepared in New York and used in Cuba under U.S. military occupation.

During the Batista years Cuba had an unusually close relationship with the United States, as epitomized by stamps praising the United States as the beacon of democracy (Scott 372), and the fact that Cuba was the second

American nation to declare war on Germany (after the United States). In 1943 a curious set of Cuban stamps (Scott 375–379) warned of the dangers of fifth column subversion from Axis agents intent on damaging the Allies' war effort. The idea for the stamps came from a U.S. diplomat with close ties to the Cuban government, and the thematic concept and proposed stamps themselves were the product of American designers.[22]

A medical controversy involving yellow fever was played out using Cuban postage stamps. At issue was the relative credit that should be given to the Cuban doctor Carlos Juan Finlay or the American Walter Reed for the discovery of the role of the mosquito in the transmission of yellow fever. The Cubans have consistently argued that the basic idea was Finlay's, and that the Americans, led by the U.S. Army major Walter Reed, borrowed his idea to eventually prove that the mosquito was the vector for the disease. In the process of testing the notion, several volunteers agreed to be bitten by diseased mosquitoes, and one of them, a young American nurse named Clara Maass, died as a result.[23] Cuban stamps over the years have supported the Finlay thesis, including pre-Castro ones in 1934 (Scott 319–320), 1954 (Scott 525), 1965 (Scott 989–995), and a souvenir sheet in 1951 (Scott C43a) overprinted with the legend "50th Anniversary of the Discovery by Dr. Carlos J. Finlay of the Agent that Transmits Yellow Fever. Honor to the Martyrs of Science. 1901–1951." During the post-1959 period the Castro regime continued the philatelic support of Finlay, issuing an extensive set of stamps in 1965 (Scott 989–995) on the fiftieth anniversary of his death, including his portrait, his microscope, and a close-up of the *Aedes aegypti* mosquito, which was proved to transmit the disease. The Cubans also honored Clara Maass with a 1951 stamp (Scott 462), which carries her portrait and shows both the New Jersey hospital where she trained and the Cuban hospital where she died. The Cuban stamp preceded a U.S. stamp honoring Maass by twenty-five years.

The nature and number of Cuban stamps changed dramatically after January 1959. Stamps were used extensively to carry themes supportive of the revolution, its goals, accomplishments, anniversaries, and principal figures. The first revolutionary stamp appeared in late January 1959 (figure 12.8), only four weeks after the "Day of Liberation" it celebrates. It features a bearded guerrilla brandishing a rifle, set against a large Cuban flag. A year later, on the first anniversary, a more detailed seven-stamp set (figure 12.9 and Scott 625–628, C200–202) laid out the main events of the revolution to that date, starting with the 26 July attack on Moncada Barracks, then the landing from the *Granma*, and several of the major battles of the 1956–1958 fighting phase of the revolution, culminating in the triumphant entry into Havana. Clandestine activities in the cities during the fighting phase are also celebrated.

The major personalities of the revolution appear frequently in the post-1959 stamps, especially if the individuals featured have died in combat or have disappeared. In the latter category Camilo Cienfuegos occupies a prominent place (Scott 647, 3171), as well as Frank País (Scott 2960). Individuals who died in the 1953 attack led by Fidel Castro on the army's Moncada Barracks are honored (Scott 742–743, 780–782), as is Castro's confidante Celia Sánchez (figure 12.10, Scott 3223; Scott 2755). The one individual who stands out in this category, reaching the status of national icon, is Che Guevara, who is featured in numerous stamps (Scott 1318, 1347–1351), culminating in the 1997 ones commemorating the thirtieth anniversary of his death in Bolivia on 8 October 1967. The day of his death is noted each year as the "Day of the Guerrilla," and the stamps issued feature Che himself, highlights of his life, and notable quotations ("Create three, many Vietnams"; "Until victory always"). Che also appears on a stamp commemorating one of his less triumphant moments: the expedition to join guerrillas fighting in the Congo (figure 12.11).

Castro himself has appeared less often; he is shown during the fortieth anniversary of the signing of the Agrarian Reform Act in 1959 (Scott 4007), during a 1960 speech at the United Nations (Scott 2354), and at the iconic moment when white doves of peace perched on his shoulders during a speech in Havana (figure 13.2, Scott 3983). In an indirect sense Castro's presence is also made known via the stamps celebrating the major events of the revolution, such as the 1964 stamp showing the cover of the text of his 1953 speech ("History will absolve me"), in which he defended his role in the Moncada Barracks attack against the then president, Fulgencio Batista (Scott 851). Revolutionary institutions are frequently honored, such as the Committees for the Defense of the Revolution (Scott 1346), the Cuban Pioneers and Young Communists (Scott 1389), and all branches of the military, including the militia (Scott 1444).

Stamps have been issued in support of guerrilla movements and the "anti-imperialist movement" worldwide. Two such stamps express solidarity with Salvador Allende and his supporters in Chile: 1974 (Scott 1919) and 1983 (figure 13.1, Scott 2605). The latter is especially striking, with a portrait of Allende off to one side against a background of the burning presidential palace (La Moneda) in Santiago. Stamps in solidarity with the Sandinista

Revolution in Nicaragua also appear on various occasions (e.g., Scott 2427 in 1981). In 2005, Cuba announced a joint Cuban-Iranian issue (though as of late 2007 it had not been issued), which may be followed by an issue that includes Hugo Chávez of Venezuela.[24] Another stamp in this class is the one commemorating Ethel and Julius Rosenberg, American Communists who were executed for spying for the Soviets in 1953 (Scott C313). Events are also marked with stamp issues: the Havana Summit of the Ibero-American Heads of State in 1999 (Scott 4052–4054), a meeting that pointedly excluded the United States; the victories of Cuban troops in Angola (Scott 3911, 4117); and a conference against the U.S. involvement in the Vietnam War (Scott 1696–1698).

Tributes to the Soviet Union have also been numerous, especially its space activities (Scott 775–779), and notable events in Soviet history and its major figures, such as Lenin (Scott 1516–1522). Cuban scientists and doctors have served at Soviet bases in Antarctica,[25] and a Cuban stamp shows a Soviet nuclear icebreaker (the *Lenin*) in Antarctica next to penguins on an ice floe (figure 13.3, Scott 1752).

Cuban stamps, like those of the Soviet Union, include significant numbers of issues devoted to art, culture, animals, natural attractions, and tourism, making them somewhat suspect as postally valid issues, since many of these stamps are in large formats, brightly colored, and apparently intended for the collector's market rather than actual postal use. Stamps used in normal internal mail are small definitive issues showing historical figures such as Martí and other heroes of the War for Independence. Many Cuban stamps are also apparently intentionally designed to appeal to other third world countries. A whole series is issued every few years on the theme of Latin American history and culture, featuring major personalities from each of the hemisphere nations, as well as musical instruments, folkloric dances, and indigenous groups (see plates 15 and 16; Scott 2887–2906, 3065–3084, 3151–3170).

A particularly irksome problem for Americans interested in Cuban stamps has been the long-standing prohibition of their importation and sale in the United States under the provisions of the Cuban Assets Control Regulations, as administered by the U.S. Treasury's Foreign Assets Control Administration, placed in effect in early 1962.[26] The prohibition was a small part of a larger policy intended to block the import and sale of Cuban goods generally, but it struck many as being petty and vindictive. An exception was made for stamps that arrive in the U.S. as part of legitimate mail from Cuba. Although the major catalogue (*Scott*) continued to list and show the stamps, no monetary value for them was posted, and it was difficult to obtain them. These provisions were loosened in early 2001, when the Treasury Department decided that used (i.e., canceled) postage stamps were "printed matter or informational material," which could be imported without restrictions.[27] Shortly afterward a major U.S. stamp firm prepared and sold a small collection of several hundred such stamps, which provide a comprehensive panorama of the history, personalities, and achievements of the Cuban Revolution, as seen from Havana. The stamps turned out to be what collectors call "canceled to order," meaning they are mint (unused) stamps that are canceled without ever being affixed to an envelope, and which have thus never carried the mail. Regardless, the Treasury Department still considered them printed informational material, and allowed their importation, without commenting on the apparent inconsistency that uncanceled stamps might also be printed informational material.

GRENADA

Stamps from this tiny Caribbean nation are of interest because of those issued during the 1979–1983 New Jewel revolutionary government, its predecessor, and its successor. The prime minister during the run-up to the 1979 revolution was Eric Gairy (depicted on Scott 549), an eccentric character who believed in the existence of flying saucers and, during a United Nations speech, tried to persuade the General Assembly to launch a serious study of the phenomenon; stamps of flying saucers were issued in support of his proposals (figure 13.4, Scott 885; Scott 883–884).[28] Gairy's corrupt and heavy-handed regime generated considerable popular resentment, and he was overthrown in 1979 by the revolutionary movement headed by Maurice Bishop, who appeared soon after on a large souvenir sheet over his motto: "Forward Ever, Backward Never." Stamps were also issued showing the achievements of his government, including free hot school lunches, housing for the poor, free health service, and progress in agricultural industry (Scott 990–993).

The New Jewel revolutionary government was not to last, and fell in December 1983 when an invasion force led by U.S. troops toppled the regime. Since then Grenada has issued a number of stamps celebrating liberation from the Bishop regime (Scott 2505) and featuring the U.S. president at the time, Ronald Reagan (Scott 1357–1358, 2603), who visited the island shortly after the invasion.

MEXICO

The postage stamps of Mexico reflect that country's rich pre-Columbian heritage and its turbulent early history as an independent and, later, revolutionary nation. They provide a large number of different designs, which lend themselves to a well-endowed in-depth set of visuals to illustrate the history, politics, economy, culture, and international relations of that nation. Mexican postage stamps have also been the subject of considerable study and reflection by both Mexicans and Americans, and there is a greater knowledge and understanding of the postage stamps of Mexico in the United States than of any other Latin American country.

Mexican postal authorities have over the years published monographs revealing a sensitivity to the multiple functions of postage stamps. A 1970 detailed analysis of the history of Mexico's postal system had this to say about postage stamps, which clearly applies to their nation: "Stamps are closely tied to the politics of the country that issues them. Furthermore, stamps are produced with intentionally political content. They are an effective publicity media. Taking advantage of their propaganda nature, countries, which have achieved an internal political stability and maturity, use their postage stamps to publicize their accomplishments achieved in matters of socio-economic welfare, culture and the arts."[29]

Other Mexican observers, especially those who are interested in stamps but are not part of the official establishment, are not so kind, describing the great difficulties they have faced with the postal system's bureaucrats in attempting to honor a particular event or individual with a postage stamp. Obregón, for example, describes the tribulations involved in advocating for a stamp celebrating the renowned engraver and woodcut artist José Guadalupe Posada (figure 13.7).[30] The stamp eventually was issued, and has been hailed as an excellent example of Mexican art on stamps, but only after many painful dealings with politically motivated bureaucrats.

Many Mexican publications, official and private, document and explain the story behind the nation's stamps. For many years of the last two decades the Philatelic Service of the postal system has put out a *Boletín Filatélico* describing the year's stamps and showing examples in well-prepared multicolor brochures. Especially significant issues merit their own single *Boletín*. In 1997 a major six-hundred-page catalogue was published with three hundred color illustrations, giving detailed information on the individual stamps, their themes, technical details, and the identity of the artist preparing them.[31] Finally, in considering postage stamps as expressions of popular culture, I note again the uniquely wry and sometimes mordant work of the cartoonist Ríus, who frequently uses postage stamps (sometimes with variants he creates) to illustrate his books, including one dedicated entirely to stamps as a form of social criticism.[32]

The early (or "classical") issues of Mexico, starting in 1856, follow the pattern already established for Latin American stamps: rather crudely printed, with an icon that portrays the major national hero of independence, Father Miguel Hidalgo (Scott 17). In 1864, however, Mexico underwent French intervention and became an empire under Maximilian. The first empire stamps show a national icon, the eagle sitting on a cactus while holding a serpent in its mouth, but the eagle wears an imperial crown.[33] Two years later the icon became the emperor's face (figure 13.5, Scott 27), in a classical pose influenced by French and British stamps of the period. By this time the area under effective control of the French was rapidly diminishing, and the stamps did not actually carry much mail.[34] In June 1867 the armies of Benito Juárez occupied Mexico City and the emperor was caught while fleeing and executed. The use of the empire stamps faded away, and postal agents used stamps left over from before the empire until a new set of Hidalgo stamps was issued in 1868.

The next period in Mexico's political postal history runs from the 1867 fall of the empire up to the revolutionary period (1910–1924), and is dominated by the long dictatorship of Porfirio Díaz. The aging Díaz was planning massive celebrations for the 1910 centenary of independence from Spain, and, as was the case with most of the Spanish-speaking nations of the hemisphere, a major commemorative set of stamps was prepared for the celebration. These were to be the last stamps issued by the Díaz administration. One mystery surrounds the departure of Díaz: the fate of his stamp collection, which was reputedly one of the finest in existence as far as Mexico and Central America were concerned. Díaz's status as president of Mexico made it relatively easy for him to obtain all the new issues, not only of his country, but also for most of the nations between Mexico and Colombia. He was not shy about asking his presidential counterparts in these countries to send him autographed sheets of new stamps. When Díaz and his entourage fled Mexico City in

1910, they were not able to take the stamp albums with them, and the albums were apparently destroyed by the mobs that invaded Chapultepec Castle and looted whatever they could find. An eyewitness account (somewhat questionable) explains that the author was at the point of talking a soldier out of the albums when a captain arrived, "and after a stupid, uncomprehending glance at the albums, tossed them through the windows and into a bonfire below—an act of vandalism rivaling, in the minds of all philatelists, that of the destruction of the records of Aztec culture by Spanish priests nearly four centuries before."[35]

The stamps of the early period of revolutionary fighting are a confused medley of overprinted and hand-stamped earlier ones, along with crudely printed issues produced by the various fighting factions, and a few original issues produced by the federal forces still in control of Mexico City itself.[36] Some of the overprints made their affiliation clear (such as "Gobierno Constitucionalista," figure 13.6, Scott 427), while others were overprinted to show their association with individual revolutionary leaders such as Pancho Villa (Scott 459) or Venustiano Carranza (Scott 574). Once the revolution stabilized and the fighting died down in the early 1920s, Mexico's stamp issues followed the pattern evident in many of the other hemisphere nations, with the added possibilities of many revolutionary themes to supplement the usual series celebrating independence from Spain. All the major events and heroes of the revolution are featured on at least one postage stamp each, and the murals of the "Three Greats" of Mexican painting of the post-revolutionary period (Rivera, Orozco, Siqueiros) provided much material for these stamps celebrating the revolution, as well as other themes which popularized Mexican history.[37] In the late 1930s, starting with the stamps commemorating the twenty-fifth anniversary of the revolutionary Plan of Guadalupe (Scott 737–739, C82–84), Mexico's stamps became increasingly sophisticated and the messages they carry much more explicit. The celebration of individuals is frequently accompanied by commemoration of significant events, such as the anniversary of the nationalization of Mexico's oil industry (Scott 1161, 1535). The fiftieth anniversary of the revolution in 1960 was also an opportunity for another major set (Scott 913–918, C253–256) celebrating its accomplishments, including agrarian reform, health, education, and the links between the guerrilla fighter of 1910 and the conventional professional military of 1960.

In the 1990s a number of conservation themes and others calling for the protection of endangered species appear on Mexico's stamps, including several spectacular souvenir sheets with up to twenty different stamps, each showing an endangered species. One of these sheets (Scott 1995) had a special design (visible only under ultraviolet light), which showed the Aztec symbols for each of the species. Economic themes included the massive "Mexico Exporta" series (Scott 1132), which featured stylized icons of major exports of Mexico. Because of inflation and minor variations, the complete set of these stamps runs to several hundred different items,[38] and as a result of the years they were in circulation, they serve as a major symbol and index of what a Mexican stamp is. The icons on the well-designed Exportas are fresh and interesting, and feature such innovations as a partial tomato slice or a quarter of a strawberry. A unique "stamp" in the contemporary period is the one posted on the Internet site of the Zapatista National Liberation Army, featuring their main leader, Subcomandante Marcos.[39] It is also available on the Web site of its creator.[40]

As indicated above, the mural tradition in Mexico provides an immense source of visuals suitable for postage stamps. A complete large mural is not readily subjected to the size restrictions of postage stamps, but fragments of murals depicting famous individuals or events are eminently adaptable to become the icon needed for a postage stamp, and the Mexican output in this dimension is by far the richest in Latin America. Chronologically the first of these stamps is based on art that goes back to pre-Columbian times, and uses portions of the early codices to create illustrations. As an example, the 650th anniversary of the founding of the Aztec city of Tenochtitlán was illustrated on a 1975 stamp with a graphic taken from the Duran Codex showing the national symbol of the eagle devouring a serpent while perched on a cactus (Scott 1087). In another clever example, the stamp celebrating the centenary of the National Chamber of Commerce is illustrated with a design from the pre-Columbian Florentine Codex showing merchants trading goods in the market (Scott 1085). Art is frequently used on stamps to illustrate literature, and chronologically this process begins with stamps honoring the first poet of the hemisphere (Scott 1144 and 1202), Nezahualcoyotl, who lived from 1402 to 1472. For understandable reasons, the colonial period was not emphasized by the muralists of the Mexican Revolution, although colonial paintings have been used to celebrate important figures such as the feminist nun-poet Sor Juana Inés de la Cruz (figure 13.8, Scott 1911). For the independence and the 1910 revolutionary period the muralists provide graphic images of all the prominent personalities (Scott 1398–1402, 1447–1455) as well as figures of the anonymous members of the underclass, such as the strikers killed during labor protests at Cananea in 1906, an event that contributed to the fall of the Díaz dictatorship, and which was brilliantly captured in a mural by Diego Rivera (Scott 1238).

A special philatelic honor is reserved for the truly best of the Mexican painters: stamps bearing their self-portraits to celebrate the painter himself or herself. Thus there are self-portraits of Geraldo Murillo, also known as "Dr. Atl" (Scott C469); Diego Rivera (figure 13.9); José Clemente Orozco (Scott 1336); and David Alfaro Siqueiros, whose dramatic self-portrait *El Coronelazo* is on a 1975 stamp (Scott C463). The most recently used painting, and one that caused some controversy in the United States, is a self-portrait of Frida Kahlo (figure 13.10, Scott Mexico 2228; U.S. 3509).

The close relationship between postage stamps and major sports events was noted in chapter 3, but bears repeating here in the specific case of Mexico. Prior to 1968, stamps bearing sports motifs had occasionally appeared, such as the Mayan ball court player stamp celebrating the Central American and Caribbean Games (Scott C222–223), but it was the 1968 Olympic Games and the Soccer World Cup the following year that really brought these themes to the fore of Mexican stamps. The main designer of the most prominent of these stamps was Lance Wyman, a New York artist working for the International Olympic Organizing Committee.[41] The Wyman trademark for the Olympic stamps featured stark silhouettes depicting different sports in a continuous pattern so that a strip of stamps would show the athletes and their characteristic equipment in a repeated design (e.g., figure 3.10 and Scott 981–985).

Wyman's Olympic work was so widely admired that he was asked to produce "something different" for the Soccer World Cup (Rimet Cup) competition to be held in Mexico in 1970. He produced two stamps, which, departing from soccer stamp tradition, focused on the fans instead of the players. But his "fans" were uniquely Mexican. For his first stamp (Scott C372) he used fifteen different dance masks of Mexico as the faces of the "spectators" surrounding a soccer ball, which appears to be heading toward the fans in the stands. His second stamp (Scott C373) uses the same concept of focusing on the spectators, but this time the spectators are the heads of fifteen different pre-Columbian pottery pieces.[42]

International themes on the stamps of Mexico display the usual features seen in the stamps of many other countries: special issues celebrating the visits of heads of state (Scott C281) or anniversaries or meetings of international organizations (Scott C263). Occasionally there is a special Mexican twist to the design, such as in the case of a 1980 stamp (Scott C635) in support of the international campaign against smoking: the icon is a José Guadalupe Posada woodcut of a skeleton smoking a cigar.

Mexico has issued a significant number of stamps relating to its northern neighbor. It was the first country to put President John F. Kennedy on a stamp, the product of an early visit to Mexico (Scott C262), and repeated the compliment to celebrate the return of the Chamizal area of El Paso to Mexico, in 1963 (Scott C282). One set of Mexican airmail stamps (Scott C5–10) has links to a monument on the barren scrub pine stands of Wharton State Forest near Tabernacle, New Jersey: it is the site of an accident that took the life of the Mexican pilot Captain Emilio Carranza, who crashed during bad weather in 1928 while attempting to make a nonstop flight from New York to Mexico City.[43]

There have also been a number of joint U.S.-Mexican stamps, usually celebrating events of importance to Mexico. These joint issues are produced with a similar design, and commemorate the same person or event. While at first glance they appear almost identical, closer inspection shows that the Mexican variant is denominated in pesos and bears legends in Spanish; in the U.S. version, the denomination is in U.S. currency and legends are in English. A prominent example is the 1960 Mexican independence issue (Scott Mexico 910, U.S. 1157) showing the bell of the village of Dolores, rung by Miguel Hidalgo to mark the start of the struggle for independence. Both Mexican and U.S. designers were involved in the project, and its official launching was the motive for travel to Mexico by a special delegation.[44] Other joint issues have included the Cinco de Mayo celebration of Mexico's defeat of the French in the battle of Puebla in 1862 (Scott 2066) and the controversial Frida Kahlo stamp of 2001.

Some Mexican stamp icons have been unusual and even startling. In 1936 a compulsory surcharge stamp (figure 14.4, RA14) designed to raise money for an antimalarial campaign featured a man being bitten by a giant mosquito in what one observer described as "a rather terrifying design."[45] Equally attention-grabbing was a stamp issued in 1977 (figure 13.11, Scott C533) to commemorate the tenth anniversary of the Treaty of Tlatelolco banning nuclear weapons in Latin America. At first glance the stamp shows the well-known Leonardo da Vinci diagram of the proportions of the human anatomy set in a circle and square, but the human being is a skeleton, and the background shows the familiar mushroom-shaped cloud signaling a nuclear explosion. The semiotics are clear: if the treaty is not respected in America, and emulated in other parts of the world, then mankind faces the possibility of nuclear annihilation.

We leave Mexican postage stamps with a final visit to the master cartoonist who has frequently incorporated postage stamps in his works of popular culture: Ríus, the pseudonym of Eduardo del Río García. He notes that postage stamps frequently serve as inspiration for his cartoons, and in his 1989 work on popular culture he used copies of real postage stamps, as well as his own invented stamps, to lampoon his favorite targets and make his major points.[46] He later published a whole book on stamps, partly a serious argument in favor of their study and collection, and partly a satirical attack on the problems of Mexican society, such as the corruption of government officials, the betrayal of the ideals of the Mexican Revolution, and the violence employed by the military and police to deal with opponents of the official PRI party (Partido Revolucionario Institucional, or Institutional Revolutionary Party).[47] Among his sharper barbs from this latter work we find a postage stamp commemorating Mexico's role in the worldwide battle against hunger; the icon shows a smiling President Carlos Salinas de Gortari enjoying a sumptuous banquet.[48] In a second "stamp" titled "Military feats" we see thugs beating up demonstrators in the 1968 "Taking of Tlatelolco." Finally, in a stamp noting the anniversary of the revolution's agrarian reform program Ríus gives us the classical iconic graphic of Emiliano Zapata. But he put a golf club in Zapata's hand and has labeled the stamp "Programa Pro-campo (de golf)," a not-so-subtle criticism of the way the rich in Mexico (who are depicted as using scarce land and water for golf courses) have deprived the poor of the land and water they need for survival.

NICARAGUA

Nicaragua's postage stamps document the sharp changes from being a country long controlled by the Somoza dynasty with close ties to the United States, to a revolutionary nation with a deteriorating relationship with the United States and a close link to Cuba. After the Sandinistas' electoral defeat in 1990 the country's postage stamps showed a return to more traditional themes. These various shifts are reflected in hiatus of new stamp issues such as the 1978–1981 gap between the last of the Somoza-era stamps and the start of the era of the FSLN (Frente Sandinista de Liberación Nacional, or Sandinista National Liberation Front). A similar phenomenon occurs between the last FSLN stamps in early 1990 (when Violeta Chamorro was elected) and the first post-FSLN stamps in April 1991. Because of the rampant inflation of the Sandinista years, Nicaragua underwent currency reform at the start of the Chamorro period and no new stamps were issued for a time. Instead, prepaid mail was hand-stamped "Franqueo Pagado."[49]

For many years the postage stamps of Nicaragua had an unhealthy reputation due to a decade of association with the Seebeck issues, in which large numbers of cheap reprints of Nicaraguan stamps flooded the market. Even years after the 1890–1899 Seebeck period there were suspicions that the metal dies held by banknote companies in the United States were surreptitiously turning out additional Seebeck stamps. To dramatize the end of the Seebeck issues, in 1951 a number of senior Nicaraguan officials witnessed the destruction of all the printing materials involved in the Seebeck issues in a ceremony held at the Security Bank Note Company of Philadelphia.[50]

Even after the Seebeck era ended in 1899, the reputation of Nicaragua's postage stamps was not helped by the large number of overprints and surcharges, which were employed to make possible the use of obsolete stamps stored in the vaults of the postal authorities in Managua. Collectors were forced to acknowledge the existence of these numerous types, but the suspicion rose that the many varieties were deliberately printed in order to increase philatelic sales. The printing quality and themes of Nicaraguan stamps up to the 1940s were not well received. A vocal American critic of Nicaraguan stamps had this to say in 1932: "Every time Nicaragua opens up one of her jerkwater railroads she issues a set of 'commemoratives.' Commemoratives have been issued for many less worthy events, but at least the stamps are usually attractive, and well produced. Not so with these Nicaraguan emissions."[51]

The Somoza period saw a considerable improvement in the quality of the stamps issued when the remaining printing contracts were transferred from local Managua enterprises to U.S. banknote companies. This period also saw the blatant use of stamps for political purposes by the Somozas. Presidents Anastasio Somoza Sr., Anastasio Somoza Debayle, and Luis Somoza all made frequent appearances on postage stamps between 1939 and the 1979 triumph of the revolution (Scott C372–376, C885). Hope Somoza, wife of Anastasio Somoza Debayle, also appeared on a 1973 stamp with a surcharge for a new children's hospital (Scott CB2). The Somozas were not above a little exaggeration or exploitation of the close ties to the U.S. at times: when President Anastasio Somoza Sr. traveled to the United States and addressed a joint session of Congress, a long set of high-quality stamps were produced with the legend "President Somoza speaks to the American Senate" (Scott C246).

Indicative of the close ties between the Somozas and the United States are a number of postage stamps honoring U.S. personalities. Will Rogers was the subject of a series of stamps commemorating his visit to Managua in 1931 after an earthquake (Scott C236–240). Cardinal Spellman was also honored this way after a 1958 visit to Nicaragua (Scott 819–823), as was a U.S. Air Force captain who died in a Managua crash during an air show (Scott 755). Also honored was a U.S. admiral who was instrumental in forcing the 1857 surrender of William Walker, the American soldier of fortune who attempted to set up a proslavery Central American empire.[52] Nicaragua was among the first nations to honor President Roosevelt after his death in 1945, issuing a series of stamps highlighting major events in the president's life (Scott 695–700), and also including one stamp showing Roosevelt the stamp collector.

When the Sandinista revolutionaries came to power in 1979, postage stamps were used to emphasize the achievements of the revolution, usually including one yearly stamp to commemorate the triumph of the revolution. The first of these carries an icon of an adult literacy class (Scott 1111); others feature heroes of the revolution, doves of peace, infrastructure development, agriculture, and key battles in the struggle for power (figure 14.1). Frequently the iconographic display features two sets of flags: the blue-and-white Nicaraguan one, and the red-and-black flag of Sandinismo and other national liberation movements (e.g., Scott 1163). In 1988, during the height of the struggle with the contras, and while the Contadora Peace process was attempting to resolve the conflict, the annual celebratory stamp (Scott 1701) carried the legend "Nicaragua fights for peace." The theme of "cultural independence" also prevails, with stamps honoring major Nicaraguan poets and the winners of the "Rubén Darío Order of Cultural Independence" (Scott 1574–1579). The Cuban Revolution and its major figures are honored (figure 14.2), although Fidel Castro shares iconographic space with Augusto Sandino, José Martí, and Simón Bolívar. The Soviet Union and its revolution are also celebrated with stamps honoring its anniversaries (Scott 1668–1670), as well as Marx (Scott 1182) and Lenin (Scott 1462–1463).

The Sandinista years coincided with a period in which many third world nations issued large quantities of stamps with little apparent relationship to their country or its culture, and Nicaragua was one of the Latin American leaders in this process. Thus we see many stamps commemorating international sports events held elsewhere, dogs, cats, paintings, insects, and so on.

Of greater legitimacy were stamps showing tourist attractions of Nicaragua (such as Scott 1177–1181); the highest value in the 1989 set features an icon of the major tourist hotel in Managua. Also favorably received were a series of commemoratives issued in anticipation of the five-hundredth anniversary of Columbus's voyage, with sets using a range of art icons such as a fifteenth-century woodcut, pre-Columbian pottery, and a series of naïf-style primitive paintings depicting the arrival of Columbus's ships. The Sandinistas were sensitive to the importance of their major icon, Augusto César Sandino (Scott 1335), and frequently attempted to strengthen their ideological and militant ties to him, even though there was no direct link between Sandino's struggle and that of the Sandinistas. A set of 1982 stamps (Scott 1175–1176) showed the icons of Sandino and other luminaries with the legend, "26th Anniversary of the Beginning of the End of the Dictatorship," thus reinforcing their claim to be the current standard-bearers of the movement begun by Sandino.

The political content of Nicaraguan stamps shifted again (and diminished markedly) when the Sandinistas lost the 1990 election to Violeta Chamorro. Religious themes made a renewed appearance, especially around Christmas time (Scott 1980a–b, 2028–2036, 2147). Her administration issued a stamp honoring her murdered husband, Pedro Joaquín Chamorro (Scott 1844), a year after her victory. During her presidency Chamorro herself appeared in a series of "famous women" stamps (Scott 2164) that also included Evita Perón. She continued to appear on postage stamps after her term ended in 1997 (figure 14.3).

In the 1990s the trend to issue large numbers of colorful and attractive stamps designed primarily for the collector's market was continued in both the Chamorro and post-Chamorro period, with many sports and animal issues including penguins (sarcastically called "the national bird of Nicaragua" by one critic), birds of New Zealand, film stars (Marlon Brando in *The Godfather*), and the like. Pushing the geographic limits for themes distant from the country's history and culture was a 1994 set of souvenir sheets showing sightings of space aliens, six in the United States and one in Argentina; each alien was described in the words of an eyewitness.[53]

URUGUAY

Uruguayan postage stamps of interest to this analysis include representative issues relating to culture, the military, the struggle with the Tupamaro guerrillas, and economic themes. One of Uruguay's most celebrated writers is José Enrique Rodó, the author of a seminal essay, "Ariel," in which he warns the youth of Latin America of the temptations of Anglo-Saxon "Nordomania" (materialism and utilitarianism), and calls on them to be true to their cultural "Latinidad." A simplistic interpretation of the essay would pit the crass and materialistic Caliban (the United States) against the more idealistic and romantic Ariel (Latin America), and the essay has frequently been presented in this fashion, although Rodó himself would probably reject this superficial level of analysis. Regardless, the essay and the author stand as important icons of Latin American culture, and offer a revealing window into how Latin Americans see the United States. Rodó has been featured numerous times on Uruguayan postage stamps (Scott 235–237, 746–747, 798, 993), and the set showing him and the monument to Ariel in Montevideo (figure 14.5, Scott 556; Scott 557–563) is one of the most aesthetically pleasing groups of postage stamps issued by any Latin American nation.

Uruguay went through a traumatic period of military dictatorships in the years when armed guerrilla movements were seen as a threat to several South American governments. The U.S. government, through various programs of military and counterinsurgency assistance, sent specialized personnel to Uruguay to work with their counterparts. One of the more controversial programs involved assistance to local police under a program run by the U.S. Agency for International Development. Through this program a U.S. civilian police chief by the name of Dan Mitrione was sent to Uruguay, only to be kidnapped and later murdered by the Tupamaros in 1970; a Uruguayan stamp honoring him (Scott C389) bears the legend "Servant of Liberty." As was the case in Argentina, during periods of military rule there are numerous stamps celebrating Army, Navy, and Air Force Days (Scott 1652, 1551), as well as honoring police who fell in the anti-Marxist struggle, but there are also stamps recognizing Uruguay's participation in a series of United Nations peacekeeping missions (Scott 1471, 1580).[54]

The death of Salvador Allende was also noted (Scott 1742), with the icon of the Chilean president set against the burning ruins of the presidential palace in Santiago in September of 1973.[55] A tragedy of another kind was commemorated in a set of 1973 stamps: the crash of a Uruguayan air force plane in the Chilean Andes carrying a rugby team on its way to a series of matches in Chile. Miraculously, sixteen survivors lived for sixty-nine days after the crash, although the crew of four and eighteen of the passengers died.[56] The human drama of the event was heightened when it became clear that a key to the survival of those who made it was the consumption of body parts of those who had already died. The movie *Alive* featured the crash, and commemorative stamps were issued not only by Uruguay (figure 14.6, Scott 871; Scott 872), but also by Chile (Scott 563) as part of a series commemorating the fiftieth anniversary of their air force.

Despite the interlude of military dictatorship, Uruguay has a long tradition of tolerance of various religious and political groups; it is the most secular of the South American nations, and Freemasonry has strong roots there. Despite the opposition of the Catholic Church, Masonic-type lodges were organized in many Latin American countries and played an important role in the nineteenth-century independence movements as an offshoot of Enlightenment currents in western Europe. This connection helps explain why Uruguayan stamps of 1989 celebrating the two-hundredth anniversary of the French Revolution featured icons of Masonic symbols such as the all-seeing eye, the plumb-line, and the tools of stone cutters and related trades (Scott 1281–1284). Explanations of these and other stamp messages are found in the Uruguayan National Postal Administration's excellent Web site, which also contains graphics of new issues since 1997.[57]

VENEZUELA

Venezuela's stamps have many of the characteristics prevalent in the countries discussed above, but with some idiosyncrasies. There are the predictable issues celebrating the important events and personalities of the independence period, including a large-format series showing the signing of the Declaration of Independence (Scott C804), maps and paintings of the major battles (figure 14.7, Scott C783), and the establishment of the Republic of Gran Colombia (Scott 959), of which it was a part, in the first years of its independence from Spain.

Peculiar to Venezuela, however, is the cult of Simón Bolívar, national hero of the country, a cult that did not begin with President Hugo Chávez.[58] Practically every contemporary portrait of the Liberator has appeared on Venezuelan postage stamps (for example Scott 1132, C1022–1033), often with numerous variations of size, color, and face monetary value. Events in the life of Bolívar, such as his birth, christening, and death (Scott 367–374), are also prominent. His exile in Jamaica is commemorated with a stamp carrying his portrait and quotations from his "Jamaica letter" (Scott C909), which set out his vision for an independent America. More so than any other independence hero, including San Martín in Argentina, Bolívar is the semiotic icon of the nation, and a symbol that can give its people an identity and a unifying tie.

An approach that caused a decline in popularity of Venezuelan stamps for collectors was the production of multiple variations along a single theme. The so-called state issue of 1951–1953 is the best example (e.g., Scott 555). For each of the twenty-four states and special federal districts a set of sixteen stamps of identical design (the coat of arms of the state) but with different face values was issued, for a total of almost four hundred stamps (and a catalogue value of over one thousand dollars) with nothing more imaginative in design than a coat of arms.

In discussing tourism and stamps previously (chapter 3), I noted that several nations emphasize tourism, to include specific tourist hotels that are readily identifiable as to name and chain. Venezuela has done this with an attractive set of stamps featuring the Hotel Tamanaco (Scott 692–702, C654) and the spectacular Hotel Humboldt near Caracas, showing its distinctive aerial gondola (Scott C1007). Sports, with an emphasis on baseball (Scott 1303), and art have made their appearance, the latter with an attractive series showing the best-known paintings of Venezuela's most notable artists, such as Arturo Michelena (Scott 899, C927) and Armando Reverón (Scott 1231–1232).

Also noteworthy are illustrations of industrial development, such as dams (Scott 1049), steel mills (Scott 855–856), and especially the oil industry (Scott 770–772). The oil stamps have an international facet, featuring OPEC (figure 14.8) and various cooperative approaches taken with other oil-producing nations (Scott 1531). One feature of Venezuela's foreign policy that appears on its stamps is its involvement in multilateral organizations that do not include the United States. OPEC is perhaps the best known, but Venezuela has also been active in SELA—Sistema Económico Latinoamericano (figure 14.9), which excludes the United States but includes Cuba. Also marked in various stamp issues are Venezuela's participation in the Andean

Parliament (Scott 1613), the Treaty of Tlatelolco (Scott 1570), and various meetings of Latin American chiefs of state, such as the Acapulco summit in 1987, whose Venezuelan commemorative stamp (Scott 1398) proclaimed it "a mechanism for political coordination."

The country's foreign relations have emphasized the Venezuelan claim on the Essequibo territory, which Guyana inherited from the United Kingdom upon independence. Map stamps appear frequently in Venezuela, and they consistently show the Essequibo area shaded in a special way to show that it is an area claimed by Venezuela (Scott 1056). Venezuela has been justly proud of the fact that it is one of Latin America's most enduring formal democracies (albeit under strains during the Chávez years), and stamps illustrating various aspects of the political process have appeared from time to time (Scott 1449, 1584), as have various appeals to good citizenship, such as pointed reminders to pay taxes on time (figure 14.10, Scott 1066).

CONCLUSIONS

The purpose of the book was to apply some basic concepts from the discipline of semiotics and the realm of politics (internal and international) to the study of the "miniature messages" carried by the postage stamps of Latin America, to include the South Atlantic Islands and (in deference to Argentina and Chile) the South American quadrant of Antarctica. The basic thesis was that this analysis would provide new insights into the politics, history, national identity, and culture of the region. By emphasizing these contributions, the book represents an interdisciplinary approach to area studies focusing on this important part of the world.

As explained in chapter 1, the use of some basic semiotic concepts (such as Peirce's typology) provided the tools for a systematic search for the messages contained in the stamps. Semiotics, especially the theoretical aspects, can be very detailed and dense, and this work does not claim to make a contribution to the more arcane aspects of semiotic analysis. But it does provide an example of how semiotics applied to a subject such as postage stamps can be a useful and systematic tool of analysis. The basic conclusion and contribution is that stamps deliver numerous semiotic messages, and that they are useful tools for understanding the culture, politics, and history of a region.

Chapter 1 also raised two basic questions: is an analysis of Latin American postage stamps academically valid, and is it popular culture? My response, as laid out in a general sense in chapter 1, and then more specifically in the chapters that follow, is yes to both questions. As far as academic validity is concerned, there is not much literature on the subject, but work such as that of David Scott on the semiotics of European postage stamps clearly has academic value, as I hope do some of my articles and conference presentations, and my extensive use of postage stamps in university courses. The academic validity of semiotic analysis of postage stamps is reinforced by the increasing acceptance of other areas of semiotic study, such as comic books, which are only now receiving respectability as legitimate fields of academic study. As far as the question of whether or not postage stamps are items of popular culture, the answer is that it depends on one's definition of popular culture. A narrow definition of popular culture as being restricted to items produced by the people (as opposed to institutions) would argue that stamps do not fit in this category since they are products of a bureaucratic government process. This book employs a broader definition of popular culture under which postage stamps are considered instruments of popular culture because they are seen and handled daily by almost all adult citizens.

Two caveats were raised at the start of this analysis. The first relates to the source of postage stamps: governments. My analysis leaves little doubt that governments from time to time have used postage stamps to further their own ideological, political, or economic ends, and that the image of the nation they attempt to present to the outside world and their own citizens can be a distorted one. Notwithstanding this concern, I conclude that postage stamps carry valuable messages in terms of the nation's self-image, even if there is a bias. Further, there is citizen input to the stamp selection process in several of the major countries, although it is difficult to evaluate how strong and effective this influence is.

The second caveat concerns whether or not the stamps examined (and the messages they carry) have actually been used to carry the mail. I have noted that although the original purpose of the stamp was to prove that postage had been paid (and thus eliminate the need for the recipient to pay it), a secondary purpose began to emerge in the early part of the twentieth century: to use postage stamps to carry messages of an economic, political, or ideological nature. Commemorative stamps issued for a short period of time have a diminished likelihood of being actually used for postage, although their impact might still be significant since they are more likely to be collected, preserved, and seen many times over the years. Apart from any political or ideological consideration, stamps bought by collectors are a free source of revenue for the government, and thus there is a tendency to issue numerous and higher value stamps with a multitude of colorful and attractive themes. This is especially noticeable in those countries where the themes portrayed have no apparent connection to the nation, and are obviously aimed at the topical or unsophisticated collector. This caveat should be kept in mind while analyzing the postage stamps of Latin America, but we should not go as far as to abandon this analysis since the stamps still represent, in large measure, the image of the nation which the government and many of its citizens seek to project.

The analysis of Latin American postage stamps over the last 150 years shows a pattern of development that begins with crude lithographed specimens that are definitive in the sense that they are used for postage for a long period of time, and whose semiotic messages are limited to portraying a modest number of national heroes or symbols such as crests and flags. This pattern begins to change with stamps issued to commemorate the one-hundredth anniversary of the independence of most of the Spanish-speaking nations in 1910. The centennial celebrations were commemorated in many of these nations with high-quality engraved portrayals of the major figures and events in the struggle for independence from Spain. After the centennial stamps had run their course, they left a legacy: the issuing of increasing numbers of commemorative stamps showing a wide range of economic, historical, and cultural themes. The shift from cheap and crudely lithographed stamps to the far more elegant and attractive engraved stamps was not without its setbacks, and I have noted how the philatelic reputation of several countries was diminished with the so-called Seebeck issues, which were produced in large numbers by the American Bank Note Company and sold to collectors after their use to carry the mails ended. More contemporary stamps show a variety of approaches to production: in some cases unattractive (but cheap) lithographed stamps continued, along with the more pleasing engraved ones, although the techniques most often used relied on modern multicolored press runs, which produced some excellent results.

These considerations suggest that stamps can (and often do) have an aesthetic value, and that well-designed and produced stamps can be a form of art in themselves. The limitations placed on the designer of aesthetically pleasing stamps are challenging, since in a very small space the stamp must deliver basic information (country index, monetary value, etc.), leaving little space for the icon that delivers the semiotic message. The stamp as a suitable means for conveying aesthetic values has given rise to stamps that are not stamps, but rather are drawings or engravings created outside of government channels, which look like stamps (although the icon sometimes is satirical, iconoclastic, and even obscene) but which cannot legally be used in the postal system.

Latin American postage stamps frequently reflect internal political realities, sometimes unintentionally. Authoritarian regimes, for example, tend to tout the glories of their administration, while personalist regimes tend to feature the individual leader, junta regimes emphasize the military as an institution, and dynastic regimes (such as the Somozas in Nicaragua or the Duvaliers in Haiti) glorify individual family members, to include (in the case of the Trujillo dynasty in the Dominican Republic) the president's brother, mother, wife, son, and daughter. Democratically elected regimes frequently present portraits of the new president, although a number of countries maintain a policy of not featuring any living person, and thus must substitute symbols of the presidency such as the presidential sash, government house, etc. A particularly original solution used by the Perón presidency in Argentina was to show the allegorical figure of Liberty swearing in Perón, with only his hand and forearm visible. When a democratically elected regime comes to the presidency after a period of dictatorship, there is often a celebratory stamp, sometimes issued with a rather frank statement celebrating the return to democracy (e.g., Scott Argentina 667).

We have also seen how the promotion of good citizenship is supported by postage stamps as well as by ink cancellations on the envelope. The cancellations also promote national identity, cultural values, political concepts, and economics, and have the virtue of being easily and quickly changed. Long-running definitive issues can often be divided into the lower-value ones, which are for internal mail (and tend to show national heroes), and higher-value ones (mainly for international mail), which tend to employ economic themes, such as the country's exports, tourism, and other attractions that might heighten interest in the country from foreigners.

Foreign influences on Latin American postage stamps crop up in a number of cases. The first stamps in the world were those of Great Britain in 1840, and many of the features of the "Penny Black" featuring Queen Victoria appear in Latin American stamps of the second half of the nineteenth century. In the first Perón administration in Argentina a team of Italian stamp designers left their mark on a series of attractive and well-designed stamps that suggest a link between Italian fascism and the authoritarian Peronista regime. In the Cuban case the Soviet influence is apparent, especially in terms of the large number of stamps that glorify the Russian Revolution, its heroes, institutions, and achievements (as the Cubans saw them). The Cuban example in turn influenced the Nicaraguan Revolution, although in the latter case the influence was limited to the 1979–1990 period, when the Sandinistas were in power.

Semiotic messages dealing with international relations can be placed in two categories: cooperative and conflictual. The cooperative ones frequently celebrate a visit to the country concerned by another chief of state or major figure, as well as anniversaries of good relations between pairs of countries. Philatelic exhibitions usually also bring the creation of stamps displaying some feature of the host and issuing country, for example Argentine stamps featuring the tango and a typical folklore dance of Thailand. More interesting from a semiotic perspective are those stamps involving disputes and even conflicts between neighboring states. These frequently employ a map that clearly shows the boundary as argued by the issuing state. Often this brings on a diplomatic crisis of lesser or greater proportion, which might include a stamp with a "countermap" showing the border as seen by the second state. The clear message is to be very careful when using a map on a stamp, especially when borders are shown. Several instances of both deliberate and inadvertent distortions of borders are documented in this book, as well as the use of stamps to assert sovereignty over islands, such as the Malvinas/Falklands and Easter Island.

Faced with the large number of Latin American postage stamps available for the analysis of semiotic messages, I selected one country (Argentina) to be addressed in a single chapter; ten others are covered in another chapter: Bolivia, Brazil, Chile, Colombia, Cuba, Grenada, Mexico, Nicaragua, Uruguay, and Venezuela. The choice of Argentina as the main focus was partly the result of my personal preferences and background, but it was a fortuitous one because there is a rich trove of Argentine stamps with their associated semiotic messages, containing many threads of information and a multiplicity of symbols. My analysis of Argentine postage stamps included a typology of their themes and statistical data on the output. The various stages in the historical development of Argentine stamps were described and presented as a pattern that was repeated by most of the other Latin American nations: the "classical" period followed by the first commemoratives at the turn of the century, then evolution to a large number of commemoratives supporting the description given above. The Argentine case was, of course, shaped by the unique features of Peronismo and the military regimes that dominated Argentine politics from the fall of Perón in 1955 to the end of the military "proceso" in 1983 after the political, economic, and human disasters of the military regimes, culminating in the humiliating defeat in the war with the United Kingdom over the Falklands/Malvinas and other South Atlantic islands.

The Argentine case study segues naturally to a semiotic analysis (chapter 6) of the stamps of the British administration of the Falklands, the short-lived seventy-four-day Argentine presence on the Malvinas, and finally the postage stamps of the British-controlled South Georgia and South Sandwich Islands. This chapter in turn transitions to a study of postage stamps issued by nations with a presence in the so-called South American quadrant of Antarctica, which is important because of overlapping sovereignty claims of Argentina, Chile, and the United Kingdom. These stamps are rich in semiotic messages, a not unexpected reality due to the need to emphasize sovereignty claims through administrative acts such as postal systems. A certain air of unreality enters here because no human beings actually live in Antarctica, unless one counts a modest number of scientists and support staff, visited by tourists in the summer. Because their actual postal use is so limited, the stamps that are issued are obviously intended for nonpostal purposes such as strengthening sovereignty claims and making known to the outside world the presence and activities of the issuing nation in Antarctica. Financial considerations are also important, as evidenced by the fact that the sale of postage stamps of the Falklands, South Georgia, and the British Antarctic Territory to collectors is an important source of revenue for the British government.

The pedagogical implications of Latin American postage stamps are brought out at several points in this work. Because they are government documents, they are in the public domain and thus not covered by copyright (with certain exceptions and conditions). Thus, they may be reproduced and used for educational purposes. The vast number of stamps and the topics they illustrate means that almost any subject in the fields of history, geography, literature, and the social sciences can be illustrated in some way using Latin American postage stamps. These illustrations can then be used by instructors of Latin American studies or students themselves to make class presentations. For faculty focusing on research who need illustrations in their publications or presentations, the postage stamps of Latin America are equally valuable.

The technology involved in making these stamp illustrations has made a quantum leap in the era of ubiquitous computers. Before around 1980, the technology was clumsy, time-consuming, and expensive. Once the desired stamp was identified, it had to be purchased and then photographed using a fairly sophisticated single-lens reflex camera. The resulting exposed film had to be sent away to be developed professionally into 35 mm slides, a process that took a week or so, and it was not until then that the instructor could be sure he or she had a useable image.[1] Presently available technology using a scanner can produce immediate results, with images available in digitized form on the computer that one can then tweak and manipulate using processing software such as Adobe Photoshop. The final image can then be easily transferred to presentation software such as PowerPoint or word-processing software such as Microsoft Word. Large collections of these images can be stored and distributed using a variety of means, including CD-ROMs, DVDs, flash drives, memory sticks, external hard drives, or email attachments.[2]

My research for this project has accumulated a visual legacy: a collection of several thousand 35 mm film and digitized images produced during my thirty-year career teaching Latin American studies, images that can now be readily distributed and accessed as needed using computer technology.

Even with the approximately forty thousand Latin American stamps I examined for semiotic content, and the two-thousand–odd images produced digitally, this project is still a work in progress, and in a sense will never be completed, as long as Latin American nations continue to produce postage stamps of interest. To cite one area where the politics and semiotics of postage stamps can make a contribution: in the first decade of the twenty-first century there has been a shift in several Latin American nations away from the free-market neoliberal model to a more nationalistic and independent model, which has not pleased policy-makers in Washington. The link between the Castros in Cuba and Hugo Chávez in Venezuela is having a considerable impact on this paradigm shift, and is influencing a globalist current in the hemisphere that is opposed to both the United States and the International Monetary Fund. It will be interesting to see how these changes will be reflected in the Latin American stamps of this period and the semiotic messages they convey.

There are Cassandras in the philatelic community who bemoan the decline of the postage stamp in the face of metered mail, email, and other forms of digital communication,[3] but the more realistic prediction is that for reasons of nationalism, propaganda, and financial returns, postage stamps will continue to be produced, and will continue to contain the kind of miniature semiotic messages addressed in this work.

NOTES

PREFACE

1 Jack Child, "Argentina as Seen through Its Postage Stamps," paper submitted for Course 33.585, Latin American M.A. Seminar, American University, Washington, D.C., 18 May 1966.

2 David Scott, *European Stamp Design: A Semiotic Approach to Designing Messages* (London: Academy Editions, 1995).

3 Garry Trudeau, *The 1990 Doonesbury Stamp Album* (New York: Penguin Books, 1990); Michael Thompson and Michael Hernández de Luna, *Stamp Art and Postal History* (Chicago: Bad Press Books, 2000); Michael Hernández de Luna, *Axis of Evil: Perforated Praeter Naturam* (Chicago: Qualitica Press, 2005). For comment on the last of these, see Alan G. Artner, "Art Review: Artists Display Sticker Shock," *Chicago Tribune*, 21 April 2005, 3.

4 Ríus (Eduardo del Río García), *Filatelia para cuerdos* (Mexico: Editorial Grijalbo, 1998).

5 Jack Child, "Researching the Politics and History of Latin American Postage Stamps at the American Philatelic Society Research Library," *Philatelic Literature Review* 52.1 (2003): 50–63.

6 Jack Child, "The Politics and Semiotics of the Smallest Icons of Popular Culture: Latin American Postage Stamps," *Latin American Research Review* 40.1 (2005): 108–137.

INTRODUCTION

1 Throughout the book, Latin American stamps will be identified at first mention by their *Scott 2006 Standard Postage Stamp Catalogue* number (e.g., Scott 280). Where no letter designation is given, the stamp is in Scott category "A" (regular postage). The letter "C" identifies it as an airmail stamp, and "B" a charity surcharge stamp. The country will be identified by name (e.g., Scott Guatemala C513) only when the text does not clearly indicate the issuing nation.

2 Darryl Fears, "Mexican Stamps Racist, Civil Rights Leaders Say," *Washington Post*,

30 June 2005, A1, A17; Darryl Fears, "White House Denounces Art on Mexican Stamps: Aide to Fox Says Cartoon is Cultural Icon," *Washington Post*, 1 July 2005, A6; Mary Lou Pickel, "For Blacks, Images Jab at Old Scars: Foreign Caricatures Revive Debate on Racial Attitudes," *Atlanta Journal-Constitution*, 27 July 2005, F1, http://www.ajc.com/. I am indebted to Caitlin Knuttel for providing copies of the Memín Pinguín comics she obtained while studying abroad in Mexico, and for the excellent analytical paper she wrote in my Latin American popular culture course.

3 Bill McAllister, "House Resolution Would Condemn Mexico's Memín Stamps as 'Racist,'" *Linn's Stamp News*, 1 August 2005, 35.

4 Enrique Krauze, "The Pride in Memín Pinguín," *Washington Post*, 12 July 2005, A15.

5 Dennis Watson, "The Stamp Selection Process: Mexico," *S.P.A. Journal*, November 1982, 167–168.

6 Bill McAllister, "Helms, Newspaper Attack Frida Kahlo Stamp," *Linn's Stamp News*, 6 August 2001, 1; John J. Miller, "The Stalinist and the Stamp," *Wall Street Journal*, 6 July 2001, 26.

7 A colleague recently pointed out that there are artifacts in Mexico that can be considered even smaller than the postage stamp: miniature carved models of household items (cooking utensils, furniture, etc.) that can be as small as a centimeter or so across. However, I would argue that while most postage stamps are larger than this, their total mass and combined surfaces in three dimensions (with the third dimension being literally "paper thin") qualify them as "the smallest icons of popular culture." In any case, they carry more significant miniature messenges than household items.

8 Scott, *European Stamp Design*.

9 Arthur A. Berger, *Signs in Contemporary Culture* (New York: Longman, 1984), 148–150. For a comment on the messages delivered by Latin American postage stamps, see José del Pozo, *Numismática, filatelia e historia de América Latina* (Montreal: G.R.A.L., 1989), 1, 19.

10 Pan American Union, "The Americas through Their Postage Stamps," *Bulletin of the Pan American Union*, June 1944, 356.

11 Ríus, *Filatelia para cuerdos*, 8.

12 Denis Altman, *Paper Ambassadors: The Politics of Stamps* (North Ryde, Australia: Angus and Robertson, 1991), 1, 3; Denise McCarty, "Michel Survey," *Linn's Stamp News*, 31 July 2006, 48.

13 James A. Mackay, *Encyclopedia of Postage Stamps* (New York: McGraw Hill, 1976), 107.

14 G. P. Murdock, "Conceptual Basis of Area Research," *World Politics* 2 (July 1950): 571–578.

15 David Bushnell, "Postal Images of Argentine Próceres: A Look at Selective Myth

Making," *Studies in Latin American Popular Culture* 1 (1982): 91–105; John Reid, "The Stamp of Patriotism," *Américas*, August 1981, 45.

16 Charles Ekker, "Stamps as Unique Primary Research Materials," *Topical Time* 20.5 (September–October 1969): 40–41.

17 Oscar Karl Goll, "The Collection of Don Porfirio Díaz," *Mexicana*, January 1975, 732–733.

18 Ernest A. Kehr, "Juan Perón, Philatelically Speaking," *New York Herald Tribune*, undated clipping, ca. 1955, Kehr clipping file, Argentina, no. 3, American Philatelic Research Library, Bellefonte, Pa.

19 Javier Pérez de Cuéllar, quoted in the *New York Times*, 23 June 1985, sec. 2, 28.

1. SEMIOTICS, POPULAR CULTURE, POLITICS, STAMPS

1 Scott, *European Stamp Design*.

2 Berger, *Signs in Contemporary Culture*, 1–2. For other general readings on semiotics and signs, see Fernande Saint Martin, *Semiotics of Visual Language* (Bloomington: Indiana University Press, 1990); Wendy Leeds-Hurwitz, *Semiotics and Communication: Signs, Codes, Cultures* (Hillsdale, N.J.: Laurence Erlbaum Associates, 1993); Marcel Danesi, *Of Cigarettes, High Heels and Other Interesting Things* (New York: St. Martin's Press, 1999); Naomi S. Baron, *Speech, Writing, and Sign* (Bloomington: Indiana University Press, 1981); Miranda Bruce-Mirford, *The Illustrated Book of Signs and Symbols* (New York: DK Publishing, 1996); and James Bunn, *The Dimensionality of Signs, Tools and Modeling: An Introduction* (Bloomington: Indiana University Press, 1981).

3 There is, of course, a rich European school of semiotics, associated with (among others) Ferdinand de Saussure and Umberto Eco. Interestingly, a recent novel by Eco (*The Mysterious Flame of Queen Loana*) involves stamps, and portrays a valuable Zanzibar stamp on the cover. See Les Winick, "Stamp from Zanzibar on Cover of Umberto Eco Novel," *Linn's Stamp News*, 5 September 2005, 15.

4 Charles S. Peirce, *Peirce on Signs: Writings on Semiotic*, ed. James Hoopes (Chapel Hill: University of North Carolina Press, 1991). Peirce's essays have been collected in a series of volumes published by the Indiana University Press.

5 Winfried Nöth, *Handbook of Semiotics* (Bloomington: Indiana University Press, 1990), 41.

6 Nöth, *Handbook of Semiotics*, 44.

7 For an explanation of these messages, see Barry Krause, "The Secret Language of Stamps," *American Philatelist* 116.5 (2002): 430–433; and Ian Urbina, "From Love to Longing to Protest, It's All in the Tilt of the Postage," *New York Times*, 15 August 2005, A1. For other comments on the semiotics of stamps, see Frank Nuessel and Caterina Cicogna, "Postage Stamps as Pedagogical Instruments in the Italian Curriculum," *Italica* 69.2 (1992): 211–213; David Scott, "Lieu de memoire," *Semi-*

otica 142.1–4 (2002): 107–124; and David Curtis Skaggs, "The Postage Stamp as Icon," in *Icons of America*, ed. Ray Browne (Bowling Green, Ohio: Popular Culture Press, 1978).

8 Nöth, *Handbook of Semiotics*, 44–45.

9 For the original description of the first postage stamps and instructions on how to use them, see "Postage Stamps," *Times* (London), 25 April 1840, no. 17341, 3.

10 David Alderfer, "Look Closely and You Can See Queen Elizabeth," *Linn's Stamp News*, 10 October 2005, 50.

11 *Scott 2006 Standard Postage Stamp Catalogue*, 770.

12 Scott, "Lieu de memoire," 28–30.

13 Ibid., 10.

14 Ibid., 9–12.

15 "The Redeemed Empire," *Time*, 29 June 1959, 6, http://www.time.com/time/magazine/article/0,9171,864652-6,00.html.

16 Kristi S. Evans, "The Argument of Images: Historical Representation in Solidarity Underground Postage, 1981–87," *American Ethnologist* 19.4 (1992): 750.

17 Jean Franco, *Critical Passions* (Durham: Duke University Press, 1999), 169.

18 See, among others, Chandra Mukerji, *Rethinking Popular Culture* (Berkeley: University of California Press, 1991); Marshall Fishwick, *Icons of Popular Culture* (Bowling Green, Ohio: Bowling Green University Popular Press, 1970); Thomas Inge, *Handbook of American Popular Culture*, 3 vols. (Westport: Greenwood, 1978, 1980, 1981); Charles M. Tatum, "Paraliterature," in *Handbook of Latin American Literature*, ed. David W. Foster (New York: Garland, 1992), 687. See also various articles in the Latin American Studies Association's *LASA Forum* 36.2 (2005): 14–19.

19 Mukerji, *Rethinking Popular Culture*, 7.

20 Franco, *Critical Passions*, 169, 179.

21 For various aspects of this approach, see William Beezley, *Latin American Popular Culture* (Wilmington, Del.: Scholarly Resources, 2000), especially xi, xviii–xx; and Altman, *Paper Ambassadors*, 3.

22 John Bryant, "Stamp and Coin Collecting," in Inge, *Handbook of American Popular Culture*, 3:459–496.

23 Susan M. Pearce, quoted in Peter Monaghan, "Collected Wisdom," *Chronicle of Higher Education*, 28 June 2002, A17. See also Pearce's comprehensive four-volume work on the subject: Susan M. Pearce, ed., *The Collector's Voice: Critical Readings in the Practice of Collecting* (Burlington, Vt.: Ashgate, 2000–2002).

24 William A. Menninger, "A Philatelic Psychiatrist on Philately," *Annals of Internal Medicine* (May 1970): 747.

25 Harold Hinds and Charles M. Tatum, *Handbook of Latin American Popular Culture* (Westport, Conn.: Greenwood Press, 1985), xi, xii.

26 Personal communication with David Bushnell, June 2002. For a sample of his work, see Bushnell, "Postal Images of Argentine Próceres."

27 Harold Hinds and Charles M. Tatum, "Instructions to Contributors," *Studies in Latin American Popular Culture* 7 (1988): v.

28 Beezley, *Latin American Popular Culture*; William Rowe, *Memory and Modernity: Popular Culture in Latin America* (London: Verso, 1991), ix, 243; Néstor García Canclini, *Transforming Modernity: Popular Culture in Mexico* (Berkeley: University of California Press, 1993); and Eva P. Bueno, *Imagination beyond Nation: Latin American Popular Culture* (Pittsburgh: University of Pittsburgh Press, 1998). All the issues of *Studies in Latin American Popular Culture*, as well as Hinds and Tatum's *Handbook of Latin American Popular Culture*, are invaluable sources.

29 Frank Nuessel, "Territorial and Boundary Disputes Depicted on Postage Stamps," *Studies in Latin American Popular Culture* 11 (1992): 123–141.

30 Jack Child, "The Politics and Semiotics of the Smallest Icons of Popular Culture: Latin American Postage Stamps," *Latin American Research Review* 40.1 (2005): 108–137; Jack Child, "The Politics and Semiotics of Argentine Postage Stamps," *MACLAS Latin American Essays* 18 (2005): 55–85.

31 Anne Magnussen, "The Semiotics of C. S. Peirce as a Theoretical Framework for the Understanding of Comics," in *Comics and Culture: Analytical and Theoretical Approaches to Comics*, ed. Magnussen and Hans-Christian Christiansen (Copenhagen: Museum Tusculanum Press, 2000), 193–207.

32 Bryant, "Stamp and Coin Collecting," in Inge, *Handbook of American Popular Culture* 3:460.

33 Ibid., 470. For his pessimistic conclusions, see 485.

34 Carlos Stoetzer, *Postage Stamps as Propaganda* (Washington: Public Affairs Press, 1953), 1.

35 Ibid., 24–25.

36 Harlan J. Strauss, "Politics, Psychology and the Postage Stamp," *Forty-First American Philatelic Congress Book, 1975* (State College, Pa.: American Philatelic Society), 162, 178–179.

37 Ibid., 16–17.

38 For a readable and well-illustrated survey of Nazi Germany's propaganda carried on postage stamps and other postal items, see Albert L. Moore, *Postal Propaganda of the Third Reich* (Atglen, Pa.: Schiffer Military History, 2003).

39 Ríus, *La cultura no muerde* (Mexico: Editorial Posada, 1968), 23. See also Jonathan Grant, "The Socialist Construction of Philately in the Early Soviet Era," *Comparative Studies in Society and History* 37 (July 1995): 487, for a comparison of Soviet stamps and those of Hitler's Germany and Mussolini's Italy.

40 Danilo A. Mueses, *De falsificaciones y falsificadores* (Santo Domingo: privately published, 1992), 136–138.

41 James A. Lees, "Italy's 1941 Rome-Berlin Axis Set," *American Philatelist* 119.8 (2005): 278.

42 Mueses, *De falsificaciones*, 137.

43 Ibid., 96; Scott, *European Stamp Design*, 23.

44 Garry B. Trudeau, "Doonesbury" (comic strip), *Washington Post*, 29 August 1986, C3.

45 Juan Moles i Carrera, "Languages on Stamps: Spain," *American Philatelist* 115.3 (2001): 222–227. See also "Filatelia-Lenguas: Federación Vasca pide incorporación euskera a sellos," EFE (Spanish news service), 18 September 2002, http://www.efe.com/.

46 Marc A. Wessels, "Storming the Cosmos: Philatelic Propaganda and the Soviet Space Program," *American Philatelist*, June 2001, 506–513. See also Karen Jean Lemiski, "The Political Significance of Philately: Imperial and National Postal Systems in Ukraine" (PhD diss., Arizona State University, 1999); and Alison Rowley, "Such Women Could Not Have Existed Before: Visual Propaganda and Soviet Women in the 1930s" (PhD diss., Duke University, 2000).

47 Brian Baur, "American Cold War Philosophy and U.S. Postage Stamps," *Scott Stamp Monthly*, February 1995, 24.

48 H. H. Tennant, "Nearly Everybody Wants to Get in the Stamp Act," *American Mercury* 76 (February 1953): 79–83.

49 Mueses, *De falsificaciones*, 138.

50 "Dominican Republic: Problem with USSR/Hungary UN Resolution Stamp," *New York Times*, 7 April 1957, sec. 2, 20.

51 These examples, and others, are found in "Stamps Serve as Anti-American Propaganda," *Linn's Stamp News*, 25 May 1987, 20; and Rick Miller, "Negative Propaganda Stamps Offer Chilling Theme for Topical Collection," *Linn's Stamp News*, 26 March 2007, 34.

52 Ralph Mendel, *The Stamp of Conflict: The Arab-Israeli Conflict through Philately* (Jerusalem: Capital Stamps, 1991), page c.

53 Barth Healey, "Philatelic Diplomacy: Palestinians Join Collectors' List," *New York Times*, 19 July 1998, http://www.nytimes.com/. For a monograph defending Palestinian national identity via the postage stamp, see Nader Abuljebain, "Palestinian History in Postage Stamps," *American Philatelist* 116.7 (2002): 669.

54 "El Rey Hussein aparecerá en un nuevo sello del correo israelí," EFE, 26 January 2000, http://www.efe.com/; "Jordania emite sellos en memoria del niño símbolo de la Intifada," *Agence France Press*, 13 August 2001, http://www.afp.com/.

55 "Postage Stamp Rekindles Old South Korean-Japan Territorial Dispute," *Agence France Press*, 13 January 2004, http://www.afp.com/; James Brooke, "A Postage Stamp Island Sets off a Continental Debate," *New York Times*, 27 January 2004, A4; Anthony Faiola, "Kicking up the Dust of History," *Washington Post*, 22 January 2004, A15.

56 Sylvia Moreno, "Stamp Backlash Worries Muslims," *Washington Post*, 24 November 2001, B1, B4; Chris L. Jenkins, "Postal Service Reissues Muslim Stamp," *Washington Post*, 18 October 2002, B3.

57 Bill McAllister, "Hobbyists and Lobbyists for Stamps Perforate the Postal Ser-

vice," *Washington Post*, 13 February 1987, A25; "Behind U.S. Pop Stamps, a Citizens' Group," *New York Times*, 1 November 1992, A48.

58 Hugo Dobson, "Japanese Postage Stamps: Propaganda and Decision Making," *Japan Forum* 14 (2002): 21–39.

59 "Comic Conspiracy," *Washington Post*, 5 April 1993, D3. See also several comic strips for that day, including *Beetle Bailey*, *Blondie*, *B.C.*, and *Peanuts*.

60 James Michener, *The World Is My Home: A Memoir* (New York: Random House, 1992), 218, 215. See also Les Winick, "Novelist Takes His Readers Inside the Stamp Advisory Committee," *Linn's Stamp News*, 6 August 2001, 22. For another insider perspective on the working of the committee, see Norman Todhunter, "Design Is the Name of the Game," *S.P.A. Journal*, July 1968, 727–734.

61 John J. Miller, "The Stalinist and the Stamp: The Wonders of Postal Diversity," *Wall Street Journal*, 6 July 2001, 11. See also "Readers' Opinions: Kahlo," *Linn's Stamp News*, 23 July 2001, 4; "Readers' Opinions: More on Kahlo," *Linn's Stamp News*, 6 August 2001, 1, 4; "Readers' Opinions: Kahlo, One More Time," *Linn's Stamp News*, 27 August 2001, 4; Les Winick, "Postal Service Thinks It Is Like McDonald's," *Linn's Stamp News*, 12 November 2001, 18; "Readers' Opinions: 34c Frida Kahlo," *Linn's Stamp News*, 11 February 2002, 4; Allison Cusick, "Three Favorite Stamps and FDCs from 2001," *Linn's Stamp News*, 11 February 2002, 30; and "Patriotic Feelings Fuel Some 2001 U.S. Poll Selections," *Linn's Stamp News*, 15 April 2002, 38.

62 "Readers' Opinions: Kahlo," *Linn's Stamp News*, 23 July 2001, 4.

63 Maurice Moffatt, "Postage Stamps, Past and Present, as Avenues of Learning," *Journal of Educational Sociology* 24.2 (1950): 110–119; Federación Argentina de Entidades Filatélicas, "Filatelia y educación," *Bibliografía de Filatelia*, no. 3 (December 1984): 9.

64 See, for example, *Scott's Monthly Journal*, January 1944, 378–379. For a sample of Kunze's views, see Albert F. Kunze, "Latin American Stamps and the Teaching of Spanish and Portuguese," *Hispania*, February 1943, 68–72.

65 "Nelson Rockefeller Distributes Stamp Articles," *New York Times*, 12 April 1942, sec. 2, 8.

66 Nancy Clark, "Sharing the Hobby: The Classroom—a Wonderful Venue!" *American Philatelist* 116.8 (2002): 687–690.

67 Ian Finlay, "The Use of Postage Stamps in Modern-Language Teaching," *Incorporated Linguist* 24.2 (Spring 1985): 117–118. See also Frank Nuessel, "Teaching Hispanic Culture with Postage Stamps," *Canadian Modern Language Review* 40.3 (1984): 429–439; Frank Nuessel and Caterina Cicogna, "Postage Stamps as Pedagogical Instruments in the Italian Curriculum," *Italica*, 69.2 (1992): 210–227; and Frank Nuessel, "Postage Stamps: A Pedagogical Tool in the Second Language Classroom," *Mosaic: A Journal for Teachers* 3.2 (1996): 12–17.

68 Asociación de Cronistas Filatélicos de la Argentina (ACFA), *Curso de filatelia*, December 1997; "Filatelia en las escuelas," *Cuadernos Filatélicos* (Uruguay), no. 40

(July 1998): 13; Gustavo Berrío Muñoz (minister of communication), "Filatelia," *Bogotá Filatélico*, no. 11 (1956): 3. Personal communication with Berrío Muñoz, Bogotá, January 1967.

69 "Law and Philately," *Linn's World Stamp Almanac*, 1989, 478–480.

70 "Stamp Embargoes," *Linn's World Stamp Almanac*, 1989, 490–491.

71 Donald Reid, "The Symbolism of Postage Stamps: A Source for the Historian," *Journal of Contemporary History* (Great Britain) 19.2 (1984): 223–249.

72 Barbara Anderson, "Stamp Artists Design Communication Devices," *Scott Stamp Monthly*, January 1994, 37.

73 See, for example: Elizabeth Gemming, *Learning through Stamps*, vol. 1, *The World of Art* (Barre, Mass.: Barre Publications, 1968); vol. 2, *Around the World* (1969); Barbara Moore, *The Art of Postage Stamps* (New York: Walker, 1979); Cornelius Vermeule, *Philatelic Art in America* (Weston, Mass.: Cardinal Spellman Philatelic Museum, 1987); Salvador Alaiga, "El arte en los sellos postales de Chile," *Life en Español*, 22 February 1960, 37; and Barbara Mueller, "The Art of the Postage Stamp," *24th Annual American Philatelic Congress Book* (1960), 41–49. See also "Postage Stamp Design," *Wikipedia*, at http://en.wikipedia.org/wiki/stamp_design.

74 For a brief consideration of the "world's ugliest stamps," see Martin Frankevic, "Not a Pretty Sight," *Scott Stamp Monthly*, June 1996, 74–75.

75 David Lidman, *Treasury of Stamps* (New York: Scribners, 1981), 76.

76 Giorgio Migliavacca, *Linn's Stamp News*, "British Stamp Wins Asiago Art Award," 23 September 2002, 2.

77 Willy Eisenha, *The World of Donald Evans* (New York: Harlan Quist, 1981), 19.

78 Ibid., 58–59.

79 Bruce McCall, *Bruce McCall's Zany Afternoons* (New York: Knopf, 1982).

80 David Jickling, *Guatemalan Philately* (Sidney, Ohio: Scott Publishing, 1991), 221. The stamp is Guatemala Scott C513, finally issued in 1973.

81 Scott, *European Stamp Design*, 9–12, 20–22.

82 Ibid., 9.

83 Winthrop S. Boggs, "Brazilian Colonization Commemoratives," *American Philatelist* 45.12 (1932): 583.

84 In July 2003 the Smithsonian's National Postal Museum opened an exhibit on art on U.S. stamps: Rebecca Dana, "American Moments Stamped into History," *Washington Post*, 20 July 2003, N7.

85 Altman, *Paper Ambassadors*, 107–108; Phil Thomas, *Washington Evening Star*, "Liberties Group Joins Fight to Mail Nude Ad," 11 March 1959, A25.

86 See Gerardo Yépiz, *Comandante Marcos*, 1997, http://jas.faximum.com/shop/stamps/sheets/sheet_45.htm (accessed 10 July 07).

87 Bill McAllister, "Stamps and Coins," *Washington Post*, 31 August 1990, D3. The *Doonesbury Stamp Album* was published by Penguin (New York, 1990) and sold for $8.95.

88 Michael Thompson and Michael Hernández de Luna, *The Stamp Art and Postal His-*

tory of Michael Thompson and Michael Hernández de Luna (Chicago: Bad Press Books, 2000).

89 Jack Mingo, "Postal Imperialism," *New York Times*, 16 February 1997, sec. 6, 36.

90 For comment on Guyana's speculative stamps, see "New Issues: Western Hemisphere," *Linn's Stamp News*, 27 September 2004, 30.

91 *Inter-Governmental Philatelic Agency Online*, 14 December 2000, http://www.igpc.net/.

2. AN OVERVIEW OF LATIN AMERICAN POSTAGE STAMPS

1 For brief treatments of the history of Latin American postage stamps, see John T. Reid, "The Stamp of Patriotism," *Américas*, August 1981, 45–48. See also Thomas P. Myers, "Latin America Offers Homegrown Classics, Seebecks, Airmails, More," *Linn's Stamp News*, 17 July 2006, 34; and various entries in James A. Mackay, *The Guinness Book of Stamps*, 2nd ed. (Enfield, Middlesex: Guinness Books, 1988).

2 Manfred Amrhein, *Philatelic Literature: A History and a Select Bibliography*, 2 vols. (San José, Costa Rica: privately published, 1992 and 1997), 2:94–99, 102, 132–138.

3 Joseph Hahn and Joseph Sousa, "El Salvador: The Seebeck Stamps," *American Philatelic Congress Handbook*, no. 43 (1977): 12; *Linn's Stamp News*, 13 June 2005, 34.

4 Danilo A. Mueses, *Seebeck: ¿Héroe o villano?* (Santo Domingo: Federación Interamericana de Filatelia, 1986), 124–125. On the cover of his book Mueses very cleverly places a photograph of Seebeck in the vignette of an El Salvador Seebeck stamp. For the Ecuadorian Seebecks, see Robert A. D'Elia and Douglas B. Armitage, *Ecuador: The Philately of the Seebeck Era* (Bellefonte, Pa.: American Philatelic Society, 2004).

5 Juan Martínez Moreno, *El descubrimiento de América en la filatelia mundial* (Madrid: Ministerio de Asuntos Exteriores, 1985).

6 Albert Kunze, "La división de sellos de la Unión Panamericana," *Ninth Annual American Philatelic Congress Book* (Washington: Pan American Union, 1943), 42–43.

7 "Correos privados en el Cono Sur de América Latina," *Cuadernos Filatélicos Uruguayos*, March 1999, 11–12.

8 "Brasil—Filatelia. Correos lanzarán estampilla con olor de café," EFE, 23 November 2000, http://www.efe.es/.

9 "A Note on New Issues for 1944," *New York Times*, 31 Dec 1944, sec. 2, 4; "A Note on New Issues for 1946," *New York Times*, 5 January 1947, sec. 2, 16; *Scott 2006 Standard Postage Stamp Catalogue*. See also Denise McCarthy, "Total New Worldwide Stamps," *Linn's Stamp News*, 29 April 2002, 28–29.

10 Denise McCarthy, "New-issue Totals," *Linn's Stamp News*, 24 May 2004, 54.

11 The 1994 data is from the *Latin American Post*, no. 1 (1996): 1556. For 1998, see *Latin American Post*, no. 2 (2000): 1868. For 2000, see *Linn's Stamp News*, 29 April 2002, 28; and 24 May 2004, 54. See also *Scott Standard Postage Stamp Catalogue* for the years 2002 and 2006.

12 The Panamanian scheme is described in Kent B. Stiles, "Panama's Series is Due

in March," *New York Times*, 20 February 1955, sec. 2, 36; "Panama: Popes Issue Planned, Not Released," *American Philatelist* 68.8 (1954): 533, 608; and Belmont Faries, "Religion Group Hits Panama Popes Set," *Washington Sunday Star*, 15 July 1956, E6. The short-lived Haitian scheme is noted in David Lidman, "Issue on Popes Planned," *New York Times*, 11 June 1972, sec. 2, 32.

13 Danilo E. Mueses, "El escándalo de las emisiones olímpicas," in *Emisiones postales dominicanas* (Santo Domingo: Banco Central de la República Dominicana, 1986), 213–216.

14 Ibid., 216.

15 Nicolás Jiménez Mendoza, "The Pirates of Philately," *Latin American Post*, no. 1 (1991): 1193–1194; "A Letter from Paraguay Offering 'Rights' to 15 Stamp Issues," *American Philatelist* 81.6 (1967): 650; Mueses, "El escándalo de las emisiones olímpicas," 213; "Peruvian Officials Deny Selling Withdrawn Stamp," *New York Times*, 17 February 1934, 9.

16 *Scott 2006 Standard Postage Stamp Catalogue*, 730–746.

17 Universal Postal Union, "International Bureau Circular 318: Argentina—Circulation of Two Miniature Sheets," 18 August 1997, http://www.upu.int/.

18 *Scott 2006 Standard Postage Stamp Catalogue*, 117. The catalogue value of $170,000 is only a guess, since there are very few of these rarities, and they seldom come on the market.

19 See, for recent Honduran stamps, the list of errors in "Interesting 'Goofs' from Honduras," *Latin American Post*, no. 2 (1995): 1508.

20 "To Err Is Divine," *Scott Stamp Monthly*, September 1995, 75.

21 F. Burton Sellers, "Two Haitian Presidents in One Uniform, or How the ABNCo Took a Shortcut," *Collectors Club Philatelist* 63.6 (1994): 349–353. For a general discussion of this problem, see Wayne Youngblood, "Resourceful Bank Note Companies Reused Good Engravings," *American Philatelist* 120.8 (2006): 716–719.

22 For accounts of the Bolivian Sun Gate issue, see Hugh Watchorn, "Bolivia's 'Gate of the Sun,'" *American Philatelist* 110.6 (1966): 707–708; Philip Mattes, "Bolivia: The Golden Sun Gate Stamps," *Collectors Club Philatelist* 41.1 (1965): 21–24; Carlos Canadell, "La Puerta del Sol," *Revista Filatélica Argentina*, July 1998, 41–46; Carlos E. Ihl B., "La Puerta del Sol de Tiahuanacu," *Chile Filatélico*, March 1971, 191–194. For a detailed record of the hearings in the Bolivian Congress that attempted to investigate the irregularities, see Eugenio von Boeck, *Bolivia: estudio de dos emisiones postales* (La Paz: Imprenta y Librería "Renovación," 1984), and *Latin American Post* 23.4 (1999): 1823–1827; 24.1 (2000): 1843–1846; 24.2 (2000): 1861–1864; 24.3 (2000): 1881–1884; 24.4 (2000): 1905–1910; 25.1 (2001): 1921–1924.

23 Von Boeck, *Bolivia*, 68.

24 For a list of these groups, see the introduction to any *Scott Standard Postage Stamp Catalogue*.

25 Hank Ketcham, "Dennis the Menace," *Washington Post*, 31 July 2005, comic section.

3. INTERNAL POLITICS

1 See, for Soviet examples, Rowley, "Such Women Could Not Have Existed Before: Visual Propaganda and Soviet Women in the 1930s"; and Debra Jean Luff, "The Utility of Philately in Comparative Education and the Analysis of Higher Education Systems" (EdD diss., University of the Pacific, 1998).

2 Mueses, *Emisiones Postales Dominicanas*, 171.

3 Provisional Presidency (Argentina), decree of 17 July 1957, in *Revista de la Sociedad Filatélica Argentina*, January 1958, 30.

4 "A Broad Brush Paints Stamps," *New York Times*, 30 March 1985, 5.

5 "La Chemanía entre el boom y la banalización," *El Nacional*, 9 October 1997, http://www.el-nacional.com/cultura/cultural.htm.

6 "Una estampilla para el Che," *Clarín Digital*, 8 October 1997, http://old.clarin.com/diario/1997/10/08.htm.

7 Héctor Arceo Trujillo, "Barrio niega que Secodam sea brazo de venganzas del gobierno," *Novedades EMEDIA* online, 13 September 2002, http://web.lexis-nexis.com/universe/document.

8 Centro Filatélico Dr. Gray, "Bandeletas puestas en circulación," *Boletín Informativo*, no. 55, March 1965.

9 "Brazil: Designation of Republic Flag, Colors, Coat of Arms," *American Philatelist* 4.4 (1899): 108.

10 "Noticias: Decreto del 2 de enero de 1957," *Revista de la Socieded Filatélica Argentina*, January–June 1957, 35.

11 "UNPA to Introduce Indigenous Art Series," *Linn's Stamp News*, 27 January 2003, 14–15.

12 "Peru: Postponed Problem," *Time*, 18 April 1969, 40.

13 David Bushnell, "Feminismo filatélico," *Boletín Americanista*, 37.47 (1997): 77–89.

14 Antonio Deluca, *Sellos y otros valores postales* (Buenos Aires: Ministerio del Interior, 1939), 253.

15 Stoetzer, *Postage Stamps as Propaganda*, 7–8.

16 H. D. Mitchell, "Philatelic Coffee Advertising in Costa Rica, 1921–23," *19th American Philatelic Congress Book* (Yorktown, Va.: H. D. Mitchell, 1953), 115–124.

17 Alfredo Grether, *Las bandeletas con leyendas del correo Argentino: catálogo ilustrado con las emitidas hasta 1961* (Buenos Aires: privately published, 1961).

18 "Brazilian Stamps to Smell like Coffee," *Linn's Stamp News*, 24 December 2001, 2.

19 "Colombia Stamp Tribute Too Candid–U.N. Rejects It," *Los Angeles Times*, 1 November 1986, sec. 1, 4.

20 Stoetzer, *Postage Stamps as Propaganda*, 4–5.

21 Richard Cabeen, *Standard Handbook of Stamp Collecting* (New York: Harper and Rowe, 1986), 284.

22 On a personal note, the author traveled to the Falklands and Antarctica on two of the ships shown in the series, *Explorer* (sunk in 2007) and *World Discoverer*.

23 "Machu Picchu—The Short Story Column," *Latin American Post*, no. 2 (2000): 1858–1859.

24 Altman, *Paper Ambassadors*, 99–100.

25 Ian White, "Ray of Sunshine," *The Herald* (Glasgow), 2 June 2001, 28.

26 See, for example, Myrtis Herndon, "The Sporting Spirit Perceptions in Philatelic Art Iconography and Sports Philately, 1896–1974" (PhD diss., Ohio State University, 1991), esp. 240–242.

27 Dale Pulver, "Several Stamps Honor Mexico's 1968 Games," *Linn's Stamp News*, 26 July 2004, 42; and Dale Pulver, "Futbol Stamps: World Cup, Jules Rimet, More," *Linn's Stamp News*, 27 January 2003, 40.

28 Rick Miller, "Hyperinflation," *Linn's Stamp News*, 9 May 2005, 38.

29 Michael Laurence, "Modern Latin American Inflation Covers," *Linn's Stamp News*, 15 October 1990, 3.

30 Discussions at the panel "Power Politics and Geography in Latin America," Latin American Studies Association Congress, Mexico City, 30 September 1983.

31 Asociación de Cronistas Filatélicos de la Argentina, *Anales de Literatura Filatélica* (Buenos Aires: Asociación de Cronistas Filatélicos de la Argentina, 1982), 48. See also Dennis Watson, "Stamp Selection Process," *S.P.A. Journal*, April 1983, 506–507.

32 Alejandro Noriega, "Comisión Asesora de Filatelia," *Revista Filatélica Argentina*, no. 205 (March 1998): 46.

33 Watson, "Stamp Selection Process," 505–506.

34 Ibid., 506.

35 David Jickling, *Guatemalan Philately, 1971–1990* (Sidney, Ohio: Scott Publishing, 1991), 3–4.

36 C. W. Hill, "The Origin of 'Opened by Censor,'" *Stamp Collecting*, 4 February 1955, 745; communication from Dr. Florene Memegalos, 27 January 2003.

37 Fritz Rosenberg, "Censored Cover Collectors Can Now Seek Answers," *Stamp Collector* (Albany, Or.), n.d., Kehr Clipping File, "Censorship," American Philatelic Research Library, Bellefonte, Pa. See also *New York Times*, "The Censor Has His Day," 7 December 1941, sec. 11, 18.

38 "Censura postal en la Argentina: Revolución de 1930," *Revista Filatélica Uruguaya*, no. 20 (November 1991): 13–19.

39 Ibid., 19.

40 Jim Cross, "The Thousand Days," *American Philatelist* 112.8 (1998): 754–755; De Almeida, *Sellos postales do Brasil*, 122–124.

4. INTERNATIONAL RELATIONS

1 This chapter relies on my past work on conflicts in Latin America, especially *Geopolitics and Conflict in South America: Quarrels among Neighbors* (New York: Praeger,

1985). Nuessel's "Territorial and Boundary Disputes Depicted on Postage Stamps," was also helpful.

2 Paul B. Goodwin, "Stamps and Sovereignty in the South Atlantic," *American Philatelist* 103.1 (1989): 43.

3 Asociación de Cronistas Filatélicos de la Argentina, *Anales* (1980), 75; Mario Raux, "Geografía Filatélica Argentina," *Revista de Correos* (Argentina), March 1948, 374; Kent B. Stiles, "War Clouds over Stamp," *New York Times*, 12 September 1937, sec. 12, 8.

4 Peter Beck, "Argentina's 'Philatelic Annexation' of the Falklands," *History Today*, February 1983, 41.

5 "Parliament's Week," *Time*, 24 February 1936, 19.

6 Mueses, "Una serie polémica: el mapita," in Mueses, *Emisiones*, 113–114.

7 Ibid., 113.

8 Ernest Kehr, "The Great Paper Wars," *Scott Stamp Monthly*, January 1982, 126.

9 *The International Geographic Encyclopedia and Atlas* (Boston: Houghton Mifflin,, 1979), 166–167. For accounts of the postal history of Clipperton, see C. Schunck, "Clipperton Island," *Topical Time*, January–February 1996, 31–32; and O. Newport, "Clipperton Island Centenary," *Gibbons Stamp Monthly*, June 1995, 45–47.

10 John Kelly, "Answer Man: In Search of Virtual Countries," *Washington Post*, 9 April 2006, C2. See also the Dominion of Melchizedek's Web site at http://www.melchizedek.com/dom/index.html.

11 Mackay, *The Guinness Book of Stamps*, 206.

12 Raymond Ireson, *The Panama Canal Story* (CD-ROM) (San Francisco: Panama Canal Study Group, 2001), frames 57–58. See also Ireson, "The Panama Canal Story," *Latin American Post*, no. 4 (2000): 1894–1897; and Wood, *This Is Philately*, 495–496.

13 Philippe Bunau-Varilla, *Panama: The Creation, Destruction and the Resurrection* (New York: McBride, 1914), 247.

14 Ibid.

15 Ibid., 249–250.

16 David G. McCullough, *Path between the Seas* (New York: Simon and Schuster, 1977), 325.

17 For identification of the individuals, see Ireson, *The Panama Canal Story* (CD-ROM), frames 124–125.

18 James G. Bradsher, "The Diplomatic Story behind a 1939 Guatemalan Stamp," *American Philatelist* 98.10 (1984): 1024–1026. See also Roland Goodman, *Guatemala: A Handbook on the Postal History and Philately*, 2 vols. (Bournemouth, England: Robson Lowe, 1974), 2:468–469, 497, 549.

19 *Linn's Stamp News*, 2 May 1983, 1.

20 Steve Pendleton, "'Jurassic Park' Island Has Postal Connection," *Linn's Stamp News*, 11 July 2005, 46–47.

21 "New Stamp to Tell World Cocos Isle Is Costa Rica's," *New York Times*, 8 October 1935, 9; Tyree Campbell, "The Pacific's Unknown Cocos Island," *Linn's Stamp News*, 10 June 1996, 35.

22 Pendleton, "'Jurassic Park' Island," 47.

23 For information on the dispute discussed in this section and the stamps involved, see A. A. Delaney, "The 1937 Stamp Design That Started a War," *Scott's Monthly Journal*, April 1970, 37–39; Irving Green, "Honduras-Nicaragua Boundary Dispute and Its Settlement," *Scott's Monthly Journal*, April 1962, 61–64; Kent B. Stiles, "War Clouds over Stamp"; Kent B. Stiles, "Issue with Map on Disputed Territory Withdrawn," *New York Times*, 6 March 1938, sec. 12, 8; and "Two Stamps Too Many," *Time*, 1 November 1937, http://www.time.com/time/magazine/article/0,9171,882884,00.html.

24 For a discussion of the conflict, and especially its resolution, see Jack Child, *The Central American Peace Process, 1983–1991: Sheathing Swords, Building Confidence* (Boulder: Lynne Reinner, 1992).

25 Corporación Venezolana de Guayana, *Guayana y su Filatelia* (Caracas: La Corporación, 1970); Kehr, "The Great Paper Wars," 124.

26 Child, *Geopolitics and Conflict*, 92–98; *Filigrana* (the magazine of the Philatelic Society of Buenos Aires), March 1942, 12–13; March 1943, 20–21.

27 Banco Central del Ecuador, *Album Didáctico* (Quito: Banco Central, 1983), 168–169.

28 Ibid., 313.

29 "Ecuador-Peru emiten sellos por aniversario de acuerdo de Cahuide," EFE, 23 May 2001, http://www.efe.es/.

30 Child, *Geopolitics and Conflict*, 85–92.

31 *Observatorio Cono Sur de Defensa y Fuerzas Armadas* (newsletter), 9 July 2005, item 1, http://www.fcs.edu.uy/investigacion/investigacion.html#unidacad (accessed 19 March 2008).

32 Rasmus Bartleson, "The Stamps of Chile Used in Bolivia and Peru During the War of the Pacific," *American Philatelist* 48.3 (1934): 172–173.

33 Mervyn G. Palmer, "The Tacna-Arica Plebiscite Issues of Peru," *Gibbons Stamp Monthly*, March 1929, 110–111; and M. Dixon, "Peru: The Tacna-Arica Plebiscite," pt. 1, *London Philatelist*, March 1990, 47–51; pt. 2, *London Philatelist*, April 1990, 83–89.

34 "Nuevas emisiones: Chile," *Filigrana*, November 1939, 20; "Isla de Pascua—Easter Island," *Chile Specialist*, 26 February 1994, 1–8. Steven Pendleton, "Exotic Easter Island Calls to the Collector," *Linn's Stamp News*, 1 September 2003, 36.

35 Denise Hatton, "Chile Issued Separate Easter Island Stamps," *Linn's Stamp News*, 15 March 1993, 8. See also "Chile protesta por sellos," *El Filotélico*, no. 85 (1991): 7.

36 "Easter Island Dispute," *Daily Telegraph* (London), 2 September 1991. See also Denise Hatton, "Unassorted Mixtures," *Linn's Stamp News*, 23 December 1991, 20.

37 "Isla de Pascua—Easter Island," *Chile Specialist*, 26 February 1994, 9.

38 Bruce Moorhouse, "Bolivia and Brazil: The Two Sides of the Acre Dispute," *Mainsheet*, November 1994, 8; Frederick Melville, *Phantom Philately* (Lucerne: E. Bertrand, 1950), 7.

39 Leopoldo Tenorio Casal, "Estado independiente del Acre: servicio postal," *Revista de la Sociedad Filatélica Argentina*, October–December 1933, 124–125; Jose Joquim Marques Marinho, *Amazonia: nossos sellos* (Manaus: privately published, 1981), 14–23.

40 For information on the Counani stamps, see Marinho, *Amazonia*, 43–143.

41 Child, *Geopolitics and Conflict*, 106–107.

42 "Bolivia-Paraguay Dispute," *New York Times*, 12 September 1937, sec. 12, 8.

43 A. Shepherd, "The Postal History of the Chaco War" (Halifax: privately published, 1981); Erwin Hershkowitz, *The Chaco War*; undated copies of exhibit pages, American Philatelic Research Library, Bellefonte, Pa.

44 "Brazil: Special Stamps Issued to Commemorate Visit of President Justo of Argentina," *New York Times*, 8 October 1933, 18.

45 "Nixon Trip," *Evening Star* (Washington), 16 May 1958, A4.

46 The importation of Cuban stamps was prohibited by U.S. law in early 1962 as part of the embargo against Cuba. The prohibition was lifted for postage stamps in 2001. The stamps in plate 15 are part of the Cuban government's 1988 stamp series "Latin American Independence Heroes." The stamps in plate 16 are part of the Cuban government's 1989 stamp series "Latin American Writers."

47 Banco Central del Ecuador, *Declaración de Santiago—soberanía de las 200 millas marítimas* (Quito: Banco Central, 1983), 295.

48 "Costa Rica solidaria con Estados Unidos a un año de atentados," EFE, 10 September 2002, http://www.efe.com/.

5. ARGENTINA

1 "Bandeletas Especiales," *Filigrana*, November–December 1960, 8; Walter Bose, "La propaganda en las máquinas obliteradoras," *Revista de Correos y Telégrafos*, February 1941, 24.

2 Walter Bose, *Literatura filatélica argentina* (Buenos Aires: Márquez, 1941).

3 See, for example, "La filatelia en las escuelas primarias," *Filigrana*, October 1939, 1.

4 Fabián Bielinsky, dir., *Nine Queens* (Argentina: Patagonik Film Group, 2002). For commentary on the film, see Stephen Hunter, "The Pro and a Con Game," *Washington Post*, 28 April 2002, G1; Stephen Hunter, "'Nine Queens': An Exhilarating Dash for Cash," *Washington Post*, 10 May 2002, C1; and Michael Laurence, "'Nine Queens': New Film Stamp Theme," *Linn's Stamp News*, 20 May 2002, 3.

5 Mackay, *Encyclopedia*, 35.

6 National Communications Commission (Argentina), *Boletín Oficial*, no. 30.539, Resolución 3956/2004, 1 December 2004.

7 Data from *Scott 2006 Standard Postage Stamp Catalogue*, 1:415–478.

8 Asociación de Cronistas Filatélicos de la Argentina, "Pintura Argentina en sellos de correo," *Anales* (1982), 83–86.

9 José Campo y Fernández, "Filatelia Gardeliana," *Revista* FAEF, September 1998, 46–53.

10 "Filatelia militar," *Revista Militar* (Argentina), no. 705 (July–September 1981): 97–98.

11 Walter B. L. Bose, *Correo Argentino: Una historia con futuro*, 2nd ed. (Buenos Aires: Manrique Zago Ediciones, 1994), 101–02. Bose, *Correo Argentino*, 101–102; "Engraved by a Baker's Roundsman," *Philatelic Magazine*, 31 October 1958, 731–732.

12 Bushnell, "Postal Images of Argentine Próceres."

13 Patricio Manns, *El corazón a contraluz* (Buenos Aires, Editorial Emecé, 1996), translated as "A Lone Horseman," in *Chile*, ed. Katherine Silver (Berkeley: Whereabouts Press, 2003), 210–224.

14 Walter Bose, "La estampilla de Tierra del Fuego," *Revista de la Sociedad Filatélica Argentina*, January 1957, 3–18; Otto Hornung, "The Man from Tierra del Fuego," *Stamp Collecting*, July 1982, 598–605; Jere Hess Barr, "History of the Tierra del Fuego Stamp," *Ninth American Philatelic Congress* (Washington: Pan American Union, 1943), 89–101; Mario D. Kurchan, *Historia postal Argentina* (Buenos Aires: All Graf S.R.L., 1994), 354–357.

15 Deluca, *Sellos y otros valores postales*, 365.

16 Ann Triggle, "The Prostitute Revenue Issues of Argentina," *Scott Stamp Monthly* 15.1 (November 1996): 16.

17 Deluca, *Sellos y otros valores postales*, 254.

18 Ibid., 270.

19 Ibid., 431.

20 "Emisión de Estampillas Conmemorativas del VI Congreso Internacional del Frío," *Revista de la Sociedad Filatélica Argentina*, January–April 1932, 10; Winthrop Boggs, "Refrigeration Congress," *American Philatelist* 46.2 (1932): 118.

21 "Sello de 10 centavos, conmemorativo de la Conferencia Interamericana de la Consolidación de la Paz," *Revista de la Sociedad Filatélica Argentina*, January–February 1937, 9; Deluca, *Sellos y otros valores postales*, 463–465.

22 Ibid., 479.

23 Ibid., 299.

24 Goodwin, "Stamps and Sovereignty in the South Atlantic," 43.

25 Deluca, *Sellos y otros valores postales*, 437.

26 Ibid., 544.

27 Barbara Tenenbaum, ed., "Perón, Juan Domingo," *Encyclopedia of Latin American History and Culture* 4:352. For discussion of the link between European fascism and postage stamps, see Strauss, "Politics, Psychology and the Postage Stamp," 167; Moore, *Postal Propaganda of the Third Reich*; and *Linn's Stamp News*, 9 December 2002, 34.

28 For examples of Mussolini-era Italian stamps, see (Scott Italy numbers) 1932, nos. 290–305 (tenth anniversary of the March on Rome and the Fascist government); 1936, nos. 355–358 (Italian industry); 1938, nos. 400–409 (Proclamation of the Empire); and 1941, nos. 413–418 (Rome-Berlin Axis; Mussolini and Hitler).

29 Robert E. Lana, "Italian Cancels Used for Ads, Propaganda," *Linn's Stamp News*, 12 August 2002, 40. For data on Argentine propaganda cancellations, see Alfredo Grether, *Las bandeletas* (Buenos Aires: privately published, 1961).

30 Bose, *Correo Argentino*, 184.

31 Ernest A. Kehr, "Juan Perón, Philatelically Speaking," *New York Herald Tribune*, undated clipping, ca. 1955, Kehr clipping file, Argentina, no. 3, American Philatelic Research Library, Bellefonte, Pa.

32 David Straight, "League of Nations Philately—a Forerunner to U.N. Philately," *American Philatelist* 119.10 (2005): 884–889.

33 "Moción Argentina sobre servicio postal propio de la U.N.," *Filigrana*, July–September 1947, 20; United Nations, "United Nations Tribute to Philately," *U.N. Chronicle* 34.4 (1997): 1.

34 "Servicio Postal Ordinario," *Filigrana*, January–June 1947, 15, and May–June 1947, 50; Kent B. Stiles, "Argentine Revolution Stamp," *New York Times*, 11 June 1944, sec. 2, 8.

35 "Argentine Remainders," *Gibbons Stamp Monthly*, undated clipping, ca. 1945, in the Kehr clipping file, Argentina, no. 3, American Philatelic Research Library, Bellefonte, Pa. See also "Argentina: San Juan Earthquake," *New York Times*, 12 March 1944, sec. 2, 4.

36 On a personal note, stemming from my birth and eighteen years of residence in Argentina, I recall vividly the serious and formal "acto de desagravio" (a ceremony of redress or amends) carried out at my English-style boarding school outside Buenos Aires after an inebriated British faculty member broke the obligatory statue of San Martín at the school and then allegedly insulted the memory of the national hero by urinating on the shards.

37 Mariano Ben Plotkin, *Mañana es San Perón* (Wilmington, Del.: Scholarly Resources, 2003), 28, 126.

38 José Omario, "Bandeletas Sanmartinianas," *Revista de Comunicaciones*, no. 288 (August 1961): 37–38, 48.

39 Bose, *Correo Argentino*, 184; "Paraguay: Perón Visit," *New York Times*, 24 October 1954, sec. 2, 10.

40 Ministry of Communications (Argentina), Decreto 23.529/46, 21 December 1946; "Estampillas sin valor postal pro monumento al 'descamisado,'" *Revista de la Sociedad Filatélica Argentina*, January–April 1947, 17; "Forum Update: Argentina—'Pro Monumento al descamisado,'" *Linn's Stamp News*, 8 January 1996, 50. See also the correspondence between H. G. Stanton (in Buenos Aires) and Ernest Kehr, for the year 1947, in the Kehr clipping file, Argentina, no. 3, American Philatelic Research Library, Bellefonte, Pa.

41 "Nuevas Emisiones," *Filigrana*, January–June 1948, 10; Ministry of Communications (Argentina), Decreto 9.379/46, April 1946; *Revista de Correos*, September 1947, 5–9.

42 Ministry of Communications (Argentina), "Emisión sello postal extraordinario con sobrecargo 'Pro Fundación Eva Perón,'" Decreto 17/586, 6 September 1951.

43 National Communications Commission (Argentina), *Boletín Oficial*, Decreto 3.399, 27 July 1952; "Eva Perón," *Revista de la Sociedad Filatélica Argentina*, July–August 1952, 97–99; "Argentina: Evita Stamps; Others Banned for One Year," *New York Times*, 28 July 1952, sec. 2, 15.

44 "Franco Stamps Obligatory," *New York Times*, 26 January 1941, sec. 10, 6.

45 Richard J. Sutton, *Stamp Curiosities* (New York: Philosophical Library, 1958), 14; Ken Wood, *This Is Philately* (Albany, Or.: Van Dahl Publications, 1982), 88.

46 José R. Merlo, "Politically Incorrect Cancel," *American Philatelist* 116.11 (2002): 1000–1001.

47 Arthur P. Whitaker, "Argentina," *Spectrum* (1964): 111; Robert A. Potash, *The Army and Politics in Argentina, 1945–1962* (Palo Alto: Stanford University Press, 1980), 141.

48 Ministry of Communications (Argentina), "Emisión: Esteban Echeverría," *Revista de Comunicaciones*, August 1956, 47.

49 Executive Branch (Argentina), "Sello postal conmemorativo de la Convención Reformadora de la Constitución Nacional," Decreto no. 9862, 22 August 1957.

50 "Emisión conmemorativa 'Transmisión del mando Presidencial,'" *Revista de la Sociedad Filatélica Argentina*, January–June 1958, 30.

51 Osvaldo Adolfo Facciolo, "La banda presidencial," *Filigrana*, July 1977, 32–33.

52 National Communications Commission (Argentina), "Emisión: Conferencia de Ejércitos Americanos," *Boletín Oficial*, 9 December 1966, 10.

53 Executive Branch (Argentina), "Sello postal extraordinario conmemorativo del 150 aniversario de la defensa de Buenos Aires," Decreto no. 3850, 17 April 1957.

54 H. González Richieri, "Matasellos sobre futbol," *Filigrana*, June 1978, 9, 13. For commentary on the stamps and political aspects of the Soccer World Cup, see "Sports: Argentina and Paraguay," *New York Times*, 19 March 1978, sec. 2, 42; and Tom Ryder, "World Cup Soccer," *Minkus Stamp Journal* 13.3 (1978): 6.

55 "Eva Perón: medio siglo de pasiones encontradas y leyenda," *CNN en Español*, 26 July 2002, http://www.cnn.com/espanol.

56 "Argentine Government Takes Over Post Office," *Linn's Stamp News*, 29 December 2003, 10. See also the comment in the *Scott 2006 Standard Postage Stamp Catalogue*, CD-ROM disk 1, p. 458; Monte Reel, "Turning the Taps Back to the States," *Washington Post*, 27 March 2006, A12.

57 Child, *The Central American Peace Process*, 105.

58 Bose, *Correo Argentino*, 189.

59 Denise McCarthy, "Hole Punched in New Stamp," *Linn's Stamp News*, 17 May 2004, 16.

60 Jose Campo y Fernández, "Filatelia Gardeliana," *Revista* FAEF, September 1998, 46–53; Luis Alposta, "Una estampilla para Gardel," Carlos Gardel Web site, http://www.gardelweb.com/.

61 *EFE News Service U.S.*, 4 November 2001, http://www.efe.com/principal.asp?opcion=0&idioma=INGLES.

6. THE FALKLANDS/MALVINAS

1 For a discussion of the Falklands/Malvinas conflict, see Child, *Geopolitics and Conflict*, 112–122. See also the entry "Falkland Islands" in Barbara A. Tenenbaum, ed., *Encyclopedia of Latin American History and Culture*, 2 vols. (New York: Macmillan, 1996), 2:535–536. A useful starting point for an analysis of the British Falkland Islands stamps is contained in "Postage Stamps and the Postal History of the Falkland Islands," *Wikipedia*, 14 June 2005, http://en.wikipedia.org/. Also Wood, *This Is Philately*, 257–259; and Reginaldo Kohlstedt, "Comienzos del servicio postal en las Islas Malvinas y primeras emisiones de sellos adhesivos," *Filigrana*, July–September 1946, 3–4. The definitive reference work is Stefan Heijtz's *Specialized Stamp Catalogue of the Falkland Islands and Dependencies, 1800–2006*, 5th ed. (Stockholm: privately published, 2006). I have profited from presentations and discussions with Heijtz at the meeting of the Falkland Islands Philatelic Study Group in Washington, June 2006.

2 Geoffrey D. Moir, *Falkland Islands History through Philately* (Croydon, England: ChrisPrint, 1993).

3 The exact number of British military stationed on the islands is not officially revealed by the authorities, but the estimated one thousand troops make the islands one of the most militarized areas in the world, with one soldier for each two or three civilians. The civilians are almost all British citizens, and no Argentine is permitted to reside on the islands. Visitors from Argentina are few, and are usually limited to family members of Argentine soldiers buried on the islands, who require special permission. I have been to the islands a number of times since 1982, and am usually required to explain to the British immigration authorities the circumstances surrounding the entry in my U.S. passport indicating that I was born in Buenos Aires.

4 Ginny Turner, "Fortunes of War in the Falklands," *Scott Stamp Monthly*, April 1984, 105.

5 "La filatelia como arma política," *Nación* (Buenos Aires), 10 May 1982, 16.

6 The population of South Georgia consists of a group of about thirty British scientists and the curators of the Whaling Museum (during tourist season); the small military garrison has now been withdrawn. South Sandwich is uninhabited, and the population of the British Antarctic Territory is limited to several scientific stations and perhaps reaches one hundred fifty in the summer, dropping to a minimal maintenance level of about thirty in the winter.

7 Beck, "Argentina's 'Philatelic Annexation' of the Falklands," 41.

8 Goodwin, "Stamps and Sovereignty in the South Atlantic," 42. Goodwin's article is a well-documented explanation of Argentine-British strains over postage stamps as part of their overall dispute. The article cites numerous documents from the British Foreign Office archives.

9 J. Andrews, "The Falklands Dispute: Argentina and the Centenary Commemorative Stamps of 1933," *Gibbons Stamp Monthly*, April 1936, 126–127.

10 Goodwin, "Stamps and Sovereignty," 42. See also "La Prensa Urges Argentina to Protest against British Issue of Centennial Stamps," *New York Times*, 11 March 1933, 9.

11 Goodwin, "Stamps and Sovereignty," 43. For the text of the recommendation of the Argentine Director of the postal system, see "El correo en la Provincia de Tierra del Fuego, Antártida e Islas del Atlántico Sur," *Filatelia Argentina online*, 29 May 2005, http://www.cpel.uba.ar/filargenta.

12 Asociación de Cronistas Filatélicos de la Argentina, "75 aniversario del primer correo antártico," *Anales de Literatura Filatélica*, 1980, 75.

13 "British Objection to Argentine 'Malvinas' Stamps," *Time*, 24 February 1936, 19.

14 Goodwin, "Stamps and Sovereignty," 43.

15 José Amilcar Romanelli, "El sabueso se prepara," *Filigrana*, April 1979, 15.

16 For commentary on the 1981 map stamps, see Lillian W. Kent, "The Falkland Islands—A Brief History," *Carto-Philatelist*, March 1992, 7–8.

17 Jack Child, *Antarctica and South American Geopolitics: Frozen Lebensraum* (New York: Praeger, 1988), 77–78.

18 Osvaldo A. Facciolo, "La soberanía en las Islas Malvinas," *Anales de Literatura Filatélica* (1982), 29–30.

19 Ibid., 30.

20 See the entry "Falklands/Malvinas War" in Tenenbaum, *Encyclopedia*, 2:536–537.

21 José Campo y Fernández, "Las Malvinas son argentinas: Aspectos filatélicos y postales," *Boletín de filatelia* (FAEF), November 1982, 52–60.

22 Ibid., 59.

23 For detailed information on Argentine postal activities on the islands from April through June 1982, see Asociación de Cronistas Filatélicos de la Argentina, *Anales de Literatura Filatélica* (1982), especially Bruno Hillebrecht, "Soberanía Argentina en el Atlántico Sur," 43–46; and Eduardo Premoli, "Las Islas Malvinas y el Correo Argentino," 71–77. See also Salvador Alaimo, "Oficina radiopostal Islas Malvinas 9409," *The Upland Goose* (quarterly publication of the Falkland Islands Philatelic Study Group), March 2002, 80–86; and Salvador Alaimo, "Soldier's Mail," *The Upland Goose*, June 2002, 118–120. For a British (Falkland Islander) perspective, see John D. Davis, *The Falkland War: Postal History and Stamps of the Argentine Occupation* (Southampton, England: Bittern Press, 1983).

24 Geoffrey Barber, "Official Argentine Post Office Instructions for Handling of Mail to and from the Malvinas (Falkland Islands), 1982–1985," *Ice Cap News*, no. 188 (March–April 1988), 76–78, and no. 189 (May–June 1988), 154–155.

25 Moir, "The Falkland Islands Conflict," 47, 50–53; Premoli, "Las Islas Malvinas y el Correo Argentino," 71.

26 Davis, *The Falkland War*, especially chap. 4, "The Propaganda War."

27 Ibid., 4–4 and 4–5.

28 A facsimile copy of the letter, postmarked 8 May 1982, was kindly provided by Stephen Pendleton (the translation is mine). The handwriting of the letter is childlike, but the address ("Soldado Argentino, Islas Malvinas, Argentina") is written in a much more adult hand.

29 For information on Vernet, see the entry "Vernet, Louis" in Tenenbaum, *Encyclopedia* 5:405. See also, "Antecedentes históricos: 1829—designación del primer gobernador argentino en las Islas Malvinas," *Argentine Marambio Antarctic Base (Air Force)*, 10 June 2005, http://www.marambio.aq/.

30 On several visits to Cape Horn Island, while acting as a guide for Antarctic and South Atlantic tour groups, I was asked to warn passengers to stay out of certain fenced-off areas due to the presence of mines placed there as defense against a possible Argentine attack. For comment on the Chilean reaction to the Cape Horn issue, see *Excelsior*, 17 June 1983, 16a. See also the entry "Beagle Channel Dispute" in Tenenbaum, *Encyclopedia*, 1:314–315; and Steve Pendleton, "Protecting the End of the World," *American Philatelist* 120.7 (2006): 634–640.

31 "Informe Chile," *Observatorio Cono Sur*, no. 177, 2 July 2005. The article referred to the just-published book by Lawrence Freedman, *The Official History of the Falklands Campaign* (London: Book Depository, 2005).

32 Premoli, "Las Islas Malvinas y el Correo Argentino," 72–73.

33 Ibid., 74. See also *Ice Cap News*, no. 188 (March–April 1988): 77.

34 A valuable source of information on current British stamps of the Falklands (as well as of South Georgia and the British Antarctic Territory) is contained in the periodic "Stamp News" sheets and first day cover inserts produced by the Falkland Islands Philatelic Bureau. The serious collector of these stamps will usually place a standing order to receive every new stamp as it is produced, and these sheets and first day cover inserts accompany the purchase.

35 Beck, "Argentina's 'Philatelic Annexation,'" 44.

36 Discussion with a Falklander at Port Stanley, January 1996.

37 Carlos Meo, *El Cóndor Traicionado* (Mexico: IDEA, 1994), 110. The theme of the recovery of the Malvinas Islands is kept alive in Argentine nationalist and political-military circles. See *Observatorio Cono Sur*, 7 January 2005.

38 August 2005 communication from John Splettstoesser, who kindly provided a sheet of the stamps.

39 José Huertos, "Un sello postal atenta nuestra soberanía," *Filigrana*, April–June

1946, 12–13; Dickon Pollard, "King George–Falklands Dependencies," *Global Stamp News*, March 1995, 46.

40 Steve Pendleton, "Stamps and Covers Mark Falklands War Service," *Linn's Stamp News*, 1 August 2005, 58–59.

41 "Quotes of the Month," *Latin American Brazil and Southern Cone Report*, April 2005, 16; "Seeking Support for Moribund Negotiations: Argentina Presses the Falklands/Malvinas Dispute," *COHA Report on-line* (Council on Hemisphere Affairs website), 16 June 2005, http://www.coha.org/.

7. SOUTH AMERICAN ANTARCTICA

1 Child, *Antarctica and South American Geopolitics*, 16, 41–43.

2 Ibid., 85–89.

3 F. M. Auburn, *Antarctic Law and Politics* (Bloomington: Indiana University Press, 1982), 39–40; Jack Child, "The Map Stamps of South American Antarctica: Geopolitics and Philately," *The New Cartophilatelist*, July 2007, 1–4.

4 Richard Bagshawe, "The Postal History of the Antarctic, 1904–1949," *Polar Record*, January 1951, 45.

5 Ibid., 78.

6 Fifth Antarctic Treaty Consultative Meeting, "Postage Stamps to Commemorate the Tenth Anniversary of the Antarctic Treaty, 1961," *Polar Record*, January 1972, 104–105.

7 Child, *Antarctica and South American Geopolitics*, 17.

8 The "Dominion of Melchizedek's" Antarctic claim is set out on its Web page: http://www.melchizedek.com/antarctica/aq_info.htm. A description of the "Dominion of Melchizedek" can be found in John Kelly, "Answer Man: In Search of Virtual Countries," *Washington Post*, 9 April 2006, C2. Contrary to the statement that the Washington phone for the "Embassy" has been disconnected, it rings constantly busy, suggesting that the phone bill has been paid but that the instrument is permanently off the hook.

9 An excellent and well-illustrated introduction to Argentine Antarctic stamps is Humberto Monzón, *Sellos postales argentinos: cien años de historia antártica* (Buenos Aires: Dirección Nacional del Antártico, 2001). Monzón divides Argentine Antarctic stamps into three categories: those that are totally Antarctic in theme, those that feature people, transportation means, and institutions involved marginally in Antarctica, and those that do not focus on Antarctica but that portray maps showing the Argentine Antarctic claim.

10 "Sector Antártico: Filatelia," *Filatelia Argentina*, http://www.cpel.uba.ar/filargenta. See also Monzón, *Sellos postales argentinos*, 5.

11 For a discussion of the early strains between Argentina and Great Britain over Antarctica, see Peter J. Beck, "A Cold War: Britain, Argentina and Antarctica," *History Today*, June 1987, 16–20. For the Argentine foreign minister's note protesting

the stamps, and the British response, see W. M. Bush, *Antarctica and International Law*, 2 vols. (New York: Oceana Publications, 1982), 1:615–619.

12 Monzón, *Sellos postales argentinos*, 3, 5, 11.

13 Argentina, Decreto 13.425, 17 May 1947, in *Revista de la Sociedad Filatélica Argentina*, May–June 1947, 50.

14 Cited in Robert J. Hardie, "Mother, Argentina and England Are at It Again!" *American Philatelist* 98.3 (1984): 240.

15 Dirección Nacional del Antártico (Argentina), *Orcadas, 80º Aniversario*, 1984, 53. See also Walter B. L. Bose, "El correo en la Antártida, factor de soberanía," *Sellos postales argentinos con historia* (Buenos Aires: M. Zago, 1981), 136.

16 Monzón, *Sellos postales argentinos*, 20–21.

17 Personal observation, Argentine Orcadas base, 1996 and 1999.

18 James Buchan, "Covers from Argentina's Antarctic Bases," *Gibbons Stamp Monthly*, November 1999, 81.

19 Monzón, *Sellos postales argentinos*, 11.

20 Personal observation, Paulet Island, January 1999.

21 Fred Goldberg, "An Antarctic Exhibit," *Ice Cap News*, no. 254 (2004): 42–46. Monzón, *Sellos postales argentinos*, 34.

22 Provisional President Aramburu (Argentina), Decreto 102087, 2 September 1957; reprinted as "Año geofísico internacional" in *Boletín de la Sociedad Filatélica*, July–December 1958, 66.

23 Monzón, *Sellos postales argentinos*, 16, 18.

24 Asociación de Cronistas Filatélicos de la Argentina, "Pionero Argentino," *Anales de Literatura Filatélica* (1980): 61.

25 Personal observation and discussion with Argentine Antarctic personnel at Almirante Brown base, Antarctic Peninsula, January 1999.

26 Monzón, *Sellos postales argentinos*, 33. Personal observation, 1986–1999.

27 A comprehensive treatment of early Chilean Antarctic philately is Sergio López Rubio, "Apuntes históricos para un estudio temático Antártico," *Memorial del Ejército de Chile*, September–December 1975, 82–117.

28 For more information, see Child, *Geopolitics and Conflict*, 52, 79. For an Argentine reaction, see "La filatelia como arma política," *Nación*, 10 May 1982, 16.

29 Child, *Antarctica and South American Geopolitics*, 111.

30 Bush, *Antarctica and International Law*, 2:327–331.

31 Ibid., 68.

32 Child, *Antarctica and South American Geopolitics*, 118–120, and the map on 119.

33 For details of the Teniente Marsh base, see Steve Pendleton, "Chilean Base Eduardo Frei Montalvo," *Ice Cap News*, October–December 2000, 109–123.

34 Buchan, "Covers from Argentina's Antarctic Bases," 82.

35 For a description of Brazil's Antarctic stamps, see Steve Pendleton, "Stamps, Covers Record Brazil's Antarctic Presence," *Linn's Stamp News*, 29 December 2004, 54.

36 The Uruguayan National Postal Administration Web page for the stamp is www.correo.com.uy/filatelia/frames/9919c.htm.

37 Steve Pendleton, "Ecuadorian Antarctic Activity," *Ice Cap News*, June 2002, 54–57.

38 "Peru-Ecuador Antarctic Rivalry," *Ice Cap News*, May–June 1988, 159.

39 Klaus Dodds, *Pink Ice: Britain and the South Atlantic Empire* (London: I. B. Tauris, 2002), 15.

40 Beck, "A Cold War: Britain, Argentina and Antarctica," 16–20.

41 Ibid., 21–22.

42 "Quotes of the Month," *Latin American Brazil and Southern Cone Report*, April 2005, 16.

43 Steve Pendleton, "South Pole Postmasters Create Postal History," *Linn's Stamp News*, 30 August 2004, 38.

44 Ibid.

8. OTHER MINIATURE MESSAGES OF NOTE

1 "Honest Opinion Forces Withdrawal of Stamps in Bolivia," *Latin American Post*, no. 4 (1995): 1547.

2 Alex Rendon, "Bolivia: A Railroad Train Story," *Aero Philatelist Annals*, January 1967, 75–77.

3 Lawrence F. Reis, "The Definitive Issues of Brazil," *American Philatelist* 106.5 (1982): 445.

4 C. W. Hennan, "As the Story Goes . . . ," *American Philatelist* 41.6 (1931): 272.

5 Statement by Brazilian Minister of Communications Euclides Quandt de Oliveira, *Selo, pequeña janela para o Brasil e o mundo* (Rio de Janeiro: Empresa Brasileira de Correios e Telégrafos, 1975), 1.

6 See, for example, Brazilian Postal and Telegraph Agency, *Brasil selos, 1991* (Rio de Janeiro: Empresa Brasileira de Correios e Telégrafos, 1991). Because the book contains the actual stamps, the Library of Congress has placed such albums in the Rare Book/Special Collections Room, making access to them somewhat difficult.

7 Bloch Editores, *Brasil atraves dos selos* (Rio de Janeiro: Bloch Editores, 1971).

8 Cícero Antônio De Almeida, *Selos postais do Brasil* (São Paulo: Metalivros, 2003), 174–175.

9 Ibid., 181.

10 Brazil, *Selo, pequeña janela*, 96.

11 De Almeida, *Selos postais do Brasil*, 120–123

12 Bloch Editores, *Brasil atraves dos selos*, 22.

13 De Almeida, *Selos postais do Brasil*, 145.

14 Brazilian Postal and Telegraph Agency, *Eco-filatelia* (Rio de Janeiro: Empresa Brasileira de Correios e Telégrafos, 1992).

15 Altman, *Paper Ambassadors*, 72.

16 Jaime Soto Aliaga, *El arte en los sellos postales de Chile* (Santiago: Editorial Pongal, 1993), 9.

17 Pozo, *Numismática*, 24.

18 Juan Mariño Sánchez, "Programas de Filatelia para Bachillerato," *Bogotá Filatélico*, no. 22 (1974): 27–29. One of the ministers of communications who promoted such programs was General Gustavo Berrío Muñoz; see his speech "Filatelia" in *Bogotá Filatélico*, no. 11 (1956): 3–5. My sources also include personal contacts with General Berrío Muñoz and other members of the Club Filatélico de Bogotá, Bogotá, 1967.

19 David Bushnell, "Regeneración Filatélica," *Revista de Estudios Colombianos*, no. 2 (1987): 27–31.

20 Jairo Londoño, "Novedades," *Bogotá Filatélico*, January–June 1955, 7–8. Interview by author with General Alberto Ruiz Novoa, Bogotá, January 1967.

21 "Fundación Botero," *Latin American Post*, no. 1 (2001): 1927; "Lanzan emisión alusiva a donación de Botero a Bogotá y Medellín," EFE, 30 January 2001, http://www.efe.es/.

22 "Cuba Plans New Stamps to Fight Fifth Column," *New York Times*, 10 May 1942, sec. 2, 8.

23 César A. Mena, "Yellow Fever: Carlos J. Finlay and Other Fighters," *American Philatelist* 92.2 (1978): 147–149.

24 "Iran and Cuba Announce Joint Issue," *Linn's Stamp News*, 5 September 2005, 2.

25 Personal observation, Soviet Bellingshausen base on the Antarctic Peninsula, 1986.

26 David Lidman, "Cuban Trade Embargo Is Emphasized Anew," *New York Times*, 4 November 1962, sec. 2, 24.

27 Denise McCarty, "Treasury Department Allows Importing of Used Cuban Stamps," *Linn's Stamp News*, 5 August 2002, 8.

28 *Scott 2006 Standard Postage Stamp Catalogue*, 885.

29 Secretariat of Communications and Transportation, *La Historia del Correo en México* (Mexico: La Secretaría, 1970), 302.

30 Emilio Obregón, *Filatelia: Timbres, sellos y estampillas*, 2 vols. (Mexico: Editorial Hispano-americana, 1963–64), 2:49–57.

31 Cynthia Palacios Goya, "Catálogo de estampillas postales de México, 1856–1996," *El Nacional*, 14 August 1997, accessed via http://global.lexisnexis.com/us, 16 June 2001.

32 Ríus, *La cultura no muerde*; and Ríus, *Filatelia para cuerdos*.

33 Dale Pulver, *Linn's Introduction to the Stamps of Mexico* (Sidney, Ohio: Linn's, ca. 1992), 3.

34 Dale Pulver, "Mexico's Short-lived Maximilians of 1866–67," *Linn's Stamp News*, 23 February 2004, 36.

35 Alvin F. Harlow, *Paper Chase: The Amenities of Stamp Collecting* (New York: Holt, 1940), 135–136.

36 Brenda Ralph Lewis, "Stamps of the Mexican Revolution," *Scott's Monthly Journal*, January 1982, 12–17.

37 Phillips B. Freer, *Mexican Journeys* (Albany, Ore.: Van Dahl Publications, 1989), 22.

38 Dale Pulver, "¡Viva Exportas!" *American Philatelist* 112.9 (1998): 834–841.

39 "EZLN stamp," EZLN Web site, http://www.ezln.org (accessed 1 June 2005).

40 Gerardo Yépiz, *Comandante Marcos*, 1997, http://jas.faximum.com/shop/stamps/sheets/sheet_45.htm (accessed 10 July 07).

41 James M. Chemi, "Stamps Aid Mexico's Olympic Venture," *American Philatelist* 82.9 (1968): 753–734.

42 James M. Chemi, "Wyman Designs Mexico's Rimet Cup Stamps," *American Philatelist* 93.9 (1970): 407–408.

43 Dale Pulver, "Capt. Carranza's Ill-fated Goodwill Flight," *Linn's Stamp News*, 9 July 1990, 12; Dale Pulver, "Various Stamps Commemorate Aviator Carranza," *Linn's Stamp News*, 28 July 2003, 24.

44 Leon Helguera, "The Mexican Independence Issues of Mexico and the U.S.A.," *Stamps*, 3 September 1960, 338.

45 Sutton, *Stamp Curiosities*, 179–180.

46 Ríus, *La cultura no muerde*.

47 Ríus, *Filatelia para cuerdos*, 42.

48 Ibid., 102–103.

49 *Scott 2006 Standard Postage Stamp Catalogue*, 1253.

50 Kent B. Stiles, "Nicaraguan Stamp Dies Destroyed in Ceremony at Philadelphia," *New York Times*, 16 December 1951, sec. 2, 19.

51 Wintrop S. Boggs, "Nicaragua: Leon Railroad." *American Philatelist* 46.9 (1932): 470–471.

52 Belmont Faries, "Nicaragua Honors U.S. Naval Officer," *Sunday Star* (Washington), 30 September 1956, E6.

53 Denise Hatton, "Nicaragua Features Space Aliens," *Linn's Stamp News*, 3 October 1994, 12.

54 Philatelic Division, National Postal Administration (Uruguay), *Correo Uraguay*, "50th Anniversary of UN Peace Missions," http://www.correo.com.uy/filatelia/frames/index_ingles.htm (accessed 13 July 2007).

55 Philatelic Division, National Postal Administration (Uruguay), *Correo Uraguay*, "25th Anniversary of the Death of Salvador Allende," http://www.correo.com.uy/filatelia/frames/allende_ingles.htm (accessed 13 July 2007).

56 "Uruguayan 'Miracle,'" *Washington Post*, 19 April 1972, A9. A gripping account by a survivor is Nando Parrado, *Miracle in the Andes* (New York: Crown, 2006).

57 *Correo Uraguay* home page, http://www.correo.com.uy/index.asp.

58 Pozo, *Numismática*, 32.

CONCLUSION

1 Jack Child, "Preparing and Using 35 mm Slides for Teaching Latin American Studies," *Hispania*, May 1987, 403–406.
2 Jack Child, "The Impact of Computer-assisted Instruction in Undergraduate Latin American Studies Courses," *Computers in the Humanities*, 1997, 389–407. See also Jack Child, "Putting Your Course Materials on a CD-ROM Disk," *MACLAS Essays*, June 1998, 133–143.
3 Wade E. Saadi, "The State of Our Hobby," *American Philatelist* 119.8 (2005): 678–679.

GENERAL INDEX

INDEX OF STAMPS

Note: In the *Scott 2006 Standard Postage Stamp Catalogue*, the prefix "B" indicates a surcharge on a stamp for charity; "C" an air mail stamp; "O" official mail; and "RA" a postal tax stamp. The absence of a prefix indicates regular first class mail.

ARGENTINA

BOLIVIA

BRAZIL

BRITISH ANTARCTIC TERRITORY

CHILE

COLOMBIA

COSTA RICA

CUBA

DOMINICAN REPUBLIC

ECUADOR

EL SALVADOR

FALKLAND ISLANDS (UNITED KINGDOM)

FRENCH POLYNESIA

GERMANY

GRENADA

GUATEMALA

NICARAGUA

PANAMA

PARAGUAY

PERU

SOUTH GEORGIA AND THE SOUTH SANDWICH ISLANDS

UKRAINE

UNITED KINGDOM

UNITED STATES

URUGUAY

VENEZUELA

JACK CHILD was born to American parents in Buenos Aires, Argentina, and lived in South America for eighteen years before coming to the United States to attend Yale University. Following graduation from Yale, he entered the U.S. Army and served for twenty years as an army Latin American specialist until his retirement as a lieutenant colonel. In 1982 he joined the Department of Language and Foreign Studies at American University, where he teaches a variety of courses (in both English and Spanish) dealing with translation and Latin American studies, with an emphasis on popular culture.

His research has focused primarily on cultural studies and conflict resolution in Latin America. He has received several grants for his research on negotiations in Antarctica and the Falklands/Malvinas, and peacekeeping and confidence-building measures in Central and South America. His interest in high latitudes has taken him on thirteen trips as a staff lecturer and guide aboard expedition cruise vessels to Antarctica and sub-Antarctic islands, including South Georgia and the Malvinas/Falklands.

Dr. Child is the author of *The Central American Peace Process, 1983–1991: Sheathing Swords, Building Confidence* (1992); *Introduction to Spanish Translation* (1992); *Antarctica and South American Geopolitics: Frozen Lebensraum* (1988); and *Geopolitics and Conflict in South America: Quarrels among Neighbors* (1985). He is the editor of *Introduction to Latin American Literature: A Bilingual Anthology* (1994); *Geopolitics of the Southern Cone and Antarctica* (1988); and *Conflict in Central America: Approaches to Peace and Security* (1986).

Library of Congress Cataloging-in-Publication Data
Child, Jack.
Miniature messages : the semiotics and politics of Latin American
postage stamps / Jack Child.
p. cm.
Includes bibliographical references and index.
ISBN-13: 978-0-8223-4179-6 (cloth : alk. paper)
ISBN-13: 978-0-8223-4199-4 (pbk. : alk. paper)
1. Postage stamps—Latin America. I. Title.
HE6185.L29C46 2008
769.5698—dc22 2007049446